THE ABUSIVE PERSONALITY

The Abusive Personality

Violence and Control in Intimate Relationships

Donald G. Dutton

THE GUILFORD PRESS
New York   London

To Antonio Vivaldi
for the Concerto in G Minor (RV-107)
I listened repeatedly to the allegro
and largo while writing this book

© 1998; Revisions for paperback edition © 2003 The Guilford Press
A Division of Guilford Publications, Inc.
72 Spring Street, New York, NY 10012
www.guilford.com

Printed in the United States of America

This book is printed on acid-free paper.

Last digit is print number: 9 8 7 6 5

Paperback edition 2003

Library of Congress Cataloging-in-Publication Data

Dutton, Donald G., 1943–
    The abusive personality: violence and control in intimate
relationships / Donald G. Dutton.
        p. cm.
    Includes bibliographical references and index.
    ISBN 1-57230-370-0 (hbk. : alk. paper) 1-57230-792-7 (pbk.)
    1. Abusive men—Psychology. 2. Object relations (Psychoanalysis)
3. Attachment behavior. 4. Intimacy (Psychology) I. Title.
RC569.5.F3D87 1998
616.85′82–dc21
                                                                98-23645
                                                                    CIP

Preface to the Paperback Edition (2003)

I have been greatly pleased by the critical acclaim given to *The Abusive Personality* since its original publication in 1998. In every one of the workshops I conducted with professionals across the United States on the development of abusiveness and its treatment implications I heard therapists who were frustrated by government-imposed models of treatment, typically feminist models such as the so-called "Duluth model." The complaint was that these models were "psychoeducational" and did not allow for therapy to occur. In some locations, the work with abusive men could not even be referred to as therapy. I do not believe that therapy with abusive men should be designed, implemented, or legislated by nontherapists—activists and bureaucrats. It should be implemented by the people who know their clientele the best: practicing therapists experienced in working with batterers and individuals with other mental health problems.

At the time of the initial publication of *The Abusive Personality*, little was known about how to bring new and different therapeutic techniques to bear on the associated aspects of abusiveness, borderline personality organization, insecure attachment, and chronic trauma symptoms. In the paperback edition, I focus on integrating treatment of these aspects with conventional cognitive-behavioral treatment (CBT). One of the treatment systems I describe in detail is Marsha Linehan's dialectical behavior therapy (DBT). DBT is capable of integration into a CBT format because both have behavioral therapy bases. DBT, however, is better at identifying "treatment-blocking" strategies and dissolving these impediments before treatment begins. DBT stresses the importance of the therapeutic bond, something completely neglected in Duluth model systems. Finally, DBT broadens the focus of CBT from anger to a wider range of emotions that can serve to generate anger, and provides skills modules similar to those used in CBT but better at focusing on impulsivity and cyclical buildups of tension.

Since fearful–angry attachment is so central to abusiveness, strategies for improving attachment style are also included in Chapter 9 of the paperback edition. These involve not only the development and maintenance of a secure base with the therapist (therapeutic bond), but also education in the concept of attachment style as an aspect of personality. A primary therapeutic goal of the former is to allow the client to reverse early dysfunctional attachment styles by relearning a secure base with the therapist. A goal of the latter is to stop the process of wife blaming for "causing" emotional reactions that are aspects of abusive men's attachment style.

Finally, since abusive men have trauma profiles that appear to have been generated by early treatment, a working through of this trauma is suggested. This process involves more than merely recoding the abysmal treatment received; it requires a working through at an emotional level until the trauma is integrated into a life course and ceases to generate symptoms. This is a lengthy process in treatment, which has been hampered by the politicizing of spouse assault. The recognition of trauma symptoms in perpetrators flies in the face of the easy victim–perpetrator distinctions of simpler views of spouse assault. It requires recognition of today's perpetrator as yesterday's victim.

The general research on the development of abusiveness as outlined in the original edition has remained unchanged, as there have been no serious empirical studies to challenge it. Again, the ego deficits described do not apply to all batterers—for example, psychopaths, where the deficit is more with conscience and empathy than with the issues described here.

Preface to the Hardcover Edition (1998)

During the last 20 years there have been remarkable advances in our understanding of the psychology of intimate rage, violence, and abusiveness. Much of this has come from the area of research known as developmental psychopathology, which charts the many microfailures in the attachment process. Rage and intimate abusiveness are closely tied to issues in early development, and understanding this connection can move our understanding beyond the "stimulus–response" models of social learning theory and enable us to chart cyclical buildups of internal tension as a key element in intimate abusiveness. Such cyclical tension is, I believe, a personality consequence of a disrupted attachment process, a pathway linking early problems with adult pathology. From John Bowlby's descriptions of insecurely attached infants "arching away angrily while seeking proximity" to the ambivalence of the abusive adult, a life-long thread appears in the psychological profiles of abusive men. This thread includes ambivalence toward the partner, dysphoria produced by intimacy, and a tendency to blame the partner for the dysphoria. The latter process spirals upward in self-amplifying ruminations that produce unbearable tension states that culminate in violence. These tension states drive thought processes into obsessional "feedback loops" and generate self-fulfilling prophecies when negative actions follow negative anticipations.

One of the goals of this book is to make explicit these pathways from early development to adult abusiveness. In so doing, I review for the professional reader both the theory and research data pointing to these pathways. I include both attachment theory and object relations since both have important points to make and we are not yet at a point where we can exclude either on the basis of available data.

The research component of this book links the psychological profiles of abusive men with their partners' reports of the form and frequency of the man's abusiveness. Once this is established, the connections of that profile to the man's recollection of early treatment are empirically established. A triad of early factors—witnessing abuse, being shamed by a parent, and being insecurely attached through unpredictable parental emotional availability—constitutes the basis of the adult abusive personality. These three components produce an emergent reaction: intimate dysphoria, blamed on the partner, and a tendency to ruminate culminating in explosive abuse. The research described links the childhood experiences to their adult sequelae. Research techniques of this sort have limitations that I describe in the text. They do represent, however, a critical first step toward understanding the development of intimate abusiveness from a life span perspective. Furthermore, they are currently being validated by longitudinal studies on children. I have included data tables and figures for the interested professional. Too many conclusions about abusiveness are not empirically founded, and there is an opportunity here to build a more solid foundation.

I have also included a treatment chapter for the clinician. Psychotherapeutic group intervention does fairly well in treating abusiveness, although certain personality constellations benefit less. Some suggestions for working with these difficult clients are included.

I would like to thank Seymour Weingarten for his encouragement in developing this book and Ardis Krueger for her valuable assistance. Basic Books, a subsidiary of Perseus Books Group, LLC, has kindly permitted me to use some material in the present work taken from my *The Batterer: A Psychological Profile* (1995), for which I am grateful.

Contents

1

Introduction

Something very profound happened to social science thinking during the 1970s. Examine, if you will, an undergraduate social psychology textbook from that era. Turn to a chapter on aggression. It's all about aggression toward strangers or enemies. It's focused on whether aggression is innate or learned. There is no description, not even an inkling of aggression toward intimates.

Or take a look at a undergraduate text on personality. Personality is described as a fixed entity, assessed at a single point in time (usually an arid psychology lab), under the most rational of circumstances, and affixed as a location on a "circumplex," a circular map of the personality styles. There is no suggestion that one's personality might be phasic, or go through predictable shifts or cycles. Or inspect the premier journal on marriage and intimate relationships, the *Journal of Marriage and the Family*; there is not one reference to "violence" from 1939 through 1969. Marriages may often have been called "conflicted," but they were never discussed as being violent.

A case in point is Robert Baron and Donn Byrne's text *Social Psychology*.[1] One of the most popular texts in the area of study, *Social Psychology* is now in its seventh edition. The 1977 version (second edition) opened its chapter on aggression with the hoary question of nature versus nurture. It reviewed research on "situational determinants" (frustration, verbal and physical attack, exposure to

1

violent role models, arousal, aggressive cues, drugs, orders, heat, and overcrowding) and concluded with a review of research on curbing aggression through punishment, catharsis, and "incompatible responses" (empathy, laughter, and lust). It reported a curvilinear relationship between sexual arousal and aggression but did not speculate about real-world examples. Individual characteristics included undercontrolled versus overcontrolled aggressors, and in an example of the latter the authors cited the story of a farmer who catches his wife in bed with another man. He does not respond, even after the interloper steals away with his truck, wife, and kids. In a second marriage, however, when he discovers another incident of infidelity, this time by the second wife, he finally explodes, murdering her and her lover. Identified characteristics of undercontrolled violent men included a need to compensate for insecurity and low self-worth, generalized mistrust of the world, and sadism. In all the social psychology texts I reviewed, this example was the only mention of intimate violence. It did not, however, go beyond the description of the killer as overcontrolled in trying to understand the dynamics of the spousal homicide.

Academic psychology tended to rely on undergraduate populations to make up its subject pools and to study aggression in university labs. Hence, inducing college sophomores to strike inflatable "Bobo dolls" or administer electric shocks to other students became the common research strategy. As Philip G. Zimbardo pointed out in his Nebraska Symposium paper on deindividuated aggression, rationale people made passive by the experimental setting were substituting for irrational proactive aggressors.[2] The result was a focus on the reaction to the microreleasers of aggression instead of on the proactive predator who seeks the situation in which those releasers reside. Eventually, this practice limited our understanding of aggression to a study of "reactions" to "aversive stimuli."

Personality theory sought to locate human personality on a dimensional map called a circumplex—a circular arrangement of 16 dimensions and 8 categories of personality. Based on some early work by Timothy Leary and his colleagues published in 1951, cited in Wiggins, the circumplex model located a person on a circle representing a circular ordering of traits in a two-dimensional space.[3] The response that led to their location was typically a self-report scale filled out in the rational calm of a campus psychology lab. To Leary's credit though, he did believe that personality assessment should be done for different "levels" (including projective tests) and the results compared to obtain a broader picture (e.g., projective results could be compared to self-reports to assess repression of undesirable impulses such as hostility). He also used psychiatric samples as his subject populations. His 1957 book, *Interpersonal Diagnosis of Personality*, was years ahead of its time. Unfortunately, the ease of using a circumplex model and self-reports of traits took over modern personality assessment. The notion that personality might undergo predictable phasic shifts was not contained in these circumplex models. The snapshot taken by the self-report scale represented personality in its totality and fixed it like a photo frozen in time rather than a dynamically shifting repetitive process.

EARLY PSYCHIATRY

Early 20th-century psychiatry tended to focus on case studies of men who had committed spousal homicide.[4] Explanations for this paradox included pathological dependency and conjugal paranoia, as well as temporal lobe epilepsy. One frequently cited study, by Snell, Rosenwald, and Robey, viewed the violence as stemming from a pathologically enmeshed system with extremes of dependency by both the male and the female.[5] Faulk's early study of 23 men who had murdered or seriously injured their wives found that 16 of these men had a psychiatric disorder. Unfortunately, Faulk generalized his profile from this rather extreme sample to all wife assaulters.[6] It remains to be seen whether all assaultive males share psychological profiles of wife killers. I suspect not.

Even when methodology was better, psychiatry would too often settle for association without explanation. Bland and Orn, for example, collected data from a large ($N = 1,200$) urban sample, assessing for antisocial personality, depression, and alcohol use.[7] All three were risk markers for wife assault, and the three together produced wife assault report rates in the 80–90% range (compared to 15% for respondents with none of the three risk markers). Unfortunately, the causal pathways among these factors were not spelled out. The reader never knew why these factors were chosen or by what model they were arranged. Were the alcoholism and depression, for example, symptoms of a deeper psychological disturbance? What was the relationship of depression to wife assault?

A more thoughtful analysis was presented by Bruce Rounsaville.[8] A psychiatrist, Rounsaville was aware of the emerging sociological literature on wife assault and attempted to answer the question of whether wife assault was "normal violence," as the sociologists claimed, or was deviant or atypical. He interviewed 31 battered women about their partners. These women were drawn from hospital emergency rooms and experienced severe and continuous violence. Rounsaville was among the first in the psychiatric literature to recognize that situational forces not masochism trapped battered women in their relationships. In his sample, 71% of the woman had been threatened with death by their partners if they left. Availability of outside resources did not discriminate those who left from those who did not. Only escalating severity of violence and fear for the children did this. As Rounsaville put it, "those who were not sufficiently motivated seemed to ignore the resources which they, in fact, possessed."[9] He also noted that "[t]he most striking phenomenon that arose in the interviews and in treatment with the battered women was the tenacity of both partners to the relationship in the face of severe abuse sustained by many of the women."[10] In 1987, Hedda Nussbaum, a woman who had been abused and tortured for years by her companion, Joel Steinberg, was charged with the beating death of their daughter, 6-year-old Lisa Steinberg. In what was to become the first of a series of high-profile televised trials involving intimate violence, Nussbaum came across as totally devoted to a man who abused, tortured, and stripped her of her essential human dignity.[11]

Rounsaville raised the question of whether wife assault was a form of psychopathology or "normal violence" as sociologists claimed. The partners of his sample had high incidences of alcoholism (45%), prior arrest (58%), imprisonment (35%), and violence outside the relationship (51%). The women described the men as extremely jealous, even preventing them from spending time with their women friends; 92% cited jealousy as a frequent cause of violent arguments. Rounsaville went on to remark that "the explosiveness of the men, the depression of the women, and the alcoholic dependencies in both may be seen as manifestations of a high level of unmet dependency needs which both are seeking to satisfy in the relationship. In such a relationship, anger frequently arises as neither partner is able to fulfill the other's unrealistic needs. The two partners handle their dependent longings in different ways. The woman devotes herself to her partner, sadly ignoring her own needs. The man angrily demands compliance lest he be refused, or fearfully projects onto the woman the desire to leave him."[12] "As evidence for the importance of intimacy issues in abuse, 44% of the women reported that the first abuse occurred either during the honeymoon or around the time of the birth of the first child. The first case usually represents an increased level of attachment, and the second a decreased level of intimacy due to the presence of the child."[13] Certain personality characteristics might be hypothesized as especially common to battering partners leading to both tenacity and the violence of the relationship. If both partners are excessively needy, they may stay together because of severe conflict, that is, because loneliness is a greater threat than abuse. A particularly volatile combination seems to be a jealous possessive man with paranoid tendencies and a counterdependent indomitable passive–aggressive woman.

Rounsaville then reviewed the sociological theories of the day, namely, that violence was modeled in the family of origin and that use of physical violence was accepted in North American society, and concluded that "[t]hese factors are unquestionably important. ... [H]owever, they are hardly specific enough to provide an explanation for the fact that wife-beating is not universal in our society but is only practiced in some marriages or relationships."[14] Rounsaville proposes a multifactorial model with features from several spheres. From the psychological sphere would be "pathological conflicts over dependency and autonomy," manifested in the men by "morbid jealousy" and controlling behavior, and an impulse control problem exacerbated by substance abuse. From the sociological sphere would be pressure to marry and distorted views of marital roles. Rounsaville's work was prescient; far ahead of its time and one of the few from the psychiatric literature to utilize psychological constructs with explanatory power and to link these, in turn, to sociological features. Rounsaville saw the importance of intimacy in wife assault, although this went largely unheeded and unrecognized for years to come. He saw the need for a multifactorial model years before a viable one was developed. His work was revolutionary. It was disregarded in the subsequent sociological tide. That sociological tide would emphasize gender dominance and power relations. But, as Rounsaville put it, "Even when the woman is in fact not of higher social status than her partner, she may be perceived as being more powerful and threatening by a man who is especially sensitive to domination by women."[15] Rounsaville saw through the facade of social power to the inner powerlessness felt in intimate relationships that was central to the abusive man.

This cycle was described as having three phases which could vary in timing and intensity for the same couple and between different couples: the tension-building phase, the explosion of acute battering, and the "calm, loving respite" behavior.

SUBTYPES OF WIFE ASSAULTERS

Do all battering relationships go through cycles? No, because there are different types of batterers. In 1988, I proposed a trimodal grouping of batterers: overcontrolled, generally violent (psychopathic), and borderline or cyclical.[16] Other researchers have also developed trimodal models, although their terminology varies, as is demonstrated in Table 1.1.

Essentially, these groups can be conceived of as existing on two dimensions of violence: over- versus undercontrolled, and impulsive versus instrumental. Overcontrolled men deny their rage while experiencing chronic frustration and resentment. Undercontrolled men act out frequently. Instrumental men use violence "coldly" to obtain specific objectives. Impulsive men act out violently in response to a building inner tension.

Only the impulsive men went through battering cycles. The overcontrolled batterers score high on avoidant personality disorders on general assessments (such as the Millon Clinical Multiaxial Inventory [MCMI], version II) which roughly map onto categories from the *Diagnostic and Statistical Manual of Mental Disorders*, third edition (DSM-III). They try to avoid conflict and deny anger. In treatment they repeatedly report having a week without anger (and consequently nothing to put in their anger log). The therapist gets them to track "irritations" and states of "subanger." The psycho-

TABLE 1.1. Batterer Classification

Hamberger and Hastings (1986)	Holtzworth-Munroe and Anglin (1991)	Saunders (1992)	Tweed and Dutton (in press)
Antisocial/ narcissistic	Generally violent/ antisocial	Type 2 (generally violent)	Instrumental/ undercontrolled
Schizoid/ borderline	Dysphoric/ borderline	Type 3 (emotionally volatile)	Impulsive/ undercontrolled
Dependent/ compulsive	Passive–dependent (family only)	Type 1 (emotionally suppressed)	Impulsive/ overcontrolled

pathic batterers also use violence outside the relationship that frequently brings them into conflict with the law. Their use of violence has an instrumental quality to it; it is used to control and intimidate. Borderline batterers, on the other hand, use violence expressively, to dispel accumulated tension. These differences are displayed in Figure 1.1.

In the first attempt to empirically establish subtypes, Kevin Hamberger and James Hastings (1986) administered the MCMI (version I) to 99 men in treatment for wife assault and factor-analyzed the results.[17] Three factors emerged which the authors called "schizoidal/borderline," "narcissistic/antisocial," and "passive-dependent/compulsive." In addition, combinations of these factor scores produced eight subgroups. Men who scored high on Factor 1 and low on the other factors, for example, were described as moody and sensitive to interpersonal slights, they were described by others as volatile and overreactive, as having a "Jekyll and Hyde" personality. The DSM-III diagnosis associated with this group was "borderline personality." These men demonstrated high levels of anxiety, anger, and depression as well as substance abuse problems. The high Factor 2 (low I and III) individuals had DSM diagnoses of narcissistic or antisocial personality disorder. Their violence was more instrumental in character and was used both inside and outside their intimate relationship. High Factor 3 (low I and II) were passive but tense and rigid. Subgroup 4 combined the angry, sullen

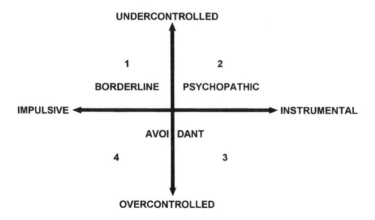

FIGURE 1.1. Two-dimensional representation of intimate abusiveness. 1, also called emotionally volatile (Saunders, 1992); 2, also called antisocial or sociopathic; 3, 4, avoidant personality loads highest on dominance/isolation.

features of Factor 1 with the aggressive, narcissistic qualities of Factor 2 to produce an extremely aggressive, psychopathic personality. Group 5 combined the sullen, moody, avoidant qualities of Factor 1 with the intense dependency needs of Factor 3 to create an extremely conflicted, frustrated, and dysphoric borderline syndrome. This group also had pronounced mood swings and periodic problems with reality testing. This group resembles the profile of men who could undergo the cyclical actions described by Walker's female respondents (see Chapter 4).

Daniel G. Saunders performed a "cluster analysis" on 182 batterers.[18] "Type 1" men reported the lowest anger levels but had the highest social desirability scores, suggesting repressed hostility. When Saunders adjusted the scores for social desirability, the Type 1 men matched the other two groups for anger and jealousy. Emotional suppression of anger was the central identifying feature of this group, making them appear clinically similar to Hamberger and Hastings's "Factor 3" men, or what we are calling overcontrolled. A later study of batterer typology by Holtzworth-Munroe and Stuart also described a trimodal categorization of batterers.[19] Included in this trilogy was a "generally violent/antisocial group" (similar to Hamberger and Hastings's "Factor 2" or subgroup 4) and a "dysphoric/borderline" group (similar to Factor 1, or subgroup 5). Unfortunately, the authors called their overcontrolled or passive–dependent batterers (Factor 3) "family only," which was somewhat misleading as most borderlines are family only batterers as well. In their typology the overcontrolled batterers came across as less pathological and with the least negative attitudes toward women. To the extent that they had any personality disorders, they were of the passive–dependent type. Clearly, they lack most of the flagrant "Cluster B" signs associated with batterers—emotional reactivity, anger, and jealousy. Just as clearly, they still erupt intermittently with violent rage. Recently, I began a study of men incarcerated for spousal homicide. I was surprised to find that 50% of the initial sample had been diagnosed by the prison psychiatrist as having "withdrawn personalities" such as schizoid or schizotypal and that few of these had any other crime record. Overcontrolled men generally try to please therapists. They are extremely cooperative in treatment, to the point that the therapist wonders how they could ever have been violent. When asked by the therapist to keep anger diaries, these men protest that they don't get angry often enough to log the events. Eventually the therapist convinces them to log their "irritations" (see Table 1.2).

TABLE 1.2. Characteristics of Overcontrolled Batterers

- Flat affect or constantly cheerful persona
- Attempts to ingratiate therapist
- Tries to *avoid* conflict
- High masked dependency
- High social desirability
- Overlap of violent and alcohol use
- Some drunk driving arrests
- Lists "irritations" in anger diary
- Chronic resentment
- Attachment: preoccupied
- MCMI: avoidant, dependent, passive–aggressive

Psychopathic batterers have the following features: a lack of the capacity to empathize; a tendency to use violence for control and instrumental gain; and, frequently, a history of antisocial actions and crime. Neil Jacobson's work at the University of Washington revealed another chilling aspect of their makeup; they demonstrate heart rate declines during heated arguments.[20] That is, despite acting in an emotionally aggressive fashion, these men, whom Jacobson called "vagal reactors," remained inwardly calm. (The term stems from the idea that excitation of the vagus nerve suppresses arousal.) The result of this autonomic suppression is to acutely focus attention on the external environment: the wife-antagonist. Jacobson found that the most belligerent and contemptuous men he studied were the ones who showed the greatest heart rate decrease. The clinical signs strongly suggest that vagal reactors are psychopaths. Indeed, this flat emotional response coupled with exaggerated control techniques are two of the defining criteria outlined in the seminal work on psychopaths by Robert D. Hare (see Table 1.3).[21] Hare describes this combination as a missing conscience and has MRI (magnetic resonance imaging) scans of brain function that demonstrate the lack of emotional response in psychopaths. Although Hare proposed a genetic basis for psychopathy, Stephen

TABLE 1.3. Characteristics of Psychopathy

- Rarely, if ever, arises de novo in adulthood (usually earlier indicator) (Lynam, 1996)
- "Vagal reactor" demonstrates heart rate decreases during intimate confrontation (Gottman et al., 1995)
- Early identification through combination of hyperactivity–impulsivity–attention deficit with conduct disorder (Lynam, 1996)
- Psychopaths commit disproportionate number of recidivist crimes (Hare, Forth, & Strachan, 1992)
- Criminal activity rises during teen years, remains high until the 40s, then declines (Hare, Forth, & Strachan, 1992)

TABLE 1.4. Characteristics of Impulsive/Undercontrolled Batterers

- Cyclical "phases"
- High levels of jealousy
- Violence predominantly/exclusively in intimate relationship
- High levels of depression, dysphoria, anxiety-based rage
- Ambivalence to wife/partner
- Attachment: fearful/angry
- MCMI: borderline

Porter had more recently suggested a "secondary psychopath," produced as a result of chronic abuse.[22]

Recently, Roger Tweed and I compared the instrumental and impulsive types of batterer (see Tables 1.4 and 1.5).[23] The impulsive men had more fearful "attachment styles" (which we will describe in detail in a later chapter) and psychological profiles more like a borderline personality.

The cyclical batterers described in this book are thus only one kind of personality-disordered batterer. But in many ways they are the most serious. The psychopathic batterers are often arrested for other, more public crimes. The overcontrolled batterers are much less frequent in their execution of the abuse (although they are a risk for spousal homicide, which is mercifully infrequent). The cyclical batterers have abuse that is frequent, predatory, and confined to their intimate relationship. They appear "normal"—even likable—in other relationships. They are hard to detect, and they are dangerous.

We will proceed in our analysis of these men in a chronological fashion, replicating the order of discovery that occurred for me. Early explanations of wife abuse were psychiatric, sociobiological, or feminist–sociological. The psychiatric explanations saw violence as essentially due to neurological dysfunction. The sociobiological

TABLE 1.5. Characteristics of Instrumental/Undercontrolled Batterers

- Violent inside and outside home
- History of antisocial behavior (car theft, burglary, violence)
- High acceptance of violence
- Negative attitudes of violence (macho)
- Usually victimized by extreme physical abuse as a child
- Low empathy
- Associations with criminal marginal subculture
- Attachment: dismissing
- MCMI: antisocial, aggressive–sadistic

perspective saw male assaultiveness as a dysfunctional form of control over contributions to the gene pool and as part of male inheritance. Sociological feminism also saw wife abuse as an expression of male power but viewed this as socially shaped. The latter two theories are broad in scope and have difficulty explaining variation in male responses. We review them in Chapter 2.

2

Early Explanations

ORGANIC BRAINS SYNDROMES AND RAGE RESPONSES

In the 1970s, academic research divided aggression into two categories: "normal" aggression, which was aggression directed either toward a stranger or an enemy, and "intimate violence," which was "abnormal," the act of madmen. Abnormal violence was viewed as having a physical basis, a structural flaw in a neural structure. In 1977, I went to an international conference of psychiatrists and criminal lawyers, noticing that some research papers were to be presented on wife assault. These papers, much to my disappointment, focused exclusively on neurological "causes" of wife assault. The complexity of intimate violence was being reduced to an electrical malfunction, a microstorm in the limbic system. The rich symbolic associations connected to the woman, associations from childhood and from cultural images, were ignored. Yet humans act on symbolism, and intimacy creates a confluence of the current intimate with idealized mother-saviors, projected mother-betrayers, whores, angels, and whatever other female imagery becomes stimulated by its onset. In effect, these psychiatrists were claiming that disturbances in a neural structure such as the temporal lobe could cause wife assault. More recently, Daniel Goleman's book *Emotional Intelligence* argues that startle responses of fear and rage (fight or flight) are generated by sensory messages proceeding first to the limbic system (thalamus and amygdala) before their subsequent processing by the neocortex.[1] This latter, "reasoned" reaction comes too late to stop the initial impulsive rage. Goleman does not, however, view limbic reactions as purely a function of "nature." Aspects of the "nurture" side of the equation also influence limbic function. Drawing on Allan N. Schore's work on early experience and brain maturation, Goleman argues that early emotional messages from parental treatment influence the development of the amygdala.[2] Psychiatrist Bessel van der Kolk had argued, in a similar vein, that separation and attachment disruption produced changes in the number and sensitivity of brain opioid receptors as well as permanent changes in neurochemistry and that "certain childhood experiences make people vulnerable to disorders of the neurotransmitter systems, which may later be activated under stress, particularly after the loss of affiliative bonds."[3] The etiology of the neurological disturbance was secondary in the theory of early psychiatry. What was essential was that neurological electrical storms caused impulsive outbreaks of rage.

An example of the original line of thought was an article by Frank Elliott, a psychiatrist at the Pennsylvania Hospital.[4] The article describes something called the "episodic dyscontrol syndrome," a term first coined by Karl Menninger, founder of the clinic named after him. Menninger had originally described episodic dyscontrol as an unconscious bodily reaction to chronic stress. It referred to episodes where a person suddenly and inexplicably went out of control, literally ran amok. It was beyond rational "ego" control and was explosive in nature. In this sense it stood out as a different level of reaction to stress, compared to the other types of stress adaptation, such as anxiety, neurotic symptoms, and psychosis. Episodic dyscontrol was listed in the fourth edition of the *Diagnostic and Statistical Manual of Mental Disorders* (DSM-IV) as one of the impulse control disorders called intermittent explosive disorder (IED) and given the official notation numbers of 312.34 (see Table 2.1). The diagnostic criteria included several discrete episodes of loss of control of aggressive impulses resulting in serious assaultive acts or destruction of property, where the degree of aggressiveness expressed was "grossly out of proportion to any precipitating psychosocial stressor (trigger)," there were no signs of generalized aggressiveness between episodes, and the episodes did not occur during the course of a psychotic disorder or other disorders (e.g.,

TABLE 2.1. Diagnostic Criteria for 312.34, Intermittent Explosive Disorder

A. Several discrete episodes of failure to resist aggressive impulses [occur] that result in serious assaultive acts or destruction of property.

B. The degree of aggressiveness expressed during the episodes is grossly out of proportion to any precipitating psychosocial stressors.

C. The aggressive episodes are not better accounted for by another mental disorder (e.g., antisocial personality disorder, borderline personality disorder, a psychotic disorder, a manic episode, conduct disorder, or attention-deficit/hyperactivity disorder) and are not due to the direct physiological effects of a substance (e.g., a drug of abuse, a medication) or a general medical condition (e.g., head trauma, Alzheimer's disease).

Note. From American Psychiatric Association (1994). Copyright 1994 by the American Psychiatric Association. Reprinted by permission.

psychopathy). In other words, the person is not psychotic and is generally not aggressive at all between "episodes" but then bursts out in a rage out of all proportion to whatever preceded it.

Elliott believed these episodes were caused by neurological firing, activity in the limbic system, that "ancient" part of the brain situated in the brain stem, underneath and behind the cerebral hemispheres. The limbic system is called ancient because it is believed to have developed far back in humanity's evolution, prior to the later development of the neocortex. It contains structures like the amygdala, the hippocampus, and the temporal lobe. These areas are believed to be the "seat of emotion," and stimulation of the amygdala in animals using microelectrodes produces rage or pleasure, depending on the exact location of the implant. Some locations will cause monkeys to press a bar repeatedly to keep the stimulation turned on. They literally press until they drop from exhaustion. Other locations cause monkeys to bare their teeth and attack.

Almost every psychology student has sat through the riveting film of Spanish neuropsychologist José Delgado, showing him dressed like a matador and being charged by a bull. The bull has received a microimplant in its limbic system that Delgado can activate by remote control. When Delgado flips the switch in a small control box, the bull stops in its tracks. Obviously, electrical activity in this area can have extensive effects on behavior associated with aggression. One kind of internally generated electrical activity in the brain is an epileptic seizure. Hence, to neurologists, this kind of epilepsy was a potential cause of uncontrollable aggression.

Elliott believed that temporal lobe epilepsy was the most common "organic" condition associated with explosive rage. Temporal lobe epilepsy, in turn, can be caused by any early trauma such as "an anoxic incident in early infancy" (the air supply is cut off) or "traumatic scars." Elliott never described his thoughts on the origin of these traumatic scars, nor did he speculate that temporal lobe epilepsy might be a consequence of childhood abuse victimization. Recent research is far more suggestive of a link. The excellent cross-generational studies by Byron Egeland have found a "transmission rate" of maltreatment from one generation to the next of 40% (meaning that 40% of adults who maltreat their children were themselves maltreated as children),[5] and psychologists Rosenbaum and Hoge have found that 61% of men assessed for outpatient treatment for wife assault had received prior head injuries.[6] The suggested causal pathway was early physical trauma (such as blows to the head) causing temporal lobe epilepsy, which in turn caused IED. Was head trauma leading to temporal lobe epilepsy the source of these outbursts? We will suggest in this book that physical trauma in the childhood of abusive men constitutes a mere "tip of the iceberg" of the sum total of traumatic victimization they sustained.

I must add that my own clinical experience has been that men come into our treatment group who do have the obvious "soft signs" of neurological disorder. These sometimes include pronounced nystagmus (jerky or saccadic eye movement) and attention deficits. One such man completed the treatment and then went on to reoffend six more times (one-sixth of all the posttreatment assaults in a group of 156 men!).

Metabolic disorders can also cause explosive rage. Elliott described a case of matricide triggered by hypoglycemia in a man who had suffered brain damage at birth or infancy. Elliott described the features of dyscontrol as being episodes of intense rage "triggered by trivial irritations and accompanied by verbal or physical violence."[7] He noted that the individual usually had a "warm, pleasant personality" but also had "a history of traffic accidents resulting from aggressive driving." More recent psychiatric explanations have maintained this focus. A study by Felthous and Bryant in 1991 is typical.[8] The authors found a subgroup of 15 men (out of 443 studied) whom they diagnosed with IED. The typical victim of their outburst was "a spouse, lover, or boyfriend/girlfriend."[9] In study after study, these neurological "explanations" seem to avoid the fact that the violence only occurs in the context of intimacy and typically in private. These contextual features suggest certain specific triggers for aggression overlooked by the focus on "uncontrollable" violence.

The literary example provided by Elliott unintentionally under-scored this problem with the entire concept of impulse disorder. Elliott cites Émile Zola's character named Jacques in his novel *La Bête Humaine*, whom Elliott describes as "a man with the symptoms of temporal lobe epilepsy who could not always control an urge to kill women who attracted him."[10] How does a neurological disorder lead one to only attack attractive women? Or, to restate our earlier question, why would these men only attack their wives and only in private? There is something else going on beside neural firing. Some neurological disorders, such as Tourette's syndrome, can be control-led by the afflicted person under specific, focused circumstances. Does this model also describe the abusive male? Or is there something in the specificity of intimacy that triggers rage? Clearly, some higher order process of mental association—some associations of the meaning of the target person to the perpetrator and the context of the violence—must direct and influence the act of vio-lence. What does the man's wife mean to him? What symbolic baggage does this man carry from his earlier days that gives shape to this meaning? Is there something special about intimacy that alters the meaning of the other person?

The insufficient nature of the activation of neural mechanisms to explain molar behavior is demonstrated by another classic study by José Delgado (as cited in Bandura, 1979). In this study, stimula-tion of an area of the temporal lobe in a dominant male monkey produced a rage response: teeth baring and attack. Stimulation of the same area in a subordinate monkey produced withdrawal: cowering and huddling in the corner of the cage.[11] To social psychologist Albert Bandura, this finding of Delgado's suggested that direct stimulation of brain systems was never a direct cause of aggression but that aggression always had learned aspects to it. The "prepotent" (most used) response at the time of the brain stimula-tion was the response that was evoked by the stimulation. That habitual response would change with the circumstances. The domi-nant monkey had learned to attack; attack was at the top of its hierarchy of responses, the one most likely to be used when neural mechanisms were kicked into action by any triggering event. Sub-missive monkeys had learned that any attempt to attack would be met by severe punishment. Their response hierarchies changed: they learned to supplicate. The dominant monkeys and submissive monkeys made opposite responses to stimulation of the same brain area. The "neural mechanism" did not have functions that were permanently fixed, and the decision to attack or curl into a ball or show the jugular vein (in an act of submission) seemed to be based in part on what expectations were generated at that time by being in a particular social status.

Years later, in a study on humans, my colleagues and I found that human emotional responses were very much determined by this same hierarchical status.[12] We measured the emotional reactions of people while they were listening to recordings of family arguments. Some of these people were assigned to low positions in a hierarchical group created for the experiment; others had high-status positions. We created "on the spot" bosses and underlings by giving "the bosses" control over the "final edit" of a report the group had to write about a family argument. People in these two status positions experienced the same family arguments differently. In these human experiments, however, greater rage was associated with low status, the opposite of what the monkey studies found. In either case, however, status mattered. There was no direct line from a neural event to broader actions like rage. The context in which rage could be acted out influences not only the choice of action but the very experience of emotion. The shortcut to the amygdala described by Daniel Goleman may only apply to "knee-jerk reactions" but not to sustained aggression.

A question was left unanswered by these early psychiatric "explanations": How do we explain the direction of rage projected outward only in specific circumstances and at specific targets (like Zola's attractive women) when the problem is attributed to either a neurological disorder or a diagnostic label such as IED? Why, for example, would the rage not be generalized to whatever targets are available—to, in effect, whomever is around at the time? Why would Felthous and Bryant's perpetrators only direct their rage toward someone with whom they were in an intimate relationship?

Neurological explanations for wife assault would suggest that the action would be expressed at random and not in selected circumstances (e.g., directed only toward an intimate and only in private). While there is some evidence that a tick disorder (such as Tourette's syndrome) can be controlled under certain social circumstances, it is unlikely that a complex action such as wife assault could be similarly repressed. The research data on wife assault suggest that this is not a random act. More is going on. Something takes over that guides the focus of rage toward the woman and is heightened by a perceived threat of loss.

The 1970s' alternative explanations were developing. Feminist analyses focused on hierarchical aspects of the social order and provided an answer for this missing context of psychiatric research, examining the power relationships between men and women. This perspective saw the use of violence by men as serving a function—that of control. At the same time, another perspective developed that supplied a motive for that control. This perspective suggested that male control, rage, and jealousy were inherited reactions to a biological mandate. The purpose of all three was to guarantee "genetic fitness," on, in other words, to ensure that no other male might be the biological father of one's children. This perspective was called sociobiology.

THE GENETIC MANDATE

Originating in the biological work of E. O. Wilson at Harvard, sociobiology came to be applied to understanding human social behavior, including cooperation and competition and intimate aggression.[13] Sociobiology is the field of study that views human social behaviors as inherited through a process of natural selection. Is violence toward an intimate partner the product of more than a million years of evolution? Are men who coerce and intimidate their wives simply playing out a sociobiological mandate handed down through natural selection? The implications of such a thought are staggering. If intimate violence is "hot wired" into our evolutionary makeup, is it then inevitable? Should we punish individual transgressors? Can we conceivably stop the violence through short-term treatment—stop in 16 weeks what took several thousand generations to develop? Is intimate violence part of "human nature"?

Beginning with Charles Darwin's idea that changes in physical characteristics were gradually acquired through natural selection, sociobiologists have argued that this acquisition happened for certain evolutionary advantageous social behaviors as well. Natural selection is that process by which those physical characteristics or behaviors that have survival value will be passed on to offspring. Those members of a species that do not exhibit such behaviors will die off. Having failed to make their genetic contribution, they will diminish in number and eventually be "selected out" of a species. Those that do exhibit them will live longer, have more progeny, and "maximize their contribution to the gene pool." This means that certain members of a species behave in such a way as to increase the chances of their having offspring who survive to further transmit their genes. This is referred to as the behavior's evolutionary function. Dominance in animal species, for example, was believed to confer two kinds of evolutionary advantage: the dominant animal took precedence over the subordinate in both mating and feeding; thus dominance itself was seen to have evolutionary benefit. The more dominant animal would eat better, mate more, and hence generate more offspring.[14]

According to the animal studies, larger, stronger animals typically became dominant and males were dominant over females. The political ramifications of where this was leading caused a lot of discomfort among people who saw it as a sort of scientific rationalization for patriarchy.[15] However, it was still a big jump to claiming that this had anything to do with human behavior. But that was coming. In 1962, in what was a predecessor to later sociobiology, W. E. Simeons, in a book entitled *Man's Presumptuous Brain,* argued that adult human emotion had sociobiological antecedents. Men, according to Simeons, had a genetic predisposition to react to sexual threat with rage.[16] How this rage might be manifested was not specified, but Simeons was painting a picture of male jealousy as a "natural" response that had evolutionary value. The "alpha" male gorilla beating its chest to deter would-be interlopers and maintain access to females in the tribe was seen as a direct predecessor of contemporary jealous display in higher primates (including human males). Later sociobiologists have been careful to argue that what is inherited is not full-blown behaviors but impulses. That is, a twinge or arousal blip may be the residual reaction of evolutionary forces. Of course, how that arousal blip is read, interpreted, or "labeled" by a person in contemporary society may have more to do with the rules of the ambient culture than with the original evolutionary payoff.

In the 1980s, the application of sociobiology to human behavior escalated with Don Symons's *The Evolution of Human Sexuality,* David Buss's *The Evolution of Desire,* and Martin Daly and Margo Wilson's *Homicide.*[17] All three books (among others) focus sociobiological analysis on human intimate relationships.

Buss explored the sexual predilections of 10,000 people in 37 cultures and found some worldwide transcultural effects, one of which was that men's sexual strategies were short term and promiscuous. They would consider sharing their genes with any woman who met their mating standard, namely, that she be young, healthy, and physically attractive. They were more likely than were women to tolerate situations where their partner formed a deep, nonsexual relationship with someone else but were subject to fits of jealousy at the prospect of sexual infidelity. Women took a longer view. When asked how many sexual partners they would desire during a lifetime, on average women say five, men say eighteen. In the ideal mate, women emphasize economic success, dependability, and commitment; men emphasize physical attractiveness.

Buss argued that both strategies made evolutionary sense. Females are guaranteed their genetic fitness because fertilization occurs internally; males do not have this guarantee. Consequently, for the male, the way to maximize genetic fitness is to have exclusive sexual access to as many sexual partners as possible—to maintain and enact a double standard (polygamy for him, monogamy for each partner). The female genetic mandate is quite different and focuses on successful bearing and care of the child. This can best be done with the cooperation of a resourceful, loyal mate who will assist her in these matters—who is, in other words, monogamous and faithful. These strategies, while both evolutionarily sound, are incompatible. Both strategies cannot be played out without conflict. Buss argues that emotions such as anger and jealousy are the inevitable signals of this sociobiological conflict. Buss also found that when men could not get women to cooperate with their sexual strategies, they tended to switch strategies to those of women. Power, in other words, plays an important part. When women are scarce (because of economic, geographic, or demographic conditions), they call the shots and monogamy prevails. When women are relatively abundant (because, say, more girls were born than boys, or wars killed many men), men are less likely to commit to monogamy.[18]

Male abuse of intimate partners occurred, according to sociobiologists, as a method of coercive control. What is crucial for the male to control, of course, is the woman's reproductive exclusivity. Hence, jealousy will be the most important precursor to intimate violence. Insults about her physical appearance generate power by undercutting the woman's self-esteem, hence, improving the chances of sexual exclusivity.[19] It is this last argument that represents the cornerstone of the sociobiological view that males try to dominate intimate females in order to guarantee sexual exclusivity. As Buss puts it, "women are more often the victims and men are more often the perpetrators of condescension and other forms of psychological abuse. . . . [V]ictims often feel that, because their mating alternatives are not rosy, they must strive valiantly to placate the current mate. . . . [M]en's motives for physically battering women center heavily on coercive control."[20]

Sociobiologists Daly and Wilson extended this view of abuse and violence as coercive control to spousal homicides. They examined homicide rates for a variety of countries and demographic groups and argued that spousal homicide represented "slip-ups in a power struggle." As they put it "although homicide probably does not serve the interests of the perpetrator, it is far from clear that the same can be said of sublethal violence. . . . Men . . . strive to control women; women struggle to resist coercion and maintain their choices. There is brinkmanship and the risk of disaster in any such contest; and homicides by spouses of either sex may be considered slips in the dangerous game."[21] Daly and Wilson then provide data on spousal homicide to attempt to prove their point. These data come from a number of countries and seem to show that males are more often the perpetrators of spousal homicide. The United States is an anomaly: the ratio there (of husband perpetrators to wife perpetrators) is about 1.3:1, compared with a 3.3:1 to 6:1 ratio in other "industrialized" countries.[22] Daly and Wilson examined in detail a sample of 1,060 spousal homicides in Canada and found that adultery and jealousy were the most frequent motives cited in police reports. For men, jealousy was mentioned explicitly by the police in 195 of 812 cases (for women, the corresponding figures were 19 out of 248). An additional motive scored as "arguments" by the police contained strong themes of sexual proprietariness.[23]

What the sociobiological perspective adds to our understanding of intimate abuse is a potential reason for its theme of jealousy. From the sociobiological perspective, abandonment is not a re-creation of earlier attachment fears but rather the immanent loss of an ability to procreate. The sexual content of verbal abuse of a female is a way of embarrassing her into submission by calling out the cultural expletives for a loose woman. All forms of emotional abuse are coercive techniques designed to generate submission. Sociobiology and feminism analyze abuse in terms of gender. Sociobiologists and feminists agree that males attempt to coerce intimate females, and sociobiologists supply a motive for that coercion—reproductive fitness. Disproportionate male jealousy stems from a lack of certainty about one's contribution to the gene pool, something that is ensured for women. This male uncertainty then generates higher rates of violence and even homicide based on jealousy motives.

Problems exist with the sociobiological view, however. In a nutshell, these have to do with the enormous variation in individual differences in the use of intimate aggression. It is important not to lose sight of the fact that the majority of men are not physically abusive during the duration of their marriages, that a smaller minority are violent once, and that a tiny minority are repeatedly abusive. How does one explain this in general statements about "genetic fitness"? Furthermore, even if they are angry, how they behave to, express the anger varies: some men simply stifle it; others direct it toward themselves; others, toward a third party; still others, toward their female partners.[24]

Buss erroneously views women as "more often the victims and men . . . more often the perpetrators of condescension and other forms of psychological abuse," a politically correct but factually incorrect claim. Marilyn Kasian and Susan Painter found that verbal abuse was more frequently committed by women than by men in a group of college-age dating couples they studied.[25] Also, a study by Gwat-Yong Lie and her colleagues (discussed later in this chapter) showed that women in lesbian relationships used physical, verbal, and sexual aggression more than did heterosexual males.[26] If verbal abuse is higher in lesbian relationships, is this serving a function of protecting "genetic fitness"? I think not. Gender differences exist not in the general level of violence committed in intimate relationships but in the greater tendency of males to use violence in response to perceived abandonment. In other words, comparisons of genders find that males are not more abusive in general than are females.[27] A gender difference exists not for overall rates of abuse but for the circumstances that trigger abuse, Males, for example, are more likely to react abusively to perceived abandonment than are females. Spousal homicide, for example, occurs much more frequently for estranged female victims than for male victims.[28] If the sociobiological mandate of reproductive fitness creates such huge gender differences why are the empirical studies obtaining these results? Even E. O. Wilson, the father of modern sociobiology, conceded that history and social context contributed to human behavior at least as much as biology. But this context is a void for sociobiologists.

In a way, there was a type of retrospective functionalism about all this. Almost anything can be seen as having served the function of maximizing reproductive fitness in retrospect. Cooperation, aggression, even hierarchy serve a purpose and, under the right circumstances, are useful and beneficial. But does that mean that the function served is the original motive for the particular behavior's occurrence? Just because we can see a case for cooperation in hindsight, does this mean that cooperation evolved through natural selection? How might it be transmitted? Is there a gene for cooperation and another for aggression? If so, they have not yet been found. And, in any event, is such animal behavior generally a good indicator of what happens in humans? Are we not far more complex? After all, we have that prolonged period of vulnerability–dependency that other species don't share. But what if that too was a product of evolutionary forces?

What's more, the logic of sociobiology is a problem. For one thing, if sexual threat is so great for males, why not turn their aggression against other men who are perceived as threats? Why do we not have a larger problem with men aggressing toward other men who are perceived as interlopers? Only 20 of 164 male–male homicides investigated by Daly and Wilson were jealousy conflicts (and we don't know how many of those may have been gay lovers). Males killing their sexual rivals occurs with much less frequency than the killing of estranged partners. Why is this the evolutionary sound response? If she may be pregnant and some other male is going to raise your child, why not move on and impregnate someone else?

How does one man become jealous over events that are meaningless to another? How do these individual differences originate? Sociobiology says that they are due to the "necessities of the environment" or "the previous history of a group."[29] But do these vague statements really explain the differences? Even if two men become equally jealous, will they both become angry? Not always. Some men get depressed as well as jealous. Why the emotional variation? Sociobiology can't answer that. In fact, if we examine men closely, we will see that they vary greatly in terms of their arousability, jealousy when aroused, and anger when jealous.[30] Buss didn't say how one group of men might come to be emotionally unstable and mistrusting while another did not. He didn't make it clear how sociobiology *could* explain this individual variation. This problem of individual variation is something that sociobiologists have not dealt with. Daly and Wilson don't even try to explain the discrepancies in spousal homicide ratios. If our inheritance from our sociobiological past is so great, why aren't we more alike?[31]

Are men really that concerned with maximizing the number of their offspring? I have a colleague with 16 children who seems to be the sociobiological ideal man. Apart from that I know very few men of my generation who either desire or have more than two children. Doesn't sociobiology confuse sex with procreation? Apart from the "macho" notion that the number of children translates into virility, is this really a major goal for most men? If most men preferred sex without procreation, would this create a difficulty for sociobiology? And if sex is the stronger motive, what psychological meaning does sex have for men? What unanticipated emotional consequences?

Finally, if we are going to have a sociobiology of gender that uses gender as a main classification system and focuses on differences in male and female behavior, let's look at one more piece of data. Suicide statistics indicate that males are far more likely than women to commit suicide. The difference exists by age 5 and increases throughout the lifetime. By age 22, males are 6 times as likely as females to kill themselves; by age 85, they are 15 times more likely.[32] Also, men are 11 times more likely to commit suicide than are women during a relationship breakup.[33] How do sociobiologists explain this? What is its evolutionary function?

One other implication from sociobiology is that social power influences behavior. As Buss puts it, men adapt a female procreation strategy when they do not have the power to impose their own. Hence, it would seem to follow that social power must interact with what we might call the "sociobiological imperative" to determine sexual strategy. If men prefer a double standard of sexual behavior and if, as feminists say, men have all the power, why then are most men monogamous?

Does this mean that I want to throw out sociobiology altogether? No. I think its broad application to gender psychology doesn't hold up. Sociobiologists assume that men are more alike and that the genders are more different than the data reveal. However, there is still one branch of influence that sociobiology has on contemporary theory. John Bowlby's connection of sociobiology to attachment, which we will examine below, seems promising to me. But what Bowlby does is to develop, through attachment theory, an idea of how subgroups may set off on their separate paths. The attachment theorists have taken pains to show how developmental

experiences of an individual can alter the direction of this sociobiological mandate. Could attachment provide a basis for a personality that manifests itself only in intimate relationships and is distinctly
different from that personality shown to the world? We will pursue
this idea below. The social contextual features that E. O. Wilson
alluded to were prominently featured in feminist–sociological explanations of abuse as male domination.

SOCIOLOGICAL FEMINISM: THE ROLE OF PATRIARCHY

In *Conjugal Crime,* author Terry Davidson outlines key contributors
and signs in the social history of wife abuse.[34] This was a history
that occurred as far as the retrospective eye could see, a history of
abuse toward women that was sanctioned by organized religion and
the law. From the Old Testament advocacy of stoning women who
could not prove their virginity, to church exhortation of men to
uphold their divine responsibility of beating their wives, to Gratian's
Decretum, a 12th-century "philosophical" basis for church law which
decreed that "[w]omen should be subject to their men. . . . [W]oman
is not made [in] God's image. . . . Woman's authority is nil. . . .
Adam was beguiled by Eve . . . not she by him. It is right that he
whom woman led into wrongdoing should have her under his
direction so that he may not fall a second time through female
levity."[35] This conception of women guided Christian ethics and
laws throughout the Middle Ages, including the infamous Inquisi-
tion and the witch trials in Europe in which 300,000 women were
burned at the stake. Fra Cherubino's *Rules of Marriage,* which was
written in the 15th century and guided the Catholic Church for
some 400 years, gave husbands the following advice on conjugal
conduct: "scold her sharply, bully and terrify her. And if that . . .
doesn't work, take up a stick and beat her soundly, for it is better
to punish the body and correct the soul than to damage the soul
and spare the body."[36] This notion of "chastisement" still appears
in the rationalizations abusive men make for their violence toward
wives.

Davidson's interpretation of gender history was that men were
terrified by the mystery of women and their inexplicable ability to
create life. They converted the terror into control (something that
batterers still do) and found sociolegal ways of repressing and
subjugating that threatening female force. This was achieved partly

by attributing various "evil" traits to women, thereby justifying the need for such repression. These included, in the Middle Ages, susceptibility to the influences of the devil, precisely described in Jakob Sprenger and Heinrich Krämer's *Malleus Maleficarum* (1486) and, in modern times, "penis envy" (Freud's assertion that women generally have feelings of inferiority and resentment because they lack a penis).[37] The institutions of religion, the law, and now psychotherapy all seem to have contributed to a male conspiracy to subjugate women. William Blackstone's *Commentaries on the Laws of England* (1765–1769), which influenced U.S. law, saw nothing unreasonable about wife beating.[38] Since the husband was to answer for her misbehavior, the law thought it reasonable to entrust him with "the power of chastisement." The Napoleonic Code, which influenced much of European law, saw the husband as the absolute power in a "strong family." The patriarchy was enshrined in the legal codes of the day. These early church codes served as recipes for abuse: husbands should have absolute power over their wives; women were inherently weak and susceptible to the influence of the devil; corrective punishment was the husbands' duty. In recent times, feminist scholars have clarified the impact of this combination of religious doctrine, self-serving superstition and legal code on the beliefs of the everyday man.

From this historical evidence, the everyday experience of women in the shelter movement, and a new feminist academic scholarship, a perspective was created that focused, on the role of patriarchy and male domination of women in perpetuating wife abuse. As Michelle Bograd put it, "All feminist researchers, clinicians and activists address a primary question: Why do men beat their wives?" she distinguishes feminists from others who ask, "What psychopathology leads to violence?" or "Why are people involved in violent interactions in families."[39] Bograd goes on to write, "feminists seek to understand why *men in general* use physical force against their partners and what functions this serves for a society in a given historical context."[40]

From this perspective, wife assault was seen as a systematic form of domination and social control of women by men. All men could potentially use violence as a powerful means of subordinating women. Men as a class benefited from how women's lives are restricted because of their fear of violence. For this reason, men have traditionally been loath to restrict other men's abusiveness. They benefit from it because of its symbolic implications for their own status vis-à-vis their wives. Wife abuse reinforces women's dependence and enables all men to exert authority and control. The reality of domination at the societal level is the most crucial factor contributing to, and maintaining, wife abuse at the individual level. The maintenance of patriarchy and patriarchal institutions is the main contributor to wife assault. Wife assault is "normal" violence stemming from commonly held beliefs that patriarchy is a "natural order," that the man is the head of the household and the use of violence to maintain this prerogative is acceptable; it is not the actions of "madmen" who are dissimilar from other men. The argument from a feminist analytical perspective, therefore, is that the use of violence to maintain male domination is accepted because it maintains the patriarchy—the status quo with men at the top of the power hierarchy. In the words of researchers R. E. and R. P. Dobash, "Men who assault their wives are actually living up to cultural prescriptions that are cherished in Western society—aggressiveness, male dominance and female subordination—and they are using physical force as a means to enforce that dominance."[41]

Clearly, sociological feminism has focused on social structure rather than individual factors as causing male abusiveness. Patriarchy is the major cause of wife assault rather than a guiding inducement that interacts with other causes. As Michelle Bograd put it, "the reality of domination at the social level is the most crucial factor contributing to and maintaining wife abuse at the personal level."[42] Domination of women is viewed, from the feminist perspective, as a cultural mandate, and violence against women as an instrument in achieving that mandate. This emphasis on the sociocultural viewpoint generated a general unwillingness to consider psychological causes of male violence, as these could serve both to exonerate male violence and to deflect the focus from necessary social change.[43] Hence, studies of psychopathology in batterers might well deflect the focus from the "normal psychological and behavioral patterns of most men"; moreover, "trait theories [of abusiveness] tend to excuse the abusive man through reference to alcohol abuse or poor childhood histories."[44] In other words, a poor psychological background is too often used as an excuse for an individual perpetrator, simultaneously exonerating him and undercutting our will to change the society that fostered his behavior.

The result of the feminist analysis of wife assault has been the acknowledgment of the powerful and complex role of social factors in creating the context in which violence occurs. It was this very

context that psychiatric explanations overlooked. Men who assaulted their wives may or may not have been suffering from
temporal lobe epilepsy, but even if they were the direction of their
rage at their wife suggested learned elements of violence.

Feminism pointed out that the learning of controlling behaviors
was a product of male sex role socialization. The need to be in
control was very much a part of the male mythos. What's more, this
control was always directed outward. Males were woefully inept at
monitoring or controlling what was within, that is, emotions like
anger or jealousy. The ensuing feminist focus was on power,
domination, male privilege, and other social context factors overlooked by the narrow focus of psychiatry. Feminists were also not
comfortable with the tone of sociobiology, which to their ears made
male dominance, philandery, and abuse sound like an inevitable
biological mandate, or a blueprint drawn by hundreds of thousands
of years of evolution.

Feminist analyses led to important research findings. Angela
Browne and Kirk Williams, two researchers at the Family Violence
Laboratory at the University of New Hampshire, showed on a
state-by-state basis how female-perpetrated homicide decreased
when criminal justice system resources became more available to
women in abusive relationships, a pattern that was distinct from
male homicide.[45] Women's homicides seemed to be based more on
self-defense against an abusive partner. When the police took an
active role and legal protection was put in place, these homicides
became fewer.

Also, feminist analysis led to a close scrutiny of the instruments
used by researchers to record abuse. The Conflict Tactics Scale
especially came under attack for simplistically equating "hits" by
males against females with hits by females. Angela Browne showed
that the Conflict Tactics Scale could not be used to compare male
and female violence.[46] Every assessed act on the Conflict Tactics
Scale is different when performed by a man. The reasons have to
do with the greater force of the action, the relative strength of the
perpetrator and target, the point of impact of the action, and the
target's ability to resist or escape. What's more, since the male
perpetrator knows that the effects of his violent actions will be
greater, this changes the assessment of the intent of male violence.
It becomes intended to hurt, control, or destroy. Female violence,
except when a weapon is used, would not have these anticipated
consequences and hence would have a different motivation.

Browne's argument shows the dangers of removing context from the measurement process and merely counting hits in comparing male and female violence. It led to a reassessment of using the Conflict Tactics Scale to compare male violence with female violence out of context. That danger, as she put it, was like "equating a head-on collision with a fender bender."

Eventually all theories have to "face the music" provided by research data. They have to bow before the God of Fact. The research data on wife assault provided a more complicated picture that any of the broad-spectrum theories like sociobiology or feminism could explain. Men who grew up in a common social context or socializing culture showed enormous individual differences in their intimate behaviors. A number of large sample surveys done in the United States and Canada from 1975 to 1992[47] used female interviewers, interviewed female respondents, and were extremely sophisticated in generating open disclosure of private actions. The results of these surveys were remarkably consistent: about 25% of women reported their spouse as using violence at some time in the marriage. Most of this was of the nature of pushing or slapping. Serious violence that could cause injury occurred in 8–12% of marriages. About 6–8% of men used serious violence repeatedly, some on a weekly basis. There was, as a social scientist put it, a "skewed distribution"; that is, a few men committed a lot of intimate violence, while most men committed none.

Just as variation existed in male physical abusiveness, considerable variation exists in family power arrangements. Diane H. Coleman and Murray A. Straus assessed marital power by having respondents indicate "who has the final say" in making decisions about buying a car, having children, what house or apartment to take, what job either partner should take, whether a partner should go to work or quit, and how much money to spend on food each week.[48] By classifying couples into whether the male or female had the "final say," four power types were generated: male dominant, female dominant, divided power, and equalitarian. Equalitarians make most decisions jointly, whereas divided power types divide responsibility or decisions. In a sample of 2,022 people from the 1975 U.S. national violence survey, 9.4% of couples were classified as male dominant, 7.5% as female dominant. The rest described their marriages as the divided power type (54%) or as the equalitarian type (29%). These results seemed to indicate that a variety of power types existed and that male dominance was more rare than portrayed in feminist views. Furthermore, a more accurate picture of physical abuse was that of a small minority of men generating a high level of repeated serious abuse. The majority of men, in the meantime, remain nonabusive.

These studies raised a question: *Why do some men become domineering and abusive while others do not?* Were they not all raised under the same socializing influences in the same society? This question is difficult for a feminist analysis to answer because feminist focus has been on gender—those socializing influences that make males and females different—not on the psychological factors that might explain why some men are abusive while most are not. Yet if men raised in the same culture exhibit such dramatic differences in their relationships with women, something else must be at work in their individual makeup. Something must have happened to these men to make some domineering and abusive in intimate relationships whereas others (the majority if we are to believe the Coleman and Straus study) are not. Whatever is driving these men to be abusive, it has to involve more than just social norms.

Even more perplexing data were to come. In the early 1990s, incidence data began to be published on lesbian violence by Claire M. Renzetti and by Gwat-Yong Lie and her colleagues.[49] The latter study was particularly fascinating. Lie and her associates conducted a survey of 350 lesbians in Tucson. Their names were drawn from a mailing list of a lesbian organization. About a third returned questionnaires.

A second sample was recruited by word of mouth through lesbian supporters of the research project in Phoenix. The women who responded were on the average about 34 years old, predominantly white and well educated. The entire sample was 170 lesbian women. Part two of the study asked the women to indicate whether they had been the target of sexual, verbal, or physical abuse "with an intimate partner." Of the sample of 170 women, 120 indicated that they had either been victimized or used aggression against an intimate partner in the past and 136 had had prior relationships with both women and men. The researchers then probed for the types of violence, the gender of the partner, etc. These women provided a rare opportunity. They served, in effect, as their own control group for what are called "within subject" comparisons. In effect, by comparing each woman's reports of being abused by men in her past with reports of being abused by women, the researchers could compare abuse victimization rates for heterosexual and lesbian relationships. Feminist theory would predict that abuse rates would be higher in the former, since intimate abuse is propagated by male domination. The surprising result was that the sample reported being abused more frequently in the past by lesbian partners than by male partners. This was true for all kinds of abuse victimization, even sexual abuse (a 42% victimization rate by men, 57% by women). This study provided a rare opportunity to separate the effects of intimacy from the effects of male domination, something that had not happened in prior research on predominantly heterosexual couples. One conclusion suggested by the findings is that some felt experience that is part of intimacy itself may play a role in generating abusiveness. That experience might be connected to the type of feelings produced in intimate relationships. Renzetti's study showed what some of these feelings might be. In her study of lesbian women, dependency and jealousy were major contributors to the use of physical violence. As we shall see below, these issues are also major contributors to violence by males against their wives and to violence by gay males against their intimate partners. What seems to be at work is a set of psychological reactions to intimate relationships that serves to generate violence. Dependency and jealousy seem to be part of this profile. Whatever this profile may be, it will exhibit variation in males. While jealousy, for example, may have origins in the protection of one's biological mandate or in perceived societal expectations about maleness, males vary in their experience of and expression of jealousy, as well as violence in response to jealousy.

Theories that can explain human variation are not broad based but more individually focused, that is, psychological. The first and most comprehensive psychological theory of aggression is social learning theory. The next chapter introduces the reader to the contributions of social learning to understanding wife assault and to its limitations.

3

Learning of Abusiveness

From 1963 to the present, psychologist Albert Bandura produced a series of research studies that showed how habits could be acquired through observation and maintained by rewarding consequences. Bandura initially found that children who watched an adult aggressively attack an inflatable "Bobo doll" and were then frustrated by the experimenter were more likely to display aggression than children who had not observed that adult aggression. This happened regardless of whether the children watched the adult live, on film, or in cartoon form.[1] Follow-up studies found that this effect was enhanced when the adult was of high status or when the children were dependent.[2] This "modeling" of aggression led to aggressive tendencies that could only be temporarily suppressed by punishment, and the suppression only occurred when the punishing parent was present. The aggression became redirected and was expressed when that parent was absent. Aggressive adolescent boys typically had physically punitive fathers. The physical punishment of these boys produced in the schoolyard the very activity the parent tried to suppress at home.

Derived from earlier learning experiments with animals, social learning theory analyzes the acquisition of habits: chronic, repeated ways of doing things. Taking learning into the human realm, social learning discovered that the principle means of human learning was through observation. From the perspective of social learning theory, physical abuse is a habit, a learned means of coping with stress. Every time it succeeds in reducing the stress or eliminating the circumstances that produced the stress, it becomes more fixed, more entrenched. That success provides the "reward" that sustains and deepens the habit.

By understanding the circumstances contributing to this acquisition, the habit can be "undone" or altered. Social learning principles, as we shall see in a later chapter, formed the basis for the first treatment groups for assaultive males. The goal of treatment was to get the males to analyze their use of anger and abuse and to learn other ways of expressing anger.

All habits have three aspects or components that help us to understand why they persist: the first is the origin of the habit; the second is the "instigator" (the event that triggers the violence); and the third is the "regulator" (reactions to the violence that either snuff it out or keep it alive). One origin of a habit can be the very body we inherit. Large muscular men inherit a higher probability that they will be rewarded for physical actions, including violence. They might learn while still boys that conflicts can be resolved through aggression. But origins such as these simply set limits or create an opportunity for reward. In this sense, reward is defined as the attainment of what is wanted or the achievement of one's objectives. Muscular people do not inherit the tendency to be physical (or violent); they inherit the body that makes physical actions more likely to succeed. Once they are rewarded for using physical actions, they are likely to repeat them. Experiments in both animal and human learning show that we repeat unconsciously the actions that are rewarded. Occasional reward strengthens the tendency to use violence, and a habit develops. Activity level, physical stature, and musculature, for example, are all inherited and are viewed as setting limits on the types of aggressive responses that can be developed and influencing the rate at which learning progresses. The inherited muscular body will not, by itself, determine aggression but only create a learning–reward opportunity. In this way, social learning theory acknowledges biological influences on behavior (see Table 3.1). Learning can be governed by physical endowment, which can influence the probability of aggressive responses being rewarded.

TABLE 3.1. Social Learning Analysis of Behavior

Origins of aggression	Instigators of aggression	Regulators of aggression

Observational learning
Reinforced performance
Structural determinants
	Modeling influences
	  Disinhibitory
	  Facilitative
	  Arousing
	  Stimulus enhancing
		External reinforcement
		  Tangible rewards
		  Social and status rewards
		  Expressions of injury
		  Alleviation of aversive
		    treatment

	Aversive treatment
	  Physical assaults
	  Verbal threats and
	    insults
	  Adverse reductions in
	    reinforcement
	  Thwarting
		Punishment
		  Inhibitory
		  Informative
		
		Vicarious reinforcement
		  Observed reward
		  Observed punishment

	Incentive inducements
	Instructional control
	Bizarre symbolic control
		Self-reinforcement
		  Self-reward
		  Self-punishment
		  Neutralization of
		    self-punishment
		  Moral justification
		  Palliative comparison
		  Euphemistic labeling
		  Displacement of
		    responsibility
		  Diffusion of
		    responsibility
		  Dehumanization of
		    victims
		  Attribution of blame to
		    victims
		  Misrepresentation of
		    consequences

Note. From Bandura (1979). Copyright 1979 by Hans Toch. Reprinted by permission.

THE ORIGINS OF AGGRESSION

Origins include our very first experiences at either observing an action carried out by someone else (observational learning) or testing the action (reinforced performance). Of course, everyone who grows up in modern "civilization" observes violence. There are thousands of murders committed every year on TV, and popular "action-adventure" films involve much violence, death, and mayhem. The observational learning aspect of acquisition remains one of the major contributions of social learning theory. It has been used extensively to argue that television can increase aggression, in that men who watched violent TV as boys are more likely to have been convicted of a serious criminal offense by the time they are thirty.[3] Of course, others argue that both the TV preferences and criminal behavior are not cause and effect but are both the results of a predisposition for violence. This predisposition may have been genetic and have led to both the selection of violent TV and later criminal activity. In response, social learning advocates argue that even in cases where exposure to observed aggression is not self-selected, subsequent violent behavior still increases. This may be due to what L. R. Huesmann calls the acquisition of aggressive cognitive scripts, literally blueprints or programs for aggressive behavior learned through observation.[4] These blueprints include evaluations of whether or not the other person can be controlled, the chances of success, and whether or not rewards or punishments might follow the use of aggression. Rewards, in the case of wife assault, typically would mean "winning a power struggle" or "blowing off steam," while punishments could include anything ranging from police intervention, to one's wife leaving permanently, to one's own emotional reaction (e.g., guilt, shame) to having used violence. There are some questions left unanswered by this approach: Why would observation of frequent violence lead to acting out more violence by hitting someone? Is such an action easily and quickly learned. Also, the "blueprint" for aggression may get distorted when someone is enraged. But studies of the social learning process, typically done only with the blessing of university research ethics committees, were not able to enrage or arouse subjects in a way that resembled the reality of intimate rage.

However, witnessing violence in one's own home between one's parents has an impact that goes beyond the impersonal violence of television. Murray A. Straus and his colleagues found in their national survey data that males who had observed their parents attack each other were three times more likely later to have assaulted their wives.[5] The reported rates jumped from 10.7 to 35% for men who had been child witnesses of violence. If the parents had been observed hitting each other, the man's chances of being a perpetrator (or victim) of violence against his wife more than tripled. The survey of Straus et al., however, simply reported a correlation or association between the two. The kids who witnessed violence had other potential causes for their adult violence: their families were poorer; they were more likely to be struck themselves by a parent; their family had poorer social support and were generally more "dysfunctional." All of these other causes were more likely to have been experienced in homes where the parents struck each other; hence, they are said to be confounded with the child's observation of violence. In addition, the child's own inherited predispositions are a possible alternative cause.[6] To those scientists who like to narrow things down, this natural "confounding" of potential causes for adult violence posed a problem. The result was a debate over the rate and meaning of what is called "intergenerational transmission," that is, the transmission of an abuse rate from one generation to the next. Do violent parents produce violent offspring by having their abusive actions observed or overheard? What if a child is the victim of abuse? Is he or she they then more likely to become a perpetrator of abuse?

The other main way that habits are acquired is through self-teaching or trial and error. Gerald R. Patterson is a psychologist who specializes in treating "unruly kids" through systematically applying social principles. Patterson and his colleagues included observational studies of naturally occurring aggression as part of their research effort. In one study,[7] they observed boys' natural "playground" interactions over time. They saw that some boys had adopted passive strategies of avoiding conflict and keeping to themselves. Other passive boys were occasionally forced to fight. Those who lost went back to passive avoidance after the fight. Those who won, however, even though the fighting was initially defensive in nature, began to initiate fights. They became predatory in their style of aggression. This "trial-and-error" learning gradually shapes habitual aggression; the reward of winning the fight leads to further fighting and more reward. Even if the reward is intermittent (win some, lose some) it is still a powerful reinforcer of the aggressive habit. In fact, intermittent reinforcement schedules are the strongest we know of—witness the tenacity of golfers and slot machine players. The habit formed becomes an instantaneous "knee-jerk" response in the situation where it seems to the perpetrator to be applicable.

Of course, trial-and-error learning is not the only origin or, as Bandura called it, "acquisition mechanism." A popular advertisement in boys' comic books in the 1940s to the 1960s was the Charles Atlas bodybuilding ad. Set up like a comic strip, the ad showed a skinny guy at the beach who gets sand kicked in his face by a muscular adversary. He goes home, builds himself up using the Charles Atlas training system, comes back, and punches out the bully. His girlfriend is impressed; she feels his bicep.

The evidence for social learning processes at work focuses on the question of what percentage of abused children go on to become abusing spouses or parents. The answer, based on retrospective studies, is about 40%. Psychologist Catherine Widom reviewed all available evidence bearing on this question and concluded that being abused as a child increased one's chances of being an abusive parent, but the pathway between the two was not simple or direct.[8] Too many of the studies done had been retrospective in nature. Starting with a group of abusive parents, they had worked backward to ascertain what percentage of them were abused as children. The rates were typically quite high. The problem with such an approach, however, is that it doesn't indicate how many abused children go on to be nonabusive parents. Since retrospective studies start with abusive parents as their sample population for study, nonabusive parents are "selected out" of the research. They don't qualify for the study. As a consequence, rates of being victimized in their childhood are unknown. To rectify this problem, Widom did a "prospective" study in which known victims of child abuse were traced years later to see if they were more at risk for adult violence. Abused children had higher subsequent rates of violent crime. This was especially true for abused male children.

Developmental psychologist Byron Egeland, at the University of Minnesota, also did a prospective study to answer this question.[9] In this study, an identified group of abused children were followed *before* they abused as adults. This is important because it eliminates the retrospective bias described above. That is, if researchers wait until the subjects Have abused and follow them back retrospectively based on their adult abusiveness, they never get to find out what percentage of the abuse victims went on to become nonabusive. Egeland found out that 40% in his prospective sample were again abusive, in the sense of maltreating their children.

Two conclusions are typically drawn from these findings: one is that abuse experiences or witnessing of abuse increases one's chances of being abusive; the other is that the majority of abused children do not go on to be abusive. This is not really the contradiction it seems, of course. It simply says that modeling or observation has an influence on later adult abusiveness, but it doesn't totally determine whether someone will become abusive or not. Social learning theory argued that people could acquire a capacity to act aggressively through observation but that this capacity would not be translated into action unless violence serves some function for them as adults. Many abused children may not have had the need or adult opportunity to engage in violence. Others may have had long lists of what are called protective factors: positive events that could mitigate against early negative experiences. By now a number of such protective factors have been identified—having one supportive adult in an otherwise hostile early environment, being in an emotionally supportive family as an adult, or involvement in psychotherapy as an adolescent or young adult.[10] There are cases I have seen where the abusiveness has been going on for at least three generations, which is as far back as most families' oral history extends.

The learning of physical violence seems relatively straightforward in that there is evidence for the learning opportunity, the exposure to the violent act. When we come to apply social learning processes to the learning of intimate abusiveness, however, some problems arise. For one thing, while it is relatively simple to learn how to make a fist and strike a blow, the intricacies of emotional abusiveness seem much more complex. How do abusers "model" how to find their particular partner's weak point, when such weak points vary from one person to the next? How in each case do they know what her vulnerabilities are? Did they observe their father exploiting the same vulnerabilities in their mother? Why do virtually all abusive men everywhere in English-speaking countries use the same four words to abuse their partners (bitch, slut, whore, cunt)? Why do most of these men never use these words in public? Why is abusiveness so often accompanied by extreme jealousy and blame avoidance? Are these personality qualities also learned? We don't know the answer to these questions, for the available evidence is inconclusive. The other problem is that there is no evidence that men learn abusiveness to women in order to fend off physical attacks. Is there some common set of feelings that a young victim of a schoolyard bully and a man arguing with his wife might feel? Both might feel powerless. In fact, men appear to feel generally powerless, threatened, and out of control in intimate conflict. But to say that an inner feeling rather than a measurable external event can trigger violence takes one step beyond the original social learning formulation.

THE INSTIGATORS OF AGGRESSION

The *instigators* of aggression include all the triggering events in the current or adult social milieu. Consider, for example, that boy (discussed above), now grown up, getting into barroom fights because someone makes fun of his weight. That insult triggers a inner state of discomfort in him called "aversive arousal." Aversive arousal is a state of excitement that feels unpleasant, uncomfortable. This state is something he would like to get rid of (hence, the aversive aspect). The perceived insult creates a felt tension that the person has an urgency to reduce or remove. Just how it gets removed depends on the learning history of the person. That learning history is likely to make him respond to aversive arousal in one of two ways: either he sees the event that caused the arousal as controllable or not. If he sees it as uncontrollable, he tries to reduce aversive arousal by escape or withdrawal from the event. Suppose the aversive triggering event is the actions of an abusive father—yelling, threatening, slamming doors, and throwing objects. Children in such households are being terrorized by the person they depend on for their survival, someone more powerful than they are, someone beyond their control. If they tried to directly confront him, things would get worse. Maybe on one occasion they did try this. They learned quickly that he could not be confronted or controlled. What options do they have to reduce the aversive arousal they feel in the face of their fathers' abusiveness? They are terrified and might try to seek cover, usually in their room, perhaps under their bed. They might play music to "tune down" their fathers' voice. But they can't escape; they are too dependent on their family. It is simultaneously their source of support and fear. The only remaining resort is to dissociate, "tune out," or self-hypnotize. These choice factors are outlined in Figure 3.1.

If they see it as controllable, the aversive arousal is converted into feelings of anger that prepares them to take action and overrides other feelings which might interfere with action. Psychologist Raymond Novaco describes anger as an "emotional response to provocation" that serves a function of overriding less acceptable emotions such as guilt or fear.[11] Anger can carry built-in rewards and so be difficult to alter or change. Furthermore, "the emotion that one experiences is a function of one's overt behavior in the situation. Physiological arousal (palpitations, sweating, etc.) will more probably be construed as anxiety if the person withdraws from or avoids the provocation and as anger if he or she challenges or approaches. In another sense, whether one experiences anxiety or anger is a function of one's coercive power relationship to the provoking person. As the perception of personal control diminishes, the arousal of anxiety during a provocation has an increased

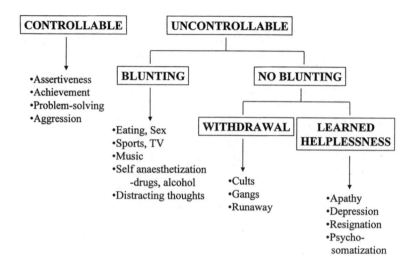

FIGURE 3.1. Responses to aversive life events. Adapted from Bandura (1973) and Seligman (1975) as cited in Stuart (1981).

probability. Indeed, the arousal of anger can be evoked to generate a sense of personal control."[12] At some point in the person's developmental reward history, anxiety/anger lead to acting out or coercive behaviors that were occasionally rewarded. When this occurred a habit of reacting with anger and coercive or punitive behaviors began to develop. This habit will become remarkably durable for several reasons. First, it was established by intermittent reward, which is notoriously difficult to extinguish. Just witness people pulling hopelessly away at slot machines (which reward on every thousandth pull), or "hackers" still pursuing the perfect golf shot (which may occur only once in a round of 100 shots), if you want to see proof of the tenacity of habits formed through intermittent reinforcement. Secondly, the *expression* of anger can be intrinsically rewarding. It both feels good by releasing body tension and by generating actions consistent with the angry man's notion of what "manliness" entails.

Novaco lists a series of functions that anger serves for the angry person: the energizing of behavior, expressive and communicative functions, and defensive functions. The energizing function increases the vigor with which we act and may increase the chances of being rewarded (termination of aversive events), especially when it enables the person to assertively confront provocation or injustice. Interpersonal problems in intimate relationships may never reach the discussion stage until one person becomes demonstrably angry. This can serve to break into a pattern of cold anger and lead to problem resolution if the anger is expressed in a problem-solving way rather than in a way that blames, hurts, and escalates a sequence of antagonism. Anger not only expresses that a problem exists but its arousal also has a self-promotional function in that it advertises potency, expressiveness, and determination. To the extent that these qualities are part of one's sex role or self-definition or are thought to be valued by the immediate group, then anger expression enhances self-image. The defensive function of anger works by short-circuiting anxious feelings of vulnerability. It is less distressing to be angry than to be anxious. In fact, one represses anger because of anxiety about its consequences. When that anxiety is overcome, anger is expressed. If this function operates successfully, angry people should feel less anxious, although this may depend on the active expression of anger, its being acted out. In this sense, anger also externalizes the conflict by directing attention to the other and hence to the nonself.

Novaco describes another function of anger: its arousal generates a sense of potency. In the words of Erich Fromm, it converts *a feeling of impotence into a feeling of omnipotence.*[13] Through this process, the entire experience of the self and the anger-provoking stimulus are transmogrified. For example, in either the personal or the political arena one's sense of alienation and self-blame are transformed into a feeling of power, self-worth and conviction while the erstwhile oppressor is vilified and becomes a worthy target for anger and violence. "The feeling that one has little control over his own destiny may lead to attempts to restore oneself as an active agent. This may involve attacking those who appear to be influencing and controlling the individual."[14] Anger arousal and the thoughts associated with it can instigate aggressive actions that are expected to change the situation (remove the aversive stimulus) (see Figure 3.2). In most cultures men are taught to override fear and take action. This tendency, called *agency,* has the effect of so shaping a man's subjective experience of emotion that the signal for fear is reduced and that for anger is enhanced. However, the anger response, that is, the action for expressing anger, varies from man to man. The mode of anger response will be whatever that individual man has discovered to work for him (to obtain reinforcement).

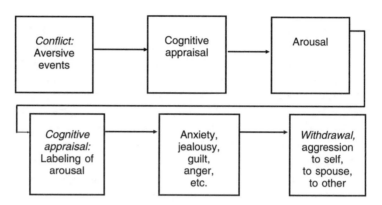

FIGURE 3.2. Relationship of aversive events to aggression.

Chronic repetitive abuse by a parent wears down the victim's will to use active strategies for reducing aversiveness. The child learns to adopt passive withdrawal strategies around the abusive parent as a means of survival and coping. The child flees to other worlds: computer games, "heavy metal," television, escape routes that focus the attention on the pursuit and off the abusive parent. Such children are still physically present, but they are emotionally and cognitively absent. In the studies of trauma victims, one response to repeated trauma that shows up repeatedly is something called *dissociation*. Dissociation is a process where a complex of thoughts is separated from the rest of a person's personality and functions independently. In some cases, the split is between an emotionally charged set of activities and one's body. Many street prostitutes had sexual abuse histories. Some sexual abuse victims learn to "watch" their own victimization from a vantage point outside their normal consciousness. They can describe, with apparent dispassion, their original sexual victimization from a "third party" vantage point (thereby removing the personal sense of being attacked). If this becomes a learned survival strategy, they will later describe a trick in this same dissociated tone. The prostitute may rattle off the facts as though she were reciting a shopping list rather than describing a sexual act in which she participated. She has learned to blunt feelings associated with sex and, when engaging in sex with a customer, to self-hypnotize, dissociate, and distance herself from it. This form of psychic numbing is a common response to an uncontrollable aversive event such as sexual victimization. Of course, when "blunting" or evasive tactics don't succeed in reducing the aversiveness of existence, victims try something more radical like running away, getting sick, or suicidal. Anything to get rid of the constant aversive arousal, the sickening tension that won't disappear. The main reason why many abuse victims don't become abusive is that they have learned other, more passive strategies for dealing with aversive arousal. In fact, using aggression against an abusive parent is likely to be punished in the extreme. The action sequence may be stored in memory, but the impulse is stifled whenever circumstances do not seem controllable. Abusers do not seem controllable; they seem to have all the power. When abuse victims do successfully fight back, they are often amazed that their former perpetrator was vulnerable.

Ironically enough, both aggression and achievement start from the perception that circumstances are controllable. They both involve direct action designed to change those circumstances. Aggression, however, is designed to control and change people. The aggressor has learned to reduce tension by being violent. If you yell, stomp and scream, and threaten and hit, circumstances will fall into place. If the violence gets rid of the tension state by changing the actions of the other, offending person, it is rewarded. The habit of violence is becoming entrenched. It is important to note that social learning theory sees the aversive arousal as being generated by current events called "aversive experiences," by external "stimuli" such as arguments or criticisms from another person. Could aversive arousal be generated internally in the absence of such aversive experiences? Could it, like water behind a dam, build up with time? If so, persons experiencing internally generated aversive states would be in a serious predicament. They would both feel bad and not have an explanation for that bad inner feeling. To what could it be attributed? Since the male orientation is to what is "out there" rather than to interior states, the explanation for the aversive arousal will probably hinge on something or somebody else. It will involve blame. Blaming someone else has another advantage: it facilitates getting angry with—maybe even yelling at—that person. This allows the tension to be discharged through anger display. Males in particular, by virtue of sex role conditioning that discourages inner awareness, are unlikely to view aversive arousal as internally caused. Trying to get males to keep daily diaries of inner states is extremely difficult. Their focus is on the environment, happenings outside themselves. Furthermore, they are raised in a society that traditionally has believed wives to be responsible for men's feelings. Hence, if the man feels "out of sorts" it must be her fault. Blaming his wife for his felt tension provides an easy, socially sanctioned explanation for why he feels that way. It also provides an excuse to get angry. The anger, directed toward the wife, allows built-up tension to dissipate.

Susan Pollack and Carol Gilligan performed a very creative investigation of gender differences in perception of threat.[15] They showed men and women Thematic Apperception Test (TAT) cards and recorded their responses. The TAT presents ambiguous pictures to people and assesses their responses as indicative of unconscious themes. Since the pictures are ambiguous, we wind up "projecting" our own themes and fantasies when we describe what we believe is occurring in the picture. Pollack and Gilligan's work found that when people perceive danger in a picture or set of pictures, they write stories with violence themes in them. By counting the strength and number of violence themes, some measure can be made of the degree of threat or danger in the pictures. Women wrote the greatest number of violence themes in response to pictures of "work situations," whereas men did so to "scenes of men and women together." The women's response was interpreted by the authors as revealing threat in achievement-related situations. The men's responses seemed to reveal threat or danger in intimacy. They suggested that this sex difference in the perception of relationship danger is a source of male–female conflict in intimate relationships, noting that men tend to be less comfortable and in control in such relationships. If this is the case, men may manifest anger, rage, and violence as a means of reestablishing feelings of control. Just as the violence works with the school yard bully by reestablishing control, so it works in the intimate scenario.

JEALOUSY AND CONJUGAL PARANOIA

Abusive men are frequently irrationally jealous about their wives. Abusive men monitor their wives' use of space and time, questioning all contact with other men. They are suspicious about any other man's interest in their wife. They seem to assume that all anyone would see in her would be sex. Some men question their wives' choice of clothes as "too sexy"; one female client of mine had a husband who checked her soiled underwear for signs that she had had sex! Of course, sociobiologists would just see this as generating control over reproduction. As was reported above, Martin Daly and Margo Wilson found jealousy to be the most frequently cited motive by police for spousal homicides. At some point, however, one has to ask how irrational perceptions maximize genetic fitness? Are baseless suspicions genetically sound? Perhaps a sociobiologist would argue you can never be too careful. In social learning terms, however, unfounded jealousy is called a "delusional instigator." Apart from giving it this title, however, social learning has little to say about how delusional instigators develop and how sudden changes in intimacy can become an "aversive stimulus."

In our therapy groups assaultive males talked a lot about jealousy and abandonment themes while trying to maintain a detached "cool" or dismissive tone about their emotional dependency on their wives. This would be expressed in a variety of ways. Men in the beginning of treatment complain a lot about their wives' behavior, partly to deflect the focus from their own abusiveness. If a man who had been complaining at length about his wife's worst habits was asked, "So why do you stay with her?," he often drew a blank. It was as though he had never considered that question. His answers were typically flimsy and transparent. He would never admit was that he needed her, found himself intensely bound to her, and found the prospect of being alone terrifying. This process is described as "masked dependency." With abusive men, the abuse serves to "keep the woman in place" while allowing the man to overlook his own masked needs. It serves the function of allowing him to maintain his illusion of detachment.

To test these intimacy-related issues with abusive men, Jim Browning and I concocted an ambitious study.[16] We endeavored to capture on videotape the essence of the conflict issues described by men in treatment. We thought that if we could have professional actors play out couples in conflict in scenarios scripted by the issues of treatment and measure men's reactions to these videotapes, we might have some evidence for the role of intimacy issues in generating fear and anger, the forerunners of abuse. We thought of a variety of ways of measuring reactions to the videotapes, ranging from self-reports, where the men fill out lists of emotion scales reporting what they are feeling, to complicated psychophysiological measurement. The latter involved strapping research subjects into a form of polygraph—popularly known as a lie detector—that measured psychophysiological indices associated with emotion, such as the "galvanic skin response" (electrical conductivity in the skin), pulse transit time, and respiration.

The first problem was to get the conflict scenarios right. We wanted one to reflect "abandonment" themes as described by the men, a second to reflect "engulfment" themes, and a third to be neutral with respect to this dimension of intimacy change. We also wanted one to be male dominant and the other female dominant. The abandonment themes included a tape on which the woman tells her husband that she wants to visit a nearby town (Seattle) for a long weekend with female friends. He reacts with outrage, telling her that they will all be "sitting ducks" in the singles bars he imagines that they will frequent. She doesn't buy it and then informs him that she will be joining a woman's "consciousness-raising" group. In the engulfment tape, the woman complains that the couple has no quality time anymore and that the man spends too much time on solitary pursuits. He says to her, in effect, "get a hobby." In the neutral scenario, the couple argues over where to spend their holidays, but since they will be spending them together in any event, the scenario is neutral with respect to changes in amount of intimacy. Each scenario had to be emotional and believable of course, for it to have the desired impact on the subjects who watched it. Fortunately, once completed, everyone saw the tapes as realistic.

The second problem came in getting a subject sample. While men were sent by the courts for mandatory treatment, there was nothing in their probation order that said they had to participate in research studies. We started by asking men in the group for volunteers, but there's something about the process of being strapped into a polygraph by psychologists who are then going to show you weird videotapes that is inherently unappealing. Images of *A Clockwork Orange* are conjured up. Eventually we settled on monetary bribes. Then, there was the problem of a control group. We decided that we needed at least three other groups: one that was maritally conflicted, one that was "happily married," and one that was violent in general. Each would provide some interesting and vital comparisons with our group of men, who were violent only in intimate relationships. The generally violent men were no problem; they too came from our treatment group. The men in the maritally conflicted group were recruited from local couples in counseling programs. It was the happily married group that proved to be the biggest problem. We ran advertisements on the sports pages of the local paper, and many men responded. Our selection procedure was to match the groups on demographic factors such as income and education and to use self-reports and partner reports of the man's use of violence on the Conflict Tactics Scale to generate group membership. The "maritally conflicted" group, for example, had as much marital conflict as the wife assaulters but did not use physical violence to resolve the conflict. To our dismay, however, about 20% of the "happily married" men's partners reported their husband as using violence! These men, needless to say, were not used in the study.

The study itself involved two lab sessions. The first was spent entirely on collecting questionnaire and self-report data. This session showed that the wife assaulters had attitudes toward women that were no different from those of the men in the other groups. They did, however, have one set of characteristics that could contribute to their abusiveness; they had both a stronger need for power over others and poorer verbal assertiveness skills. They did not, in other words, have the verbal capacity to satisfy their power needs. The second was used to show the subject each videotaped scenario and after each to record his self-reports of emotion and his perceptions of the conflict. The anger ratings are demonstrated in Table 3.2.

The emotion self-ratings showed a difference between the groups of men. The wife assaulters reported the greatest anger and anxiety to the scenarios in general and the highest ratings of all to the abandonment scenario. There was something about this group that made them especially emotionally reactive (about two and a half times as reactive), and more rejection or abandonment sensitive than the happily married men, the generally violent men, and the maritally conflicted men. For some reason, none of these differ-

TABLE 3.2. Means and Standard Deviations (in Parentheses) for Anger Ratings

			Intimacy condition		
Group	Dominance	Prerating	Abandonment	Engulfment	Neutral
Wife assaulters	Male	6.05 (4.61)	18.64 (6.10)	9.80 (5.90)	12.60 (6.70)
	Female	5.36 (3.05)	16.90 (5.90)	10.60 (6.10)	12.10 (6.20)
Generally assaultive	Male	6.00 (4.61)	13.00 (6.10)	10.33 (5.90)	13.44 (6.70)
	Female	5.22 (3.05)	15.22 (5.90)	11.00 (6.10)	12.67 (6.20)
Maritally conflicted	Male	8.22 (4.61)	15.78 (6.10)	13.11 (5.90)	14.78 (6.70)
	Female	5.11 (3.05)	14.78 (5.90)	12.67 (6.10)	11.78 (6.20)
Happily married	Male	5.78 (4.61)	12.22 (6.10)	11.11 (5.90)	10.67 (6.70)
	Female	3.78 (3.05)	8.33 (5.90)	6.11 (6.10)	6.67 (6.20)

Note. Scale range = 1–9.

TABLE 3.3. Relevance of Intimacy Issue Portrayed to Own Relationship

Group	Condition		
	Abandonment	Engulfment	Neutral
Wife assaulters	78%	58%	42%
Generally assaultive	54%	66%	40%
Maritally conflicted	39%	72%	56%
Happily married	29%	56%	0%

Note. χ^2 = 38.3, *df* = 6, *p* < .001.

ences showed up in the physiological measures. But these men saw themselves as more angry and anxious. They also said they would have been more likely to use violence to resolve the conflict presented if they had been the man in that situation. They perceived the man as being humiliated by the wife's demands. The other men hardly even saw them as demands. The wife assaulters also saw the intimacy issues portrayed in the videotapes as more relevant to their relationship than did the other men (see Table 3.3).

This study was an important first step in getting "inside the head" of the wife assaulter. We now knew that he saw intimate conflict differently than other men, men who had been raised under the same socializing culture as he had. The abusive man saw more threat, felt more anxious and humiliated, and reacted with more anger than other men, even men who were violent in outside relationships. There was a distinct emotional and perceptual response from the men whose violence was relationship specific. It began to appear that more than mere imitation of actions sustained abusiveness.

At that time, we could not account for the origin of these differences, and we did not know that they might be part of a larger psychological picture; we could only say that they existed. We knew nothing then, as we do now, of what we now call the "abusive personality." Instead, we couched our description of wife assaulters in the vernacular of the day: social learning theory.

NEUTRALIZING THE CONSCIENCE AND THE REGULATION OF VIOLENCE

The last category in social learning analysis is what is called the regulators of aggression. Since behavior is shaped by the immediate reactions it generates, regulators include the external rewards and punishments that occur after aggression (i.e., the reactions of others) and "self-rewards and -punishments" (i.e., the way we think about what we have just done). In this category is what some would refer to as conscience. Two learning principles in the regulation of violence are especially important. One is that, in the absence of overt punishments from others, the violence is rewarded. Males who act violently are automatically rewarded through the means described above: ending aversive tension and producing a feeling of agency and domination. These feelings are enough to regenerate the violence at a later time. Secondly, these feelings only have to occur occasionally to sustain the habit; if the violence is intermittently rewarded, the habit will be sustained. Nevertheless, according to Straus's surveys, about one-third of men who assault their wives do stop being violent without the police getting involved. What happened in these cases to generate this "spontaneous desistance" is unknown. The woman may have convinced the man that if he ever did that again she would leave, or the man may have been upset by his own reaction to what he did.

With assaultive men aggression propagates a variety of responses from their partner, including calling the police, leaving, staying away for some time, threatening to leave the relationship, being fearful and sexually guarded, etc. Many of these responses, if taken seriously, generate punishment to the abuser. They may not be taken seriously, however, if they have been made before without follow-up action. They become "idle threats" without sanctioning power.

There are great differences in conscience or the self-punishment aspect of abuse (see Figure 3.3). Psychopathic men, of course, do not suffer pangs of conscience. Most normally socialized men who are not psychopathic do go through some remorse for abusing their wife. The remorse, of course, feels bad, and to avoid it men go through what Bandura called the "neutralization of self-punishment." In social learning terms, conscience is the ability to punish the self for violating one's own standards of conduct. In men with conscience, feelings of guilt or shame would follow the use of aggression against a loved one. The so-called "contrition phase" that Walker described would be generated by conscience. Of course, pangs of conscience are painful, so people find ways to "neutralize" this self-punishment by mentally reconstructing a "reprehensible" action that one has committed. Perhaps the most famous neutrali-

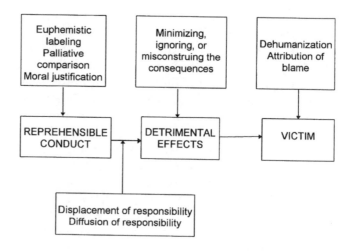

FIGURE 3.3. Mechanisms through which behavior is disengaged from self-evaluative consequences at different points in the behavior process. From Bandura (1979). Copyright 1979 by Hans Toch. Reprinted by permission.

zation is Adolf Eichmann's proclamation that "I was only following orders," stated at his trial, as so thoughtfully recounted by Hannah Arendt in her *Eichmann in Jerusalem: A Report on the Banality of Evil*.[17]

In the case of intimate aggression, this mental reconstruction of the act includes blaming the victim for having provoked the aggression ("If she hadn't nagged me so much this wouldn't have happened; I told her not to make me angry"), ascribing the aggression to external factors such as alcohol consumption ("I only get that way when I drink"), and minimizing the severity of the act both through the language used to describe it ("the night we had our little incident") and the comparisons made ("most men are as violent as I am"). I have routinely asked court-mandated men to estimate what percentage of men in the general population are as violent as they are. Their average estimate is 85% (the real incidence is about 3–4%). Ironically enough, wife assaulters and feminists both adopt causal models of wife assault that ascribe it to social factors. For the wife assaulter, this exonerates him from personal responsibility for his violence. He uses the inflated incidence as "evidence" that he is only following social dictates. Table 3.4 shows some frequently used excuses.

TABLE 3.4. Neutralizing Self-Statements

1. *Moral justification*: "The Bible [Koran, etc.] says I am the head of the household and she must submit."
2. *Palliative comparison*: "I'm not a real batterer because I never used a weapon."
3. *Displacement of responsibility*: "I was so drunk, I didn't know what I was doing."
4. *Diffusion of responsibility*: "It happens in every marriage." "It's no big deal in my culture."
5. *Dehumanizing the victim*: "My old lady deserves everything I dish out."
6. *Attribution of blame to the victim*: "She drove me to it." "If she didn't keep nagging me, none of this would have happened."
7. *Minimization/selective memory*: "I got mad at her only once."

While all or some of these aspects of denial may be present in most wife assaulters, victim blaming is by far the most prominent. Men in treatment groups regularly begin their contribution to group process—literally introduce themselves—by listing their litany of grievances with their wife.

Social learning theory had one big advantage over previous theories of wife assault; it can account for individual variation. For a long time social learning theory seemed to be the best way to think about explaining wife assault. With its extensive research base, it could relate wife assault to a large body of general studies on aggression. However, these were still problems; for one thing, social learning, largely as a result of its research methods, views people as "responding to stimuli," so that violence is always triggered by an external event. Like a rat in a cage (the model whence social learning theory developed), the wife assaulter is viewed as responding to external events. He has no "inner life" apart from how he decides an "aversive stimulus" is controllable or not and his conscience-like reactions to his own behavior.

This portrait is very unlike the one offered by battered women. Their descriptions portray the man as generating tension and arousal in the absence of objective changes in his environment. He "becomes irritable for no apparent reason" and reacts with escalating verbal abuse and then physical abuse. He is pathologically jealous, drawing ludicrous conclusions about nonexistent affairs. He externalizes blame for everything. He is never wrong. He experiences sleep disturbances, anxiety, and depression. He goes through building tension cycles that are unrelated to his surroundings. These cycles suggest inner tensions and an inner life that is much more complex than social learning depicts and, to a large extent, incapable of being "modeled," as it is interior and private. Batterers do not merely react to external stimuli but create a different view of the world where emotional bumps become earthquakes. Neither social learning nor feminist theory nor the psychiatric labels we have mentioned so far can account for these syndromes of rising and falling tensions, and shifting phases of emotion, perspective, and attitude. A more comprehensive disturbance is evident, one that draws from the deeper levels of the man's essential character.

4

The Psychology of
the Cycle of Violence

As I look now at the interview notes I took from women partners of our clients, the phrases jump off the page at me: "He's like two different people," "He's like Jekyll and Hyde," "He's completely different sometimes," "His friends never see the other side of him; they think he's just a nice guy, just one of the boys," "I never know which one is coming in the door at night." There are over 200 files with the same statements in them, all offered up spontaneously to my request for a description of their husbands. It wasn't just those phrases either; it was the repetition in the descriptions of the men: moody, irritable, jealous, changeable. As one women put it, "He's like living on an emotional roller-coaster." It was always the same.

In 1979, psychologist Lenore E. Walker wrote her seminal description about the experiences of battered women. Based on 120 women interviewed in Denver, Colorado, *The Battered Woman* was an early and important combination of vivid description and quantitative analysis of victims of battering.[1] The descriptions of the abuse experience reported by these women served as the platform for Walker's later development of the notion of a battered woman syndrome and its subsequent use as a legal defense. The battered woman syndrome was a constellation of reactions common or typical to the experience of being victimized by chronic intimate abuse. For our present purposes, however, another aspect of the descriptions given by these women is of interest. They described a cyclical buildup up tension and abusive release that typified the behavior of their abusive partners. Walker referred to this pattern as the "battering cycle."

This cycle was described as having three phases, which could vary in timing and intensity for the same couple and between different couples: the tension-building phase, the explosion of acute battering, and the "calm, loving respite." In the tension-building phase, the man escalates whatever form of abuse he has been using: possessive smothering, verbal harangues, "gaslighting" (or undercutting the woman's view of reality), or physical brutality. The woman typically goes into a survival mode and caters to his every whim in a desperate attempt to avoid the inevitable. She swallows her own anger. He becomes hypervigilant for signs of defiance. Since he projects so much of his own anger onto others, he may misperceive it even when its not being expressed. The tension buildup continues to the point of the battering incident. Sometimes, sensing that it is inevitable, she defies him just to get it over with.

According to reports from battered women, only batterers can stop the violence, once initiated. Social psychologist Philip G. Zimbardo calls this process "deindividuated violence" and sees it as responsive only to internal cues from the violence perpetrator. In other words, it is unresponsive to cues from the victim.[2] Zimbardo's analysis was discussed in Chapter 1. He described a psychological mechanism, reward from proprioceptive cues that generates spiraling rage. The process feeds on itself specifically because each act of aggression, each blow or punch, is rewarding. The source of reward is the feedback from the body (proprioception) and tension release. Hence, during the battering phase, batterers continue punching and kicking harder and faster to the point of exhaustion. The release of energy lowers tension levels, and the batterer becomes addicted to this form of release. Its the only way he knows how to get rid of the bad feelings building up inside, the so-called aversive arousal.

Although Zimbardo focused on social features that increased the likelihood of deindividuation occurring, there is a parallel process for some men where breakdown of individualized constraints occurs within their own psyche. For some reason, they lose the ability to imagine another's fear or pain or the dreadful circumstances that might follow abuse. Some, whom we call psychopaths, have permanently lost this human function. Others lose their ability to empathize in a cyclical or intermittent way.

Psychologist Roy F. Baumeister refers to the "tunnel vision" that occurs just before people commit suicide as "deconstructed thinking" (see Figure 4.1).[3] This is a type of thought that is focused on concrete acts and has no sense of an extended future. Baumeister had carefully analyzed suicide notes to see what clues to the thinking of the person were left by the linguistic aspects of the note. It occurred to me that this kind of narrowly focused thinking process precedes intimate abuse.[4] The profile of murder-suicides, for example, indicates a prior long-term intimate relationship with a history of abuse, separations, and reconciliations. Perpetrators of murder-suicide have histories of substance abuse and depression. They are described as experiencing "morbid jealousy," a type of endless rumination also called "conjugal paranoia" and common in batterers. The depression deepens with the perceived "final" separation and this state triggers the murder-suicide.[5, 6] Both sets of perpetrators possess this ruminative tendency. Men in treatment groups call it "playing the bitch tape." Murder-suicide perpetrators undergo an "incubation" period where they become preoccupied with simple sets of thoughts such as "She can't leave me, I'll show her" or "If I

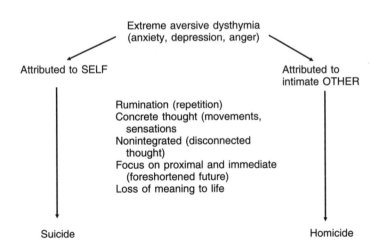

FIGURE 4.1. Deconstructed thinking. Adapted from Baumeister (1990). Copyright 1990 by the American Psychological Association. Adapted by permission.

can't have her, no one else will." As the tension mounts and these thoughts obliterate every other thought from consciousness, the urge to destroy the partner becomes overwhelming. Obviously this evidence comes from both reconstructing the lives of completed murder-suicides and from interviewing men who completed the murder and failed at the suicide attempt. We will return to this subject below in the section entitled "Catathymic Crisis."

Typically friends and coworkers overlook the signs of a tension buildup that precede abusive outbursts. These are described in the quotidian vernacular as "moody" and not understood as originating from within the man. It was this split between the public and private forms of behavior that led to the notion that all abusiveness was planned and deliberate. The male seemed to pick his spots to be abusive. He seemed to be able to monitor and control himself if he needed to. In other cases, though, there would be some leakage of the private irritation into the public world. Tension-building phases demonstrate some leakage in group sessions (see Figure 4.2). Men seem, at first, more serious, preoccupied, tense, always distracted, as if they are somewhere else. Each man in this phase tends to

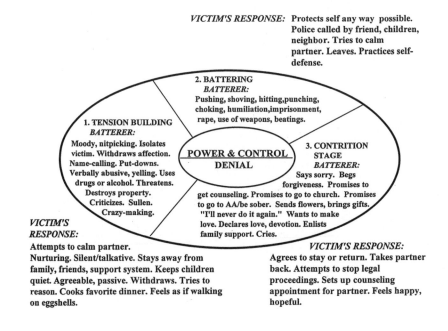

FIGURE 4.2. Cycle of violence.

complain more than usual about whatever social group is on his emotional hit list for that week. Small issues assume great weight and importance.

The "contrition phase" of the cycle follows the tension release from the acute battering phase. The batterer has alienated his wife and now seeks to "woo her back" to the relationship. He promises reform and recruits others (e.g., her mother, the parish priest, mutual friends) to persuade her to return. He promises to get counseling, to join Alcoholics Anonymous (AA), to mend his ways. He promises never to be violent again. He brings her flowers. He works on her guilt: she is the only thing he has; only she can save him; he'll recover if she sees him through it; love can conquer all. He may threaten suicide if his pleas fall on deaf ears. She gets hooked on her need to rescue him and her sense of hope of a possibility for the relationship. She becomes aware of his despera- tion and alienation from meaningful human contact, and this appeals to her nurturance. Religion, traditional female socialization, and guilt conspire to keep her in the relationship. Temporarily, she is given all the relationship power.

Walker's respondents describe what sounds like two different people in the tension-building and contrition phases. These two people are so different that we forget they inhabit one skin. Decades of research in trait psychology have led us to believe that people are basically alike from day to day. That notion, a product of the snapshot methodology of personality assessment, is misleading when it comes to intimate abusers. They have a split between their public and private selves and a split between their tense and contrite selves. Each "self" is constructed around a phasic need to reduce anxiety stemming from an unbearable intrusion (during the tension- building phase) or an unbearable foreboding of aloneness (in the contrition phase).

When I set out to gain some understanding of a cyclical or phasic personality, I hit a dead end right away. Academic psychology was more preoccupied with finding a spot on a map to locate the one dominant (and public) personality everyone was believed to possess. This map was called a circumplex because the personality types studied by academics were believed to arrange themselves in circular fashion like a pie chart divided into quadrants.[7] The top-left-hand quadrant of this circular map contains arrogant– calculating people who are self-assured at best and coldhearted at worst. Antisocial personalities also fall into this quadrant, and so do narcissistic, self-absorbed people who feel they are "special" and the rest of the world is beneath them. Most celebrity batterers would fit here, as would many abusive professional men and all abusive would-be gurus. Directly across on the top-right-hand quadrant are the flamboyant personalities, warm and gregarious at best, histrionic at worst. Below this group, in the lower-right-hand quadrant are the dependent types, warm and agreeable at best, clingy at worst. Finally, across from them on the lower left are the aloof, introverted people, sometimes called schizoid or avoidant. Most of the overcontrolled abusive men come from this category. They really want to be alone and resent all attempts to make them remain, socially at least, in the everyday world. Intimate relationships make just this demand. Mathematically, this circumplex represents what is currently believed to be the structure of personality, the map by which personality theorists order humanity. By having thousands of college students fill out hundreds of thousands of questionnaires and mathematically analyzing the results to find what response patterns hang together, these four quadrants continually reappear. They serve as a guide to the personality—a chronic way of experiencing and behaving in the world. Academic researchers measure this personality in public, and research subjects respond to the measure with a description of their public self at one point in time. This "snap shot" is something like a portrait. The subjects often put their best face on. They may not even know at this stage of their life that they have an abusive side in intimate relationships. If they do, it does not figure into the descriptions of themselves that they give the researchers. To get at that abusive aspect, something else has to be assessed.

The search was stalled for an understanding of the type of man who would do the things described by the battered women in Walker's study. Personality research wasn't particularly interested and didn't have much to offer. I needed a discipline that had studied not just a snapshot of personality but regarded it as a dynamic process, capable of undergoing predictable changes or phases. I turned to the clinical literature, especially to the psychiatric journals. I had read a copy of psychiatrist John G. Gunderson's book called *Borderline Personality Disorder.*[8] In that book I made a startling discovery; what Gunderson called a "borderline personality" was a type of personality that went through three dramatically different phases; that is, it didn't always stay the same, the way the "snapshot" researchers had assumed (see Table 4.1).

TABLE 4.1. Gunderson's Three-Phase Defense Structure of Borderline Personality

Phase 1	A "dysphoric stalemate." Intimacy needs are unmet and the requisite motivation, insight, and skills to assert those needs are nonexistent.
Phase 2	The relationship is perceived as possibly lost. The defense structure expresses itself as anger, devaluation of the significant other, or open rage.
Phase 3	Occurs when the relationship with the significant other is lost. The borderline personality engages in behaviors designed to ward off the subjective experience of aloneness (e.g., impulsive substance abuse and promiscuity).

Note. From Gunderson (1984). Copyright 1984 by American Psychiatric Press. Reprinted by permission.

Gunderson described a defense structure of borderline personality with three different levels that produced sudden shifts in their entire world view. This meant that their preoccupation's perspective on their intimate relationship, emotions, and behavior would all shift from one phase to another, leading to a repetitive or cyclical form of personality. One of the essential features of this cyclical personality was that they experienced repeated dissatisfactions with whomever they were attached. Their personality changed in a predictable way over time.

These phases sounded to me very much like the phases of the cycle of violence described by Walker's women respondents. It was this type of understanding of personality that I had been looking for—one that described predictable shifts, that altered cyclically and with time, not just a dot on a personality map that remained fixed and immutable. What's more, the descriptions of personality Gunderson gave were remarkably like the descriptions of actions that Walker's battered women gave. It was as though one could be mapped onto the other—could, in effect, provide an explanation for the descriptions of Walker's respondents. Phase 1 of the borderline individual's shifting personality consists of an internal buildup of tension; Gunderson called this a "dysphoric stalemate" in which the person feels depressed and irritable but doesn't know how to verbalize the psychic discomfort. In relationships, the borderline personality caught in a dysphoric stalemate is trapped in a deepening downward spiral of bad feelings, urgently in need of soothing and intimate connection but not able to recognize or express this need.

The dysphoric stalemate is made even more problematic by another essential clinical feature of borderline individuals—that the intimate other serves the function of integrity of the self. Whereas nonborderline persons can maintain their own self-integrity, the borderline individual requires another person to sustain this process. Thus, the loss of the other carries a risk of feeling a loss of self. In the vernacular, this is described as "coming unglued" or "coming apart at the seams." It is experienced as a profound terror with no distinct origin. The borderline person converts this into abuse through (1) the belief that the intimate partner should be able to ameliorate the bad feelings and (2) conversion of the terror into rage. As the distancing builds, borderline individuals act in a way that self-fulfills their "prophecy" or belief about being alone or abandoned. They become increasingly withdrawn and verbally abusive, generating in their partner self-protective withdrawal ("walking on eggshells"), the opposite of what the borderline wants but is unable to detect or ask for. Underneath the increasing anger is an intense demandingness, the plea for self-survival. John Bowlby used the phrase "arches away angrily while simultaneously seeking contact" to describe the actions of separated children upon reunion with their mother. Borderline adults appear to recreate this intimacy conflict. This first stage, I believed, was the "tension-building" phase of the abuse cycle, during which frustrations increase. Walker's respondents had simply described what it was like to be on the receiving end of a relationship with someone like this.

According to Gunderson, the unexpressed irritability builds until the borderline person erupts into an angry outburst (Phase 2)—in others words, the abusive outburst. If the angry outburst drives away the significant other, the borderline personality engages in desperate attempts to "ward off the feeling of aloneness" (Phase 3). Binge drinking, drugs, and promiscuity are examples of such attempts most frequently cited. It seemed to me that the contrition phase of the abuse cycle also fits this category. The abuser promises anything to get her back. These behaviors persist until the woman has tentatively returned; then gradually the man's attempts to appease her subside, and the cycle eventually repeats itself.

Borderline personality organization is a clinical category developed in the psychiatric literature for clients who were neither psychotic nor neurotic. As Gunderson describes the borderline personality (see Table 4.2), the essential defining criteria (in order

TABLE 4.2. Essential Characteristics of the Borderline Personality

1. A proclivity for intense, unstable interpersonal relationships characterized by intermittent undermining of the significant other, manipulation, and masked dependency

2. An unstable sense of self with intolerance of being alone and abandonment anxiety

3. Intense anger, demandingness, and impulsivity, usually tied to substance abuse or promiscuity

Note. From Gunderson (1984). Copyright 1984 by American Psychiatric Press. Reprinted by permission.

of importance) are as follows: (1) involvement in intense and unstable relationships in which the significant other is undermined and manipulated; (2) intolerance of being alone combined with increasing abandonment anxiety; and (3) *intense anger,* demandingness, and impulsivity, often linked to substance abuse or promiscuity. This sounded exactly like the husbands of the battered women I have known and those that Walker described. It was only the prevailing opinion of the time that prevented family violence researchers from searching for a personality explanation for these men. The emphasis was on "male violence" in general, as described in Chapter 2, not on the personality profiles of particular males. In 1977, psychiatrist Otto Kernberg estimated that 11–15% of the general population exhibited signs of borderline personality organization; of these, only some 10–25% might be diagnosed as having borderline personality disorder, the more severe form. A personality type is classified as a disorder when it is so rigidly fixed as to cause repeated interpersonal difficulties. Personality disordered individuals cannot escape from themselves. Even less severe forms of some personality types can be problematic, and just when the condition becomes classifiable as a "disorder" is somewhat arbitrary,[9] usually based on a comparison of the person's score on a scale with those of clients diagnosed with the disorder. My own approach has been to eliminate this arbitrary classification of disorder and simply to examine a continuum of scores on the key aspects of borderline personality.

Psychiatrists have been more interested in the more severely disturbed clients and generally focused on women with borderline personality simply because the bulk of their clinical outpatients were women. Women seek help more easily; men get into trouble. Some of these troubled men wound up in our study. Borderline men, overlooked for so long, frequently appeared to be cyclical wife abusers.

The term "borderline personality organization" is fuzzy and misleading, causing some researchers, such as psychologist Theodore Millon, to argue that the borderline category should be called the *cyclical personality* as it was in earlier times.[10] Cyclical describes the central feature of the personality better than the term borderline, which meant originally that these clients existed on a "border" between psychosis and neurosis. Millon is right that the cyclical aspect is what is salient, and Gunderson's description of the three phases captures this particular aspect. In any event, I began to test wife assaulters for borderline personality organization using a self-report instrument devised by psychiatrist John Oldham and his colleagues in 1985. This questionnaire measured three aspects of the borderlines personality: "identity diffusion" (an unstable self-concept); lapses in "reality testing" (not knowing sometimes whether sensations come from outside or within); and "primitive defenses" (like the tendency to split women into "all good" [Madonnas] or "all bad" [Whores] categories without integration) or "projection" (the tendency to project all unacceptable impulses onto the other person). Men with borderline personalities typically experienced a lot of ambivalence (dependency and hostility) toward intimates and a lot of expressed anger. To me, this sure sounded like a group that might become intermittently abusive.

Writers in both science and literature have always recognized the coexistence within a single person of intense and divergent moods such as euphoria, irritability and depression. Millon traced the historical antecedents of the current "borderline" label back to the 17th century when the emphasis was on the impulsive and erratic moods of the borderline that later came to be called *cyclothymia*. The psychiatrist Emil Kraepelin called this circular personality "manic-depressive insanity" and saw it as due to metabolic dysfunction.[11] This "excitable personality," as it was also called, was characterized by irritable temperament, unstable relationships, and impulsivity. Later descriptions of what was then called the "labile personality" also described an impulsive, preoccupied personality type.

Millon saw the "depth and variability of moods" as central to the borderline personality. These moods are *"unpredictable and appear prompted less by external events than by internal factors."*[12] The borderline predisposition is in place from early childhood and is noticeable from what Millon describes as a kind of merry-go-round of repeated failures at coping with no evidence of learning from mistakes. As he puts it, "the borderline patient goes round in circles, covering the same ground as before, getting nowhere, and then starting all over again." Borderline individuals go through "transient periods" in which irrational impulses are exhibited and "fears and urges that derive from an obscure inner source take over and engulf them in an ocean of primitive anxieties and behaviors." He continues: "Unable to grasp the illusory character of these inner stimuli, they may be driven to engage in erratic and hostile actions or embark on wild and chaotic sprees they may only vaguely recall. These episodes of emotional discharge serve a useful homeostatic function since they afford relief from mounting internal pressures."[13] For these reasons, borderline persons have unreliable work/school histories, tending to exhibit extreme unevenness in fulfilling normal social responsibilities.

Millon wrote a description of the "borderline cycloid" in 1975 for the third edition of the *Diagnostic and Statistical Manual of Mental Disorders* (DSM-III) Task Force personality subcommittee that included the following description: "This pattern is typified by intense, variable moods and by irregular energy levels, both of which appear to be unrelated to external events. There is a notable fear of separation and loss with considerable dependency reassurance required to maintain psychic equilibrium. Strong ambivalent feelings, such as love, anger and guilt are often felt toward those upon whom there is dependence."[14]

Millon's diagnostic criteria were the following (any three of which were present to a notably greater degree than in most people and were not limited to discrete periods or necessarily prompted by stressful life events):

1. *Intense endogenous moods*—Repetitive failure to be in a normal mood, and this failure is not readily attributable to external sources; an emotional state noted by recurring periods of dejection and apathy interspersed with spells of anger, anxiety, or euphoria.
2. *Dysregulated activation*—Experiences wavering energy level and irregular sleep–wake cycles.
3. *Self-condemnatory conscience*—Reveals recurring self-destructive thoughts; redeems moody behavior through self-derogation.
4. *Dependency anxiety*—Preoccupied with securing affection and

maintaining emotional support; reacts intensely to separation and reports haunting fear of isolation and loss.

5. *Cognitive-affective ambivalence*—Portrays a repeated struggle to express attitudes contrary to inner feelings; experiences conflicting emotions toward others, notably love, rage, and guilt.

With the exception of criterion 3 above, these all seem consistent with what describes abusive men. If you changed criterion 3 to read "redeems moody behavior through derogation of a significant other," you would have a description of wife assaulters. Millon describes the "most striking characteristic of borderline [individuals] is the intensity of their affect and the changeability of their actions."[15] He referred to impetuous, unpredictable, impulsive mood shifts. Borderline persons find it extremely difficult to maintain a stable sense of self and hence lack purpose or direction. Their identity depends strongly on their surrounding social group. A consequence of this is a tendency to become extremely dependent on others, a need for protection and reassurance. People with borderline personality disorders suffer from intense separation or abandonment anxiety, dreading potential loss while chronically anticipating it, "seeing it happening, when in fact it is not."[16] Here the characteristics of borderline adults clearly relate to attachment or separation–individuation issues, which we will explore in a later chapter. And, in a male population, their dependency will be masked and transformed into controlling actions—actions designed to ensure the woman's constant availability. This control masks a fear of abandonment.

Millon goes on: "Since most borderlines devalue their self-worth, it is difficult for them to believe that those upon whom they depend could think well of them. Consequently, they are exceedingly fearful that others will depreciate them and cast them off. With so unstable a foundation of self-esteem, and lacking the means for an autonomous existence, borderlines remain constantly on edge, prone to the anxiety of separation and ripe for anticipating inevitable desertion. Events that stir up these fears may precipitate extreme efforts at restitution such as idealization, self-abnegation, and attention-gaining acts of self destruction or, conversely, self assertion and impulsive anger."[17]

People with borderline personality disorder are also intensely conflicted regarding dependency needs. In their quests for self-identity, they are often subjected to ridicule and isolation, producing feelings of intense anger toward others. Moreover, they cannot avoid being ambivalently anxious. They neither can trust others nor hope to gain the security and affection they need. Should their anxiety about separation lead them to submit as a way of warding off or forestalling desertion, they expose themselves to even further dependency and thereby an even greater threat of loss. Moreover, they simultaneously experience intense anger toward those upon whom they depend, not only because they are ashamed of their dependency and weakness but also because they resent the other person's power in having "forced" them to yield and acquiesce. This very resentment then itself becomes threatening. When they feel forced to appease others to prevent abandonment, they must take pains to ensure that their mounting anger stays under control. Should this resentment be discharged, even in innocuous forms of self-assertion, their security will be severely threatened. They are in a terrible bind. Should they "strike out" alone, no longer dependent on others who have expected too much of them or have demeaned them, or should they submit for fear of losing what little security they can gain thereby?

When I read Millon's description of the "borderline cycloid," I sensed the origins of controlling behaviors and masked dependencies in abusive men. But these underlying feelings are strongly disguised by the urge to control, to act out, to aggress, and to vilify the other as both a release from and a reaction to personal tensions. If a borderline male can blame his wife for these tensions and vague feelings of personal deficiency, he need not confront them or deal with them, a process that might well undermine his carefully constructed "macho" self-image or persona.

CATATHYMIC CRISIS

As I read further in the clinical literature, other personality explanations for the cycle of violence began to appear. Eugene Revitch and Louis B. Schlesinger, a psychiatrist and psychologist, respectively, developed the notion of what they called a "catathymic crisis."[18] Originating in psychodynamic theories of violence, a catathymic crisis was a process of "delusional thinking with the patient being driven to a violent deed without a rational motive, with the act having a symbolic meaning and the victim not counting as a person, but as part of an overwhelming image."[19] This process developed within "ego-threatening relationships" and was divided by the authors into three stages, which they called the incubation stage, the violent act, and the relief stage. These stages again sounded to me like the phases of the cycle of violence. The authors themselves offer the observation that "the most common catathymic murder occurs within the boyfriend–girlfriend relationship" and cite the following case: a man murdered his girlfriend, who for a period of 6–8 months was the subject of the perpetrator's obsessive preoccupations; this was coupled with homicidal and suicidal fantasies.[20] Eighteen years later, while on parole for this crime, he killed his second girlfriend and then committed suicide.[21]

In such cases, the authors argued, the incubation stage could last from several days to close to a year. During this stage the future offender is obsessively preoccupied with the prospective victim. This preoccupation is accompanied by depression and loose schizophrenia-like thinking (loose associations). Thoughts of suicide eventually intermingle with fantasies of murder of the "ego-threatening subject." The homicidal impulse eventually becomes dominant, and suicidal thoughts usually completely disappear after the murder. Both the homicidal act and the inner experience of the incubation period is perceived by the perpetrator as unreal and "ego-alien." The feeling is one of anxiety, combined with a sense of an impending loss of control or a need to commit violence. Often the perpetrator discloses these feelings to a professional or close friend. His warning is usually misunderstood and ignored. The criminal act may impress the jury as planned and deliberate. However, the offender perceives the seeming premeditation not as a plan but as a thought divorced from action.[22]

Revitch and Schlesinger said that jealousy or the victims loss of interest were usually cited by the press as the cause of the murder. This brings to mind a study by Maria Crawford and Rosemary Gartner that showed that 45% of women killed were murdered by recently estranged husbands or boyfriends.[23] Revitch and Schlesinger see the extreme jealousy as preceding (and causing) the victim's attempt to leave the relationship. As they put it, "The cooling off of a relationship is actually due to the perpetrator's obsessive preoccupations, ambivalence, and pathological jealousy. . . . [I]t is the very relationship that shatters the perpetrator's psychological homeostasis so that the released affect disrupts logical thinking."[24]

The authors saw the accumulation of affect as occurring in relationships where transference occurred and early conflicts (usually oedipal conflicts) were restimulated.

Psychologist J. R. Meloy developed this line of thought further.[25] Meloy described catathymic violence as sudden, overwhelming emotion having symbolic significance that is unconscious at the time of the violence. In acute (single-attack) incidents, the perpetrator is overwhelmed by intense autonomic arousal, overwhelming anger during the violence, has a perception of the victim as an imminent threat to the ego structure, and simply wants to reduce that threat and return to "intrapsychic homeostasis." Meloy's description is consistent with the descriptions of deindividuated violence by Philip G. Zimbardo and the notion of deconstructed thinking described by Roy F. Baumeister. When we put the three together, we see that the symbolism of loss or impending loss generates extreme rage, agitation, and tunnel vision. In this state, the future perpetrator ruminates consistently on the woman's malevolence, driving their arousal and rage even higher. When they finally vent the rage, it is uncontrollable. They stab or shoot until they are exhausted or the gun is empty of bullets. They want to annihilate the victim.

In the chronic form of catathymic violence as described by Meloy, two types of incubation period are possible. In the first, which Revitch and Schlesinger described, the incubation is ego-alien or, as clinicians call it, ego-dystonic and is experienced as an impending loss of control—feeling that the center cannot hold, to borrow from William Butler Yeats's "The Second Coming." In others, however, the homicidal ideas generate a pleasurable and anxiety-free sense in the future perpetrator. Rehearsal for the future homicide occurs, including practicing at a shooting range, experimenting to find the most suitable weapon, and attempting to construct alibis or form alliances with others that would mitigate responsibility after the offense. This latter form of catathymic buildup might be experienced by psychopaths or "vagal reactors," as Neil Jacobson described them above in Chapter 1. The ego-alien incubation process, as Revitch and Schlesinger described it, seems more like that experienced by borderlines individuals. This connection was not lost on Meloy, who saw chronic catathymic violence as requiring either borderline or psychopathic traits. Meloy's connection of incubation processes with the psychopathic personality has another implication. In nonlethal ebbs and flows of abusiveness both psychopathic and borderline perpetrators might experience some form of violence cycle.

The foregoing descriptions of cyclical personalities provided by Gunderson, Millon, Revitch and Schlesinger, and Meloy offer a rich insight into the abuse cycle. The original research by Walker was descriptive; it did not seek to explain the origin of cyclical violence. The clinical material described above is rich in possibilities for such an explanation, a virtual roadmap into the heart of darkness of the intermittently abusive man. It led me to attempt to search for the existence of cyclical personalities in assaultive males. We needed research studies to establish a link between cyclical personality in men and their partners' reports of their abusiveness. How would we prove this connection, and what if, despite the promising appearance of a psychological profile for abusiveness, it simply was not there? We now turn our attention to this empirical expedition.

5

The Structure of the Abusive Personality

I have shown above how strong similarities exist between descriptions of abusive men and descriptions of cyclical or borderline personality. The test for the connection would involve assessing both borderline personality and abusiveness and then ascertaining if the two are reliably related. As Thomas Henry Huxley once put it, "Sit down before the god of fact and be prepared to give up every preconceived notion."[1] As we have seen by now, there are a lot of preconceived notions about the causes of abuse. We have also seen that most of these theories stumbled on some facts of abuse: that lesbians are as abusive as heterosexual couples; that certain situations involving real or symbolic abandonment trigger rage and violence; that anger seems to build from within, in the absence of any real stressors. The apparent similarity between borderline personality organization and the cycle of violence could be just another theoretical resemblance without fact or substance.

At this point I should remind you again that I am not arguing that all abusive men fit into the borderline category. I outlined above three profiles of intimate abusiveness. The one that I believe conforms to a borderline profile is the man who is chronically and intermittently abusive but only within the family. He has a split between his public persona and his private personality. He does not get into brawls with other men like the psychopathic abuser. He is also very emotional, experiencing high levels of depression, anxiety, and anger. Unlike the overcontrolled abuser, who erupts after long periods of unexpressed rage and whose anger is usually a buildup of frustration to external events, the borderline batterer is repeatedly erupting to buildups of internal events, the cyclically occurring tension described in the last chapter. It is the cyclical personality on whom we focus, the personality that drives the actions known as the cycle of violence.

I should also point out that borderline personality was only the first step in building a model of abusiveness. Other qualities common to the profiles of abusive men will be added as our journey through the data progresses. You shall see this step-by-step unfolding of what I now call the abusive personality in the coming chapters.

One always begins these empirical quests with some anxiety based on the very real probability of being wrong. The day when the data are finally in the computer and about to be analyzed is a day fraught with tension, not unlike dramatist's reaction to the opening of his or her play. Social scientists watch the data collections the way that politicians watch polling results and investors read stock reports. Like anyone who has built a model airplane, we want to know, "Will it fly?" We started the studies of what we came to call the borderline personality organization (BPO) by amassing the necessary ingredients: valid and reliable questionnaires to measure BPO and the reactions theoretically associated with it, namely, anger, jealousy, blaming "attributional styles," and alcohol use. We called these the "associated features" of abusiveness. Later on, we were to add another associated feature: the chronic experience of trauma symptoms. Our task was to measure these aspects in both abusive and nonabusive men. Then we needed to take the crucial step of finding out whether these personality reports related to actual abusiveness. This crucial step would be taken by measuring both the man's self-reports of abusiveness and, more importantly, his intimate partner's reports of his abusiveness.

First, the most important measure—that of BPO itself. How could we measure it when psychiatrists themselves could not agree on the diagnostic criteria? Psychiatrist John Oldham and his colleagues solved this problem for us by surveying various definitions of borderline personality and developing a self-report scale, one the men could complete themselves, based on three characteristics of borderline males for which there was already some research evidence (Figure 5.1).[2] Borderline men suffer from identity disturbances, they use "primitive" defenses, and they experience transient psychological states during which they are unsure what is real.

These characteristics were assessed by writing items for each that could be directly reported as personal experiences or feelings that a particular man had had. These feelings and experiences could, Oldham and his colleagues agreed, be assumed to be manifestations of unconscious processes. In other words, the scale was a way of translating the inner experience of these men into a measurable score on a self-report scale. The identity disturbance aspect, for example, includes a diffuse sense of identity, a changeable sense of self, or a lack of stability in the sense of self. Items that reflected this characteristic included the following: "I see myself in totally different ways at different times"; "I find it hard to describe myself"; "It is hard for me to be sure about what others think of me, even people who have known me very well." All of these items assess an insecurity or uncertainty about the self. Another item, "I feel empty inside," taps another important dimension, a sense of inner vacuity. Would someone who was insecure and struggled against a gnawing sense of emptiness experience greater anxieties about intimacy? Would they have greater expectations of their partner, ultimately expecting the relationship to fill the emptiness? Another item reads, "I feel that I'm a different person at home compared to how I am at work or at school." This item, although it has different meanings, taps into another central theme of abusiveness—that the abuse is private and that the abusive man appears quite differently to his workmates. This aspect of the BPO Scale, referred to as the Identity Diffusion subscale by Oldham and his colleagues, originally had 58 such statements used to assess it. Eventually, only those 10 items that were most closely mathematically related to each other were kept. That is, if someone answered "3" on a 5-point scale on a given item, he would tend to make similar answers to the other related items. This is called the internal consistency of the scale. Of course, having a consistent scale isn't much good unless the scale measures what it purports to measure, in this case BPO. Oldham and his colleagues gave the scale to patients who had already been diagnosed to ensure that this was so. This was done by ensuring that those in the diagnosed borderline group scored differently on the scale than did those in other clinical groups. Thus, the Identity

For each of the statements below, please indicate how true it is about you by *circling* the most appropriate number beside each statement:

1	2	3	4	5
never true	seldom true	sometimes true	often true	always true

1. I feel like a fake or an impostor, that others see me as quite different at times. 1 2 3 4 5
2. I feel almost as if I'm someone else, like a friend or relative or even someone I don't know. 1 2 3 4 5
3. It is hard for me to trust people because they so often turn against me or betray me. 1 2 3 4 5
4. People tend to respond to me by either overwhelming me with love or abandoning me. 1 2 3 4 5
5. I see myself in totally different ways at different times. 1 2 3 4 5
6. I act in ways that strike others as unpredictable and erratic. 1 2 3 4 5
7. I find I do things which get other people upset, and I don't know why such things upset them. 1 2 3 4 5
8. Uncontrollable events are the cause of my difficulties. 1 2 3 4 5
9. I hear things that other people claim are not really there. 1 2 3 4 5
10. I feel empty inside. 1 2 3 4 5
11. I tend to feel things in a somewhat extreme way, experiencing either great joy or intense despair. 1 2 3 4 5
12. It is hard for me to be sure about what others think of me, even people who have known me very well. 1 2 3 4 5
13. I'm afraid of losing myself when I get sexually involved. 1 2 3 4 5
14. I feel that certain episodes in my life do not count and are better erased from my mind. 1 2 3 4 5
15. I find it hard to describe myself. 1 2 3 4 5
16. I've had relationships in which I couldn't feel whether I or the other person was thinking or feeling something. 1 2 3 4 5
17. I don't feel like myself unless exciting things are going on around me. 1 2 3 4 5
18. I feel people don't give me the respect I deserve unless I put pressure on them. 1 2 3 4 5
19. People see me as being rude or inconsiderate and I don't know why. 1 2 3 4 5
20. I can't tell whether certain physical sensations I'm having are real, or whether I am imagining them. 1 2 3 4 5
21. Some of my friends would be surprised if they knew how differently I behave in different situations. 1 2 3 4 5
22. I find myself doing things which feel okay while I am doing them but which I later find hard to believe I did. 1 2 3 4 5
23. I believe that things will happen simply by thinking about them. 1 2 3 4 5
24. When I want something from someone else, I can't ask for it directly. 1 2 3 4 5
25. I feel I'm a different person at home as compared to how I am at work or at school. 1 2 3 4 5
26. I am not sure whether a voice I have heard, or something that I have seen, is my imagination or not. 1 2 3 4 5
27. I have heard or seen things when there is no apparent reason for it. 1 2 3 4 5
28. I feel I don't get what I want. 1 2 3 4 5
29. I need to admire people in order to feel secure. 1 2 3 4 5
30. Somehow, I never know quite how to conduct myself with people. 1 2 3 4 5

FIGURE 5.1. Borderline Personality Organization Scale. From Oldham et al. (1985). Copyright 1985 by American Psychiatric Press. Reprinted by permission.

Diffusion subscale originated. It measured "*a poorly integrated sense of self . . . reflected in a subjective experience of chronic emptiness, or in contradictory perceptions of the self, contradictory behavior that cannot be integrated in an emotionally meaningful way.*"[3] This was manifested through difficulties in describing the self, uncertainty about career or goals, contradictory behaviors, and instabilities in intimate relationships. Borderline individuals do not confuse themselves with other persons the way that psychotic people might, but they have a "split" in self-perceptions. Part of themselves just cannot be fit or integrated with other parts. Naturally, I had to wonder if this split might be related to the Dr. Jekyll and Mr. Hyde descriptions given by the wives of abusive men.

The second and third subscales of the self-report instrument to assess BPO were developed in an identical fashion: numerous items were written and then "boiled down" mathematically to the 10 items in each subscale that were most closely related to each other and best distinguished already diagnosed borderline persons from others (see Figure 5.2). The second subscale was called Primitive Defenses, so called because the defense styles it measured are believed to develop very early on (around the age of two in what is called the pre-Oedipal period).

One such defense mechanism is called "splitting" and refers to the division of the self and significant others into "all good" and "all bad" aspects. Although we all may do this to a degree, the borderline individual is incapable of integrating the two aspects at all. In the case of the significant other, that person becomes either idealized or devalued. I remembered how batterers would flip-flop from one week to the next in describing their wives. One week she was impossible, life with her was living hell. The next week, everything had changed—she was a "good woman," and it was he who was wrong. Batterers could not hold and integrate their partners' positive and negative qualities. In the cycle of violence, men in the contrition phase idealize their mates and devalue themselves. In the tension-building phase, they seem to devalue their mates. I didn't know how they feel about themselves at this point, but they act with a sort of false omnipotence, a sense of entitlement as if they were a king or infallible. This self-absorbed ego inflation always explodes into a deflation and sense of unworthiness, like a bubble being blown up, over and over again. On the face of it, the scale was again tapping into our clients.

Another aspect of Primitive Defenses is called "projective iden-

Identity Diffusion Items

- I feel like a fake or an impostor, that others see me as quite different at times.
- I see myself in totally different ways at different times.
- I feel empty inside.
- It is hard for me to be sure about what others think of me, even people who have known me very well.
- I'm afraid of losing myself when I get sexually involved.
- I find it hard to describe myself.
- I don't feel like myself unless exciting things are going on around me.
- Some of my friends would be surprised of they knew how differently I behave in different situations.

Reality Testing Items

- I feel almost as if I'm someone else, like a friend or relative or even someone I don't know.
- I find I do things which get other people upset and I don't know why such things upset them.
- I hear things that other people claim are not really there.
- I've had relationships in which I couldn't feel whether I or the other person was thinking or feeling something.
- People see me as being rude or inconsiderate and I don't know why.
- I can't tell whether certain physical sensations I'm having are real, or whether I am imagining them.
- I believe that things will happen simply by thinking about them.
- I am not sure whether a voice I have heard, or something that I have seen, is my imagination or not.
- I have heard or seen things when there is no apparent reason for it.
- Somehow, I never know quite how to conduct myself with people.

Primitive Defenses Items

- It is hard for me to trust people because they so often turn against me or betray me.
- People tend to respond to me by either overwhelming me with love or abandoning me.
- I act in ways that strike others as unpredictable and erratic.
- Uncontrollable events are the cause of my difficulties
- I tend to feel things in a somewhat extreme way, experiencing either great joy or intense despair.
- I feel that certain episodes in my life do not count and are better erased from my mind.
- I feel people don't give me the respect I deserve unless I put pressure on them.
- I find myself doing things which feel okay while I am doing them but which I later find hard to believe I did.
- I feel I don't get what I want.
- I need to admire people in order to feel secure.

FIGURE 5.2. Identity Diffusion, Reality Testing, and Primitive Defenses items from the BPO Scale. From Oldham et al. (1985). Copyright 1985 by American Psychiatric Press. Reprinted by permission.

tification," a process first described by Anna Freud.[4] Projective identification means perceiving in the other person those aspects of ourselves that we can't face in ourselves. We deny them in ourselves and project them onto someone else, usually someone close with whom we have some psychological connection. They become like a blank screen for our movie, but we write it and direct it. For abusers, this means, among other things, perceiving aggression in their wives while denying their own aggression. It means seeing their wives as flirtatious while denying their own philandering. The identification part does not mean that the abuser "identifies" in any sympathetic way with the other person. Rather, because he has an intimate relationship with her, she becomes the screen for his own projections, expectations, and fears—all of which developed long before he ever met her. Some items that were retained to make the final version of the scale included the following: "I act in ways that strike others as unpredictable or erratic"; "I tend to feel things in a somewhat extreme way, experiencing either great joy or intense despair"; "It is hard for me to trust people because they so often turn against me or betray me"; "People tend to respond to me by either overwhelming me with love or abandoning me."

A final defense tapped by the Oldham BPO scale is called "primitive denial" and is defined as *their being aware that their perceptions, thoughts and feelings about themselves . . . are opposite to those they may have at other times, but this awareness has no emotional relevance for them.*[5] In other words, the split itself may be detected or brought to conscious awareness but it is emotionally denied. For example, the item "I act in ways that strike others as unpredictable and erratic" taps this tendency. Although most people sense contradictions about themselves, this is not enough to generate a high score on the Primitive Defenses subscale. Borderlines endorse scale items in the extreme, far beyond a mere recognition of inconsistency. There is one aspect of the Primitive Defenses subscale that should be mentioned before moving on to the final subscale. That is, the two strongest items (those most strongly associated with total scores for the scale itself) measure themes of trust and abandonment ("It is hard for me to trust people because they so often turn against me or abandon me"; "People tend to respond to me by either overwhelming me with love or abandoning me"). Clearly, the scale assesses fear of abandonment, another characteristic of abusive men.

The final subscale of the Oldham BPO scale is called Reality Testing. To a certain extent, this subscale distinguishes borderlines from psychotic personality types. While psychotic individuals experience constant difficulty with reality testing, borderline persons have only "transient psychotic states" during which they have difficulty distinguishing internally originating perceptions from those that originate externally ("I can't tell whether certain physical sensations I'm having are real or whether I am imagining them").

Another feature of reality testing is the inability to differentiate the self from the nonself ("I've had relationships in which I couldn't feel whether I or the other person was thinking or feeling something") and to evaluate one's behavior in terms of social criteria of reality ("Somehow, I never know quite how to conduct myself with people").

The final version of Oldham's BPO scale contained only the 30 items with the strongest associations to the subscale scores, boiled down from a much larger original pool. The average total score on the scale by a group independently diagnosed as borderline was 73, that by a nonborderline group was 59 (with a standard deviation of 14). In other words, the nonborderline group didn't score all that differently from the borderline group. The average nonborderline score was 81% of the average borderline score. Could such a small difference really account for abusiveness?

The next step was to get the scale completed by men coming into treatment for wife assault. I approached the therapists in two treatment programs, one dealing almost exclusively with court-mandated men and another with "self-referred" men. The court-mandated men had been convicted in court of wife assault and were sent to treatment as a condition of their probation. Their motivation to participate in treatment and to complete psychological tests was mixed to say the least. The typical "self-referred" man had shown up largely at the behest of his wife, who had basically drawn a line and insisted that, if the husband didn't get treatment for his abusiveness, she was leaving. We came to call these the "wife-mandated" men. These men were easier to work with in some ways then the others. They had at least got to the point of seeing that they had a problem.

On the other hand, they often seemed more maladjusted than the court-referred men, more angry, more jealous and depressed. At first my cotherapists wouldn't agree to mandatory assessment of the men. They felt it was unethical to force men to complete questionnaires. So we made sure to let them know that questionnaire testing was voluntary. The outcome was that not many of the men (maybe about half) ever completed the tests. They would take them home half-heartedly but would then "forget" to fill them out, concocting various excuses for noncompliance. Eventually, I was able to convince everyone that if we were going to do the research properly, we were going to have to make the assessments mandatory. Only in this way would we get everyone referred to the program to fill out the questionnaires instead of a self-selected few. However, if we were going to tell the men that the assessment was mandatory, we were going to have to use the assessment and give the men some feedback on their test scores. In other words, we would make it a real assessment instrument as well as a research measure. How were we going to tell someone that they were a borderline personality?

There were still other problems such as the assessment of honest reporting. Was it possible to see through the objective of the questionnaire and answer in a "socially desirable" way? Social desirability refers to completing a questionnaire the way that will make you appear "good" to the researcher. Fortunately, there are ways to measure just how much respondents are "faking good" and ways to mathematically adjust their scores to take this into account.[6] With the scores corrected in this way, a new picture emerges and one sees the measures and issues that were most concealed. Table 5.1 reports correlations of various measures with social desirability.

By finding out what the men are most embellishing about themselves or, conversely, what they are hiding the most, one gets a snapshot of their conscience and of their sense of guilt and shame. Self-referred men, you will notice, underreport their high levels of

TABLE 5.1. Correlations between Social Desirability and Other Measures

| | Whole sample ($N = 78$) | Referral source | |
		Court ($N = 38$)	Self ($N = 40$)
BPO total	−.40***	−.17	−.48***
Anger total (MAI)	−.42***	−.39*	−.38**
Trauma (TSC-33) total	−.23*	.13	−.43**
Jealousy	.05	.17	.44**
Dyadic adjustment	.28**	.11	.38
EMBU			
Father/rejection	−.29**	−.57***	−.08
Mother/rejection	−.49***	−.58***	−.43**
Father/warmth	.38***	.49**	.17
Mother/warmth	.43***	.47**	.36**
CTS			
Verbal abuse	−.26*	−.01	−.39**
Physical abuse	.15	.16	.17

Note. None of the between-groups comparisons of correlation coefficients were significant at the Bonferroni-adjusted level. MAI, Multidimensional Anger Inventory; TSC-33, Trauma Symptom Checklist; EMBU, Egna Minnen Beträffande Uppfostran (Swedish: "Memories of My Upbringing"); CTS, Conflict Tactics Scale. From Dutton and Starzomski (1994). Copyright 1994 by Sage Publications. Reprinted by permission.

*p < .05; ** p < .01; *** p < .001.

anxiety, sleep disturbance, and depression, probably because these levels are so extreme that they feel "unmanly" reporting such high scores. Notice the high negative correlations between parental rejection and social desirability (and high positive correlations between parental warmth and social desirability). Court-referred men tend to idealize their parents. They do not derogate their parents as a way of excusing their own abusiveness.

You will also notice that Table 5.1 includes scales measuring anger (the Multidimensional Anger Inventory, MAI), jealousy, trauma (the TSC-33), and recollections of parental treatment (the EMBU). All of these scales are important in fully understanding the development and structure of intimate abusiveness. All will be fully described below.

One of the tests for social desirability is called the Marlowe–Crowne Social Desirability Scale (MC). Another is called the Balanced Inventory of Desirable Responding (BIDR; see Table 5.2).[7] The former measures "impression management," that is, attempting to persuade the test giver that you are really a decent, responsible person. The latter goes a step beyond that and assesses self-deception as well. Self-deception involves both the claim of positive attributes and denial of negative attributes beyond their actual level.

TABLE 5.2. Correlations between Social Desirability Measures and CTS, and PMWI Scales for Perpetrator Sample

	MC	BIDR: IM	BIDR: SD	SD: E	SD: D
CTS					
Reasoning					
You	−.05	−.29	.06	.01	.08
Partner	−.17	−.10	−.14	−.24	−.01
Verbal aggression					
You	−.38**	−.41**	−.31*	−.26	−.27
Partner	−.37*	−.35*	−.26	−.11	−.31
Violence					
You	−.20	−.32	−.10	−.06	−.10
Partner	−.01	−.15	−.09	.03	−.18
PMWI					
Dominance/isolation	−.57**	−.45**	−.56**	−.38*	−.58***
Emotional/verbal abuse	−.50**	−.33	−.40*	−.30	−.37*

Note. CTS, Conflict Tactics Scale; MC, Marlowe–Crowne Social Desirability Scale; BIDR, Balanced Inventory of Desirable Responding; IM, Impression Management; SD, Self-Deception; E, Enhancement; D, Denial; PMWI, Psychological Maltreatment of Women Inventory. From Dutton and Hemphill (1992). Copyright 1992 by Springer Publishing Company, Inc. Reprinted by permission.

*p < .05; **p < .01; ***p < .001.

This would obviously include the denial of abusiveness. People who score high on self-deception are fooling themselves; those who score high only on impression management are trying to fool the researcher. My graduate students Kenneth J. Hemphill and Andrew Starzomski and I conducted studies of these tendencies in groups of abusive men, working on the assumption that high associations of measures with these social desirability scores indicated some sense on the part of the respondent that whatever the scale measured was a "bad attribute"—in other words, that these scales could be used to give us a window into his sense of guilt or shame about himself (see Table 5.3). People would only deny, after all, those aspects of themselves that they suspected were unacceptable to others. The results were quite strong. The aspect most related to the tendency to engage in impression management was the man's reports of his anger, especially his "hostile outlook" and his tendency to let his anger out, followed by his own reports of emotional abusiveness and then by reports of his physical abusiveness. Self-deception related most strongly to his reports of the range of situations that made him angry, to his hostile outlook, and to his emotional abusiveness. It was almost as if anger was harder to admit than abusiveness!

We interpreted the self-referred batterers' scores as indicative of a "pure" group of assaultive males. These men were more likely

TABLE 5.3. Correlations between Social Desirability Scales and Multidimensional Anger Inventory Subscales

MAI	MC	BIDR: IM	BIDR: SD	BIDR: D	BIDR: E
Anger					
Frequency	−.44**	−.31*	−.38**	−.44**	−.22
Duration	−.36**	−.28	−.27	−.30*	−.16
Magnitude	−.34*	−.25	−.36*	−.34*	−.28
Total mode of expression	−.44**	−.32*	−.40**	−.43**	−.26
Anger–in	−.30*	−.30*	−.31*	−.35*	−.16
Anger–out	−.48***	−.68***	−.46**	−.48***	−.33*
Guilt	−.01	−.11	−.25	−.22	−.20
Brood	−.45***	−.31*	−.23	−.26	−.13
Discuss	.18	.10	.01	.00	.04
Outlook	−.60***	−.49***	−.56***	−.60***	−.36*
Range	−.58***	−.47***	−.59***	−.57***	−.44**

Note. MAI, Multidimensional Anger Inventory; MC, Marlowe–Crowne Social Desirability Scale; BIDR, Balanced Inventory of Desirable Responding; IM, Impression Management; SD, Self-Deception; D, Denial; E, Enhancement. From Dutton and Hemphill (1992). Copyright 1992 by Springer Publishing Company, Inc. Reprinted by permission.
Two-tailed significance: *$p < .05$; **$p < .01$; ***$p < .001$.

to enlist for treatment during a "contrition phase" bargain with their wives. The court-referred men, on the other hand, were more of a mixed bag. Since the criminal justice system works in occasionally capricious ways, we would have a mixed sample of men who were repeatedly violent, men who had had one loud altercation that the neighbors overheard and reported to the police, and career criminals who got dumped on the treatment group out of court desperation. It was not surprising that the psychological profile of this group was varied.[8]

For about a year the self-reports of clients in the treatment groups came trickling in. It was hard work. Not only were many of the men unreceptive, but many of their partners were hard to find: some had left after the violence; others wanted nothing to do with the man, his treatment, or some psychologists with questionnaires. Others, however, were grateful for the chance to talk and disclose their perceptions of the abuse. As the numbers began to reach an acceptable level, we decided to get a control group for purposes of comparison. Since most of the men in treatment were blue-collar workers, we obtained some blue-collar control data by getting 45 members of a local union (and their wives) to fill out the same questionnaires.

Finally, with the data collected and entered in the computer, we were ready see the results. The initial data runs started. Would our theories be verified? Would the suspected connection of BPO to abusiveness appear in the data. The first thing we looked at were the scores on Oldham's BPO self-report measure. The score for the independently diagnosed borderline group had been reported as 73; for the "normal" nonborderline group, 59. What would assaultive males, as a group, look like? The scores that came out for our group were as follows: controls, 61; court-referred batterers, 66; self-referred batterers, 74. The court-referred abusive men as a group scored about halfway between the normal group and the diagnosed borderline group. The self-referred men scored just like the diagnosed borderline men.

The next step was to directly measure the strength of the associations between BPO scores and other aspects of abusiveness not assessed by the BPO scale. Was BPO associated with other central clinical features of abusiveness such as anger and jealousy? To do this a measure called a correlation was computed. A correlation directly assesses the strength of a relationship between two measures. The higher the correlation, the more strongly associated are the two measures. A correlation, however, does not prove that either measure caused the other. Your age, for example, is positively correlated with the earth's population. As one increases, so does the other. But the cause-and-effect relationship is unknown. In our initial data, the BPO scales correlated significantly with the men's self-reports of abusiveness on the Conflict Tactics Scale (CTS) devised by Murray A. Straus at the University of New Hampshire in 1979. The first hurdle had been crossed.

The schema shown in Figure 5.3 is a representation or summary of the set of associations obtained from our abusive sample of men. In our sample of all the control and assaultive men combined, we found strong correlations between BPO scores and self-report measures of what we called the "associated features" of abusiveness. These are the feelings and perceptions that set the stage for someone to be abusive. The features that were strongly related to borderline scores were anger (+.62) and jealousy (+.41) and tendencies to blame women for any "negative" event in a relationship (see negative attributions in Table 7.2). These were certainly consistent with the clinical descriptions of borderline males. Another feature appeared, however, that was unexpected and serendipitous. The higher the BPO score, the more the men experienced "trauma symptoms" (depression, sleeplessness, anxiety attacks). We will say more about these below. But suffice it to say for now that common sense had suggested that only

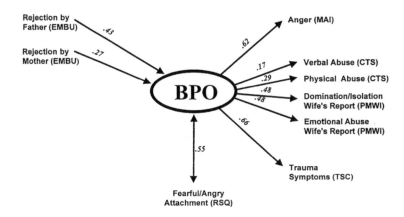

FIGURE 5.3. The centrality of BPO in an assaultive group of males ($N = 160$): $r > .52$, $p < .00001$; $r > .26$, $p < .01$; $r > .15$, $p < .05$. RSQ, Relationship Style Questionnaire.

assault victims suffered trauma symptoms and not assault perpetrators as well! Also, the higher the BPO score, the greater the problems
with alcohol. We wondered if these men drank to blot out the bad
feelings that welled up inside them.

The jealousy, which they also experience to the extreme,
seemed to me to be a fear of abandonment—that one will be left
for another, sexually more desirable person. The high-BPO men
also reported more abuse toward their partners, both physical and
emotional. The higher the BPO score, the greater the overall
psychological and physical abusiveness, even in a sample that was
abusive to begin with. Given the profile of these other characteristics, we weren't surprised. Again, let me emphasize that these
associations held up after the data were corrected for socially
desirable responding. It wasn't just a case of abusive men having a
response style that led to their increased disclosure. Even if that had
been the case, this was no reason to believe that they would report
more anger or abuse than they had actually experienced. Why make
up something like that? In any event, we measured the man's
tendency to disclose anger and abusiveness, his tendency to manage
the impression he believed he was making, and even his level of
self-deception. With all these sophisticated measures accounted for,
the relationship of BPO to other key feelings and actions held up.
It was robust. The BPO profile appeared to have passed its first test.
BPO was strongly related to a constellation of abuse features:
feelings like anger and jealousy; perceptions of blame, and actions
such as telling a woman she was unattractive and that no one else
would want her, or of controlling her use of space and time, or of
hitting her.

The second and bigger test for the data was the wives' own
reports of the man's abusiveness. The ultimate corroboration of his
abusiveness lay in her reports. We already knew that the women
were pretty honest in these reports, so they constituted the confir-
mation of the men's self-reported correlations between BPO and
abusiveness (see Table 5.4).[9] We examined the data for the man's
abusiveness supplied by the wives and female partners of the men
in our sample. We measured abusiveness using both the Straus CTS
and something called the Psychological Maltreatment of Women
Inventory (PMWI; see Figure 5.4) developed by Richard Tolman at
the University of Michigan in 1989. The former concentrates primarily on physical actions such as pushing, shoving, kicking, punching, beating up, and threatening with or using a weapon.

TABLE 5.4. Correlations of BPO and Anger Scales with Victims' Reports of Psychological and Physical Abuse

	PMWI		CTS physical abuse	
	Dominance/ isolation	Emotional abuse	Total	Severe
BPO total	.58***	.55***	.29**	.19
Identity	.55***	.52***	.21*	.14
Defenses	.53***	.53***	.33**	.11
Reality	.56***	.50***	.30*	.29**
Anger total	.52***	.48***	.07	.24*
In	.58***	.50***	−.07	.18
Out	.06	.00	.01	.27*
Duration	.32**	.30**	.20	.13
Magnitude	.63***	.56***	.12	.18
Frequency	.49***	.43***	.13	.28*

Note. From Dutton and Starzomski (1993). Copyright 1993 by Springer Publishing Company, Inc. Reprinted by permission.
*p < .05; **p < .01; ***p < .001.

The PMWI measures frequency of two general factors of emotional abusiveness. The first is called *dominance/isolation* and has to do with a man controlling his partners use of time and space. It includes items like "restricted my use of the telephone," "refused to let me work outside the home," "was stingy in giving me money," as well as about 25 other such items. The other factor, called *emotional/verbal abuse,* contains items such as "put down my physical appearance," "insulted me or shamed me in front of others," "said something to spite me," as well as about 25 others. The PMWI is the most comprehensive measure of emotional abusiveness that we have.

We wanted the answer to the following question. How did the men's BPO scores relate to the scores their wives gave them on the CTS and the PMWI? The result was vivid: both verbal and physical abuse were strongly statistically related to BPO scores (see Table 5.5). Men who scored high on BPO were the ones whose wives rated them as highly abusive and vice versa. Now, as was noted above, correlations do not prove causality. However, numerous studies have shown that BPO seemed to be produced by early experiences. We will examine the role of early factors in chapters to come, but previous studies indicated that BPO had early origins. A man didn't become high in BPO later in life (although he might become abusive). The BPO scores, in other words, probably had been around for some time; they preceded the abusiveness, which by definition couldn't have started until the man was in an intimate

For each of the following statements please indicate how frequently *your partner* did this
to you during the last year by circling the appropriate number:

0	1	2	3	4	5
not applicable	never	rarely	occasionally	frequently	very frequently

1. My partner put down my physical appearance.   0 1 2 3 4 5
2. My partner insulted me or shamed me in front of others.   0 1 2 3 4 5
3. My partner treated me like I was stupid.   0 1 2 3 4 5
4. My partner was insensitive to my feelings.   0 1 2 3 4 5
5. My partner told me I couldn't manage or take care of myself   0 1 2 3 4 5
   without him.
6. My partner put down my care of the children.   0 1 2 3 4 5
7. My partner criticized the way I took care of the house.   0 1 2 3 4 5
8. My partner said something to spite me.   0 1 2 3 4 5
9. My partner brought up something from the past to hurt me.   0 1 2 3 4 5
10. My partner called me names.   0 1 2 3 4 5
11. My partner swore at me.   0 1 2 3 4 5
12. My partner yelled and screamed at me.   0 1 2 3 4 5
13. My partner treated me like an inferior.   0 1 2 3 4 5
14. My partner sulked or refused to talk about a problem.   0 1 2 3 4 5
15. My partner stomped out of the house or yard during a   0 1 2 3 4 5
    disagreement.
16. My partner gave me the silent treatment, or acted as if I wasn't 0 1 2 3 4 5
    there.
17. My partner withheld affection from me.   0 1 2 3 4 5
18. My partner did not talk to me about his feelings.   0 1 2 3 4 5
19. My partner was insensitive to my sexual needs and desires.   0 1 2 3 4 5
20. My partner demanded obedience to his whims.   0 1 2 3 4 5
21. My partner became upset if household work was not done   0 1 2 3 4 5
    when he thought it should be.
22. My partner acted like I was his personal servant.   0 1 2 3 4 5
23. My partner did not do a fair share of household tasks.   0 1 2 3 4 5
24. My partner did not do a fair share of child care.   0 1 2 3 4 5
25. My partner ordered me around.   0 1 2 3 4 5
26. My partner monitored my time and made me account for where 0 1 2 3 4 5
    I was.
27. My partner was stingy in giving me money.   0 1 2 3 4 5
28. My partner acted irresponsibly with our financial resources.   0 1 2 3 4 5
29. My partner did not contribute enough to supporting our family.   0 1 2 3 4 5
30. My partner used our money or made important financial   0 1 2 3 4 5
    decisions without talking to me about it.
31. My partner kept me from getting medical care that I needed.   0 1 2 3 4 5
32. My partner was jealous or suspicious of my friends.   0 1 2 3 4 5
33. My partner was jealous of friends who were of his sex.   0 1 2 3 4 5
34. My partner did not want me to go to school or other   0 1 2 3 4 5
    self-improvement activities.
35. My partner did not want me to socialize with my same sex   0 1 2 3 4 5
    friends.
36. My partner accused me of having an affair with another   0 1 2 3 4 5
    man/woman.

(Figure 5.4 continued on next page)

FIGURE 5.4. Psychological Maltreatment of Women Inventory (PMWI). From
Tolman (1989). Copyright 1989 by Springer Publishing Company, Inc. Reprinted by permission.

37. My partner demanded that I stay home and take care of the children.   0 1 2 3 4 5
38. My partner tried to keep me from seeing or talking to my family.   0 1 2 3 4 5
39. My partner interfered in my relationships with other family members.   0 1 2 3 4 5
40. My partner tried to keep me from doing things to help myself.   0 1 2 3 4 5
41. My partner restricted my use of the car.   0 1 2 3 4 5
42. My partner restricted my use of the telephone.   0 1 2 3 4 5
43. My partner did not allow me to go out of the house when I wanted to go.   0 1 2 3 4 5
44. My partner refused to let me work outside the home.   0 1 2 3 4 5
45. My partner told me my feelings were irrational or crazy.   0 1 2 3 4 5
46. My partner blamed me for his problems.   0 1 2 3 4 5
47. My partner tried to turn our family, friends, and/or children against me.   0 1 2 3 4 5
48. My partner blamed me for causing his violent behavior.   0 1 2 3 4 5
49. My partner tried to make me feel like I was crazy.   0 1 2 3 4 5
50. My partner's moods changed radically, from very calm to very angry, or vice versa.   0 1 2 3 4 5
51. My partner blamed me when he was upset about something, even when it had nothing to do with me.   0 1 2 3 4 5
52. My partner tried to convince my friends, family, or children that I was crazy.   0 1 2 3 4 5
53. My partner threatened to hurt himself if I left him.   0 1 2 3 4 5
54. My partner threatened to hurt himself if I didn't do what he wanted me to do.   0 1 2 3 4 5
55. My partner threatened to have an affair with someone else.   0 1 2 3 4 5
56. My partner threatened to leave the relationship.   0 1 2 3 4 5
57. My partner threatened to take the children away from me.   0 1 2 3 4 5
58. My partner threatened to have me committed to a mental institution.   0 1 2 3 4 5

FIGURE 5.4 (*continued*)

relationship. In the correlational schemata in Figures 5.3, 5.5, and 5.8, you will note an association with a scale called the EMBU (see Table 5.1). We will discuss this developmental aspect below.

With our men, we would have to make the case for cause and effect on theoretical grounds. BPO, for example, had a large and independent set of studies indicating that it was initiated early in life. The work of psychiatrist Bessel van der Kolk, among others, indicated that this was the case. Van der Kolk and his associates found that early physical abuse was more frequent in the histories of borderline adults than in other clinical groups studied.[10] Moreover, excessive separations, losses, or disruptions were more likely in the lives of borderline patients and federal prisoners convicted of crimes of violence. This was especially true for those convicted of family violence. Van der Kolk and colleagues suggest that early physical abuse causes long-term problems in modulating emotion

TABLE 5.5. Correlations of BPO Subscales with Conflict Tactics Scale Subscales

	Verbal/symbolic aggression	Physical aggression
Reality testing	.28**	.22*
Primitive defenses	.33**	.26*
Identity diffusion	.29**	.24*
Total	.32**	.24*

Note. From Dutton (1994a). Copyright 1994 by Elsevier Science. Reprinted by permission.

$*p < .05; **p < .01.$

and aggression and, especially in males, may well lead to chronic anger. These problems are manifested first as affective numbing and constriction, sometimes called "alexithymia," or the inability to recognize emotional reactions and make use of them. This stage is followed by hyperarousal (with an extremely strong pulse, sometimes visible as a bulging neck vein, sudden and rapid actions, and profuse sweating) culminating in aggressive outbursts. The form of the aggression apparently is influenced by sex roles: abused boys generally identify with the aggressor and subsequently act out; abused girls often later turn to self-destructive acts.[11] Psychologist Catherine S. Widom found that childhood victimization (by physical abuse) increased overall risk for violent offending, particularly for males.[12]

Although anger and jealousy may germinate at an early age, the adult forms of these feelings and the issues to which they become attached appear to be shaped much later. The origins of the private personality appear to precede the later social "persona" that people carry through life. Likewise, the psychological seeds of abusiveness are sewn early in childhood. The full development of the abusive personality may be a gradual process that occurs over years, but the path direction—the way in which the abusive personality creates itself—is set early on. However, we are getting ahead of ourselves; at this point we merely want to establish the connection between BPO and abusiveness.

Why do these men get so angry and abusive in intimate relationships? The answer may lie in part in the meaning of intimacy to them. For men high in BPO, intimate relationships serve the well-nigh unachievable task of gluing together their shaky ego integrity. With an unstable sense of self and an inability to tolerate aloneness, these men depend on their relationship with their female partner to prevent their fragile selfhood from disintegrating and to dissipate the pervasive anxiety that they feel. It is for this reason that earlier studies of abusive men had reported a "masked dependency" on the victim. Yet that very relationship which they needed so desperately was fraught with "dysphoric stalemates": inability to communicate intimacy needs, abandonment anxiety, and extreme demandingness. The intimate relationship of the high-BPO scorer is asked to do the impossible, and when it fails, or appears in his eyes to fail, extreme anger results because his very sense of self is threatened and because his use of projection as a defense tells him that it is *her fault* that it is failing. He views her, at that phase of the relationship, as "all bad." If that impasse resolves, he then tends to view her as "all good" and himself as bad, and enters the contrition phase of the abuse cycle.

In other words, the borderline male has an ego held together tenuously, an arrangement that threatens at any time to fail and with much at stake—his very sense of ego integrity, of himself as whole. With a volatile combination of ego needs, an inability to communicate them, chronic irritability, jealousy, and a blaming perspective, this man is programmed for relationship destruction.

Thus, anger is an unavoidable aspect of intimacy for borderline males and carries with it a high likelihood of blaming the partner and projection of unacceptable impulses onto her. These men think this way. Their personality scores on BPO also relate to measurable tendencies to blame the woman when things go wrong in intimate relationships (see negative attributions in Table 7.2). And to them, things are always going wrong. By setting nearly impossible standards for others, the abusive personality ensures that things will always go wrong. As their tension mounts, the need of these men for perfect control in an imperfect world generates inevitable failures.

BPO also correlated with abusiveness in our blue-collar control group (see Figure 5.5), but only with emotional abuse, suggesting that they may have learned a different style of abusiveness. The mood cycles which characterize borderline men are essential features of the disorder, but the behavioral forms of abuse may be learned reactions—not just to external stress but to the internal cues of dysphoria. It is for this reason that victims of the abuse describe it as self-generated by the perpetrator.

We also collected data for two other comparison groups. A clinical outpatient sample of males referred for any problem except

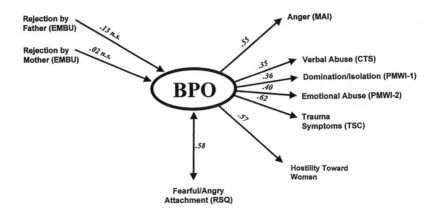

FIGURE 5.5. The centrality of BPO in a nonassaultive group of males (N = 46): $r > .40$, $p < .0001$; n.s., no shows.

intimate abusiveness revealed the same pattern of associations with anger and abusiveness (see Figure 5.6). These men, however, as with our blue-collar sample, were not physically abusive. BPO scores for them correlated with psychological abusiveness. The difference seems to have been that both the blue-collar and outpatient samples were less likely to have witnessed physical abuse in their families of origin. Both, however, experienced psychological abuse.

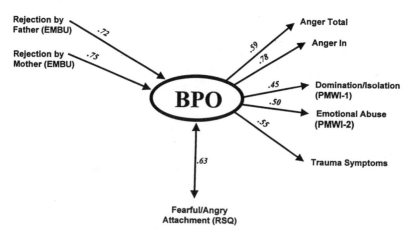

FIGURE 5.6. The centrality of BPO in clinical outpatient males (N = 45): $r > .41$, $p < .0001$.

The gay sample again replicated the basic pattern of prior groups. Of interest here is the notion that intimacy, per se, generates abusiveness in borderline men, regardless of their sexual orientation (see Figure 5.7). Partner assault here is not an issue of "male dominance," it is an issue of intimate anger.

As the tension and dysphoria build, the BPO men unconsciously require their partners to take it away, to soothe them, to make them feel whole, to make them feel good. But they do not express this—indeed, are unaware of it and so *cannot* express it. For this reason, communication skill-building exercises with these borderline males is not enough. Even if they had the skills, they couldn't identify the message. Instead, they begin to act counterproductively, uttering hurtful words and generating actions that distance their partners. These build to a crescendo with the acute abusiveness episode.

THE MINDSET OF THE ABUSER

Of course, the way the abusive man thinks about the situation also paves the path toward abuse. Recall that John Oldham's discussion of borderline individuals said they engaged in a "primitive defense" called projective identification. This involved blaming all of one's

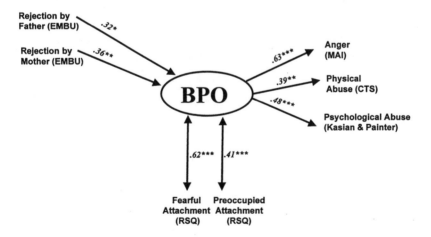

FIGURE 5.7. The centrality of BPO in a sample of gay men ($N = 104$): *$p < .01$; **$p < .001$; ***$p < .0001$ (two-tailed). The "psychological abuse" scale is from Kasian and Painter (1992).

own negative attributes onto one's partner. My graduate student
Andrew J. Starzomski examined how borderline males interpret
intimate events by examining middle class university students (see
Figure 5.8) who had been in serious intimate relationships.[13] These
20-year-old males were assessed using the same psychological tests
as those used with the batterers we studied, and then they listened
to audiotapes of intimate couples arguing. After hearing each tape,
they filled out a questionnaire called the Relationship Attribution
Measure (RAM), which assesses how they perceived intimate conflicts to be caused. Specific words were replayed from the conflicts,
and the students were asked why he or she had said that.

The male students who had higher BPO scores had a more
"blaming orientation" to the conflicts. They saw the female as being
to blame for the conflict and saw her as intending to hurt her
boyfriends' feelings. They thought she would continue to act this
way in the future. They saw her personality as the cause of the
problem. They also indicated that was how they saw problems with
their own girlfriends. This "blaming mindset" maintains their anger
and operates against negotiation in resolving intimate disputes. The
high BPO has thoughts (blaming) and feelings (anger) about intimacy that mutually reinforce each other and set the stage for

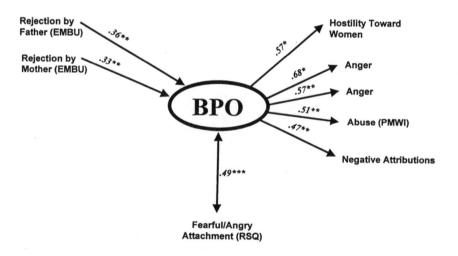

FIGURE 5.8. The centrality of BPO in two groups of college students: *N =
72 (Starzomski, 1993); **N = 77 (van Ginkel, 1995); ***both studies. Here
r > .33, p < .001; r > .29, p < .01; r > .22, p < .05.

abusiveness. It's a short step from anger and blaming to overt abusiveness. It's possible to be angry with someone crucial, to blame them for conflict and your own unhappiness, and not be abusive, but it's unlikely. Once the feelings and mindset are in operation, the chances of abuse go way up.

The high-BPO college students also had more negative attitudes toward women in general and much higher self-report scores on anger. A lot is made of how misogynistic attitudes "cause" violence. I think that both misogynistic attitudes and abuse stem from one common source, BPO. I imagine borderline teenage boys (like many teenagers) enter and leave numerous intimate relationships. The borderline youngster, however, sabotages each with his own impossible demands and anger. When each relationship breaks up, he blames it on the female. After many breakups, this generalizes to "women." Borderline men have more negative attitudes toward women than do matched control men. Some of the college men we assessed are the abusive husbands of the future. They have inchoate abusive personalities. If we assessed these dimensions in teenaged boys, and got them into the right kind of treatment, we might prevent the worst.

Another measure was thrown into our assessment package almost as an afterthought. Psychologists John Briere and Marsha Runtz had developed something called the Trauma Symptom Checklist (see Figure 5.9), which, as the name suggests, gets respondents to report the frequency with which they experience certain psychological symptoms.[14] These symptoms, Briere and Runtz found, are more frequent in people who have been traumatized in their past. In fact the frequency of these symptoms can accurately discriminate people who have been victims of childhood sexual abuse from a nonvictim group. This works for both females and males. The symptoms that the scale measures are depression (e.g., crying, sadness, feelings of inferiority), anxiety (e.g., tension, trouble breathing, panic attacks), sleep disturbance (e.g., restless sleep, nightmares, early morning awakenings), dissociation (spacing out, flashbacks, dizziness, out-of-body experiences), and "post-sexual abuse trauma—hypothesized" (sexual problems, fear of the opposite sex, memory problems). This latter category is just what it says, hypothesized, it cannot be used to "prove" the existence of sexual abuse. Nonabused people score only at a much lower frequency of symptoms than do abused people. Crisis center clients, for example, generate scores of about 44; university students, about 20. Males report lower scores than females, about 16 versus 27 in nonabused samples and 20 versus 40 in abused samples. Our first surprise were the scores in our respondents: the control group men scored at 19; the batterers, at 26. For males, this was a very high score, 6 points higher than the normal score for an abused sample of males.

As we investigated further, some interesting patterns came to light. One was that BPO scores were highly related to trauma symptoms. Borderlines, it seemed, suffered more frequently from every aspect of trauma symptoms; depression, anxiety, sleep distur-

How often have you experienced each of the following in the last 2 months? Please circle the appropriate number:

0	1	2	3
never	occasionally	fairly often	very often

1. Insomnia (trouble getting to sleep)		0 1 2 3
2. Restless sleep		0 1 2 3
3. Nightmares		0 1 2 3
4. Waking up early in the morning and can't get back to sleep.		0 1 2 3
5. Weight loss (without dieting)		0 1 2 3
6. Feeling isolated from others		0 1 2 3
7. Loneliness		0 1 2 3
8. Low sex drive		0 1 2 3
9. Sadness		0 1 2 3
10. "Flashbacks" (sudden, vivid, distracting memories)		0 1 2 3
11. "Spacing out" (going away in your mind)		0 1 2 3
12. Headaches		0 1 2 3
13. Stomach problems		0 1 2 3
14. Uncontrollable crying		0 1 2 3
15. Anxiety attacks		0 1 2 3
16. Trouble controlling temper		0 1 2 3
17. Trouble getting along with others		0 1 2 3
18. Dizziness		0 1 2 3
19. Passing out		0 1 2 3
20. Desire to physically hurt yourself		0 1 2 3
21. Desire to physically hurt others		0 1 2 3
22. Sexual problems		0 1 2 3
23. Sexual overactivity		0 1 2 3
24. Fear of men		0 1 2 3
25. Fear of women		0 1 2 3
26. Unnecessary or overfrequent washing		0 1 2 3
27. Feelings of inferiority		0 1 2 3
28. Feelings of guilt		0 1 2 3
29. Feelings that things are "unreal"		0 1 2 3
30. Memory problems		0 1 2 3
31. Feelings that you are not always in your body		0 1 2 3
32. Feeling tense all the time		0 1 2 3
33. Having trouble breathing		0 1 2 3

FIGURE 5.9. Trauma Symptom Checklist. From Briere and Runtz (1989). Copyright 1989 by Sage Publications. Reprinted by permission.

bance, and dissociation. Even more surprising was the finding that abusive men had a psychological profile similar to men in other studies who had been diagnosed with posttraumatic stress disorder. This finding suggested another common early origin of BPO, one that we shall explore in detail in a later chapter. This origin suggests that, for assaultive men, some kinds of traumatic early experiences have lasting effects—effects that are far beyond the copying of violent actions. Every aspect of the man's "intimate personality" is affected: how he sees his wife, how he feels, how he thinks about the causes of his problems.

But for now we had a picture slowly coming into focus. The abusive male scored high on BPO, which meant he had difficulty in maintaining a strong, clear self-image. To a certain extent, he expected his relationship to answer that question of who he was. The problem was, for reasons he couldn't understand, he kept feeling bad in intimate relationships. He would intermittently feel tense, anxious, irritable, "off center." He would start to get angry easily, over little things. He knew his partner was to blame for this. He tunneled in on her faults. They grew until they filled the screen of his consciousness. She was to blame for his feeling this way. "If only, she didn't. . . . " You can fill in the blank. His strange "ego-dystonic" feelings increased; he had trouble sleeping; he was depressed. He ruminated more on her faults. He began yelling at her, snapping over little things. He wanted to push her away. But sometimes he wanted her to come and get him, make him feel better, soothe him. That feeling passed so quickly he hardly noticed it. He went back to feeling that he wanted to push her away, a feeling that stayed with him. She was such a bitch. If only he could get free of her, he would finally be happy. He started to drink more heavily. The alcohol seemed to dull the dysphoria. The problem was, he got less restrained, more aggressive. Sometimes it scared him, this energy from within. He felt that it might overwhelm him. Friends found him occasionally a bit withdrawn.

6

The Primitive Origins of Rage

As we saw in the previous chapter, the BPO scale has a section called "Primitive Defenses" on which abusive men score high. These "primitive" defenses assessed on this scale include projection, splitting, and denial. That is, they deny aggressive and sexual impulses in themselves, project them onto their partners, and view their partners intermittently as either flawless or wicked. When psychiatrists refer to a defense as "primitive," they mean it formed very early in life, even before the "Oedipal stage" of development. Whereas Sigmund Freud emphasized the "Oedipal" around age 3, later psychiatry has focused on the "pre-Oedipal" period as having great importance for the formation of personality. During this earlier phase, our basic notions of selfhood develop, as we wander for the first time from the embrace of our mothers. During this initial sojourn it gradually dawns on the infant that it is a separate entity from its mother. This dawning has been described by psychiatrist Margaret Mahler and her colleagues as the "psychological birth of the human infant."[1] It is also during this stage that rage is born and temper tantrums appear.

Men who are abusive experience extreme anger in an intimate context. They also experience extreme anger and fear at anticipated abandonments, yet they act in such a way as to drive their partners away. These men are literally at their wives' knees or at her throat.

We began the search with the men themselves, bearing in mind that any answers they could provide would only be clues for further study. The men's own recollections might not be accurate measures of what really happened in their family of origin. Instead, they could be self-serving fictions invented to rationalize their current abusiveness.

We knew before we started the research that boys raised in families where they experienced parental violence were more likely to become abusive themselves. The social learning explanation for this was that the boy observes the violence and models it. The propensity for violence is in his repertoire. When stress or conflict occurs to him as an adult, he responds with what he already knows. Clearly, we were going to have to measure whatever violence had transpired as the men we studied were growing up. From the beginning of the research, however, I had a notion that something more than the modeling or copying of abusive behaviors was occurring. I wanted to get beyond merely counting hits between family members and assess the emotional climate of the household. Somehow, I felt that some men in treatment reacted as though their very sense of selfhood was threatened by events that, to an outsider, did not seem that threatening. I suspected that there had been emotional assaults on the self of these men at an early age.

Punishment of the self creates what psychiatrist Leonard Shengold describes as "soul murder."[2] Also referred to as psychic murder, this term refers to the "shutting off of all emotion, often by using autohypnosis," which occurs in abused children largely to defend themselves against their hurt and rage at the perpetrator.[3] The rage must be defended against, as any indication of it in the presence of the perpetrator could prove lethal. Although Shengold refers in general to cases of severe ongoing sexual or physical abuse, it may be that shaming attacks on the self generate similar responses. By comparison, punishment that was neither public, random, nor humiliating did not seem to carry such a permanent imprimatur.

Clearly, there was more than mere modeling going on in abusive families. There was an entire climate that seemed to destroy the soul, a climate whose message was the unworthiness of the self. It began to become clear why identity diffusion was an aspect of the abusive personality. The "self" of these men was not being nurtured. A stable, positive sense of who one was could not develop. My imagination asked the following question: What if this climate had persisted since birth for this boy? This was not far fetched, for as the data of Straus and Gelles indicates much violence begins early in the relationship.[4] What other psychological processes that underlie the regulation of rage could be jeopardized by growing up in such a climate? Would any of these processes help in the understanding of intimate rage with all its aspects; intermittency, private expression, tension phases, etc.?

THE EARLY DEVELOPMENT OF THE SELF AND THE ORIGINS OF RAGE

I began to read the literature on two major theories that have informed the search for an origin of rage, the theories of object relations and of attachment. Both contain explanations for ambivalence in intimate relationships originating in the intermittent frustration of attachment needs. We will examine the theory of object relations in this chapter and attachment theory in the next. Object relations is the psychiatric theory about how infants first form relationships with others, usually called "attachment objects." It provides a basis for another theme that predominates in the abusive personality—a split that views women in the extreme as Madonnas or Whores. This split is related to the abuse cycle. Men in the dysphoric phase ruminate on the concept of their wife as a Whore: unfaithful, sexually promiscuous, malevolent, and unloving. After the release of tension during abuse, their entire pattern of perceptions of their wife and women in general changes. What's more, it changes literally overnight. They become temporarily docile, almost servile, and she is a Madonna, idealized and put on a pedestal. (I am reminded of Gloria Steinem's dictum: "A pedestal is as much a prison as any other small space.") This intermittent treatment creates extremely strong bonds in the woman, bonds that make it extremely difficult for her to leave the relationship.

In object relations, the rage that follows upon frustration by the all-powerful mother is "split off," as expressing it risks annihilation. She is, after all, the source of all, she is life sustaining. The rage becomes dissociated to a "bad object" that remains separate from the "good object" (mother). Wives become later representations of that "good object," but the fear of the "bad object" and of one's own rage keeps haunting the male whose object relations are disturbed.

In their book *Love, Hate and Reparation*, psychiatrists Melanie Klein and Joan Riviere developed the basis of object relations theory.[5] According to them, the initial relationship between the infant (self) and mother (object) provides the origins of rage. As they state, "For the infant child, the mother is the original and most complete source of satisfaction of the totality of wants and pleasures. Yet, this total pleasure is inevitably frustrated."[6] Infants experiences this frustration as a threatened destruction of the entire self since their existence at this level depends on the object (mother, breast) upon which they are totally dependent. Frustration with such severe consequences generates strong reactions, notably rage, hatred, and a wish to annihilate the "bad object." These destructive fantasies and impulses must be defended against, however, since their expression could jeopardize the relationship with that same needed object (mother, breast). So-called primitive defenses originate at this stage, to defend against these strong emotions. One survival mechanism basic to psychological growth is that of splitting or dividing the object into good and bad parts. By preserving this distinction, fantasies of rage toward the "bad object" can be entertained without risk of destroying the "good object." In normal development, the two aspects are eventually integrated. Sometimes this process gets derailed, however, and when it does, this integrated view of the mother does not develop. What remains are two segregated views of a the object: the "good" one (breast, mother), who is ideal and nourishing, and the "bad" one, who is punitive, withholding, and thus destructive.

In her first section of the aforementioned book, Joan Riviere described the development of projection at this early stage of development. "The first and the most fundamental of our insurances or safety measures against feelings of pain, of being attacked, or of helplessness—one from which so many others spring—is that device we call projection. All painful and unpleasant sensations or feelings in the mind are by this device automatically relegated outside oneself. . . . [W]e blame them on someone else. [Insofar] as such destructive forces are recognized in ourselves we claim that they have come there arbitrarily and by some external agency. . . . [P]rojection is the baby's first reaction to pain and it probably remains the most spontaneous reaction in all of us to any painful feeling throughout our lives."[7] These early reactions, according to Klein and Riviere, are the origin of rage and appear to occur as early as the pre-Oedipal stage of development (18 months to 3 years).

Abused women often describe their husbands as having tantrums. Rage in intimate relationships, whether it is expressed through violence or sexual acting out, appears out of all proportion to what triggered the action, as though the perpetrator's very life was threatened. This type of rage is usually found when one's essential identity feels threatened. Hence, the origins of such rage appear to originate during that developmental period where identity issues are first formed. As Klein and Riviere put it:

> A baby at the breast is actually dependent on someone else, but has no fear of this, at least to begin with, because he does not recognize his dependence. In fact a baby does not recognize anyone's existence but his own (his mother's breast is to him merely a part of himself—just a sensation at first) and he expects all his wants to be fulfilled. . . . [B]ut what happens if these expectations and wants are not fulfilled? In a certain degree the baby becomes aware of his dependence; he discovers that he cannot supply his own wants—and he cries and screams. He becomes aggressive. He automatically explodes, as it were, with hate and aggressive craving. If he feels emptiness and loneliness, an automatic reaction sets in, which may soon become uncontrollable and overwhelming, an aggressive rage which brings pain and explosive . . . choking bodily sensations; and these in turn cause further feelings of lack, pain and apprehension. . . . The baby's world is out of control . . . and this is because he loves and desires. . . . The hate and aggression . . . felt and expressed by grown up people are all derivatives of this primary experience.[8]

Rage toward the "good object" must be split off, for otherwise the risk of losing that all-nourishing object is too great. The original rage has to be controlled because to express it or even feel it risks annihilation. The good nourishing object, if it detects the rage, could sever the lifeline. This splitting off of the unacceptable rage leads to dissociative splits of the everyday self from this rageful, bad, or shadow self. Thus, this splitting of the original object into unintegrated parts may constitute the later split of the Dr. Jekyll (good, unaggressive, socialized self) from the Mr. Hyde (bad, aggressive, abusive, uncontrolled self). The two parts of the self are not integrated, and, to the extent that they appear in different situations, leave one (and one's partner) with the confusing task of reconciling two different selves. As battered women frequently say, "He's like two different people." The result is a failure to complete the developmental tasks of object constancy: a stable, consistent, positive sense of self and a stable inner representation of a comforting person that is sufficient to sustain ordinary periods of separation from a primary caregiver.

In persons without this sense, a vague but deep terror of disintegration is a constant experience. Aloneness is terrifying, and any prospect of abandonment is horrific. At the same time, for a boy being socialized into a male culture where such feelings are unacceptable, the terror is submerged and stifled until it becomes a distant presence—the proverbial Hounds of Hell, locked in the basement of the subconscious, tearing at the lock on the flimsy door to the main floor where everyday life is lived. No wonder later the adult male experiences sleep disturbances, nightmares, and feelings of vague "dysphoria." This man vaguely senses something isn't right; he feels this diffuse tension but can't name it, can't find the words. His emotional lexicon is limited; "weird" might come to mind, or "bummed out." If asked, he is likely to draw a blank about himself. But his wife, he complains, cannot do anything right. She doesn't keep the house clean, nor does she fix the meals properly, nor dress the kids as she should. If only she did, everything would be OK between them, he says. He wouldn't have to yell at her or hit her, as he sometimes does. These violent outbursts enable him to get rid of the dysphoric feelings temporarily. The tension he was accumulating dissipates. If he drives her away, though, the terror gets worse, manifesting itself in extreme actions to get her back including threats of suicide. Several independent studies have shown that such threats are not merely manipulative—that men with these disturbances of self are prone to suicide during threatened abandonments.[9]

Psychologist David Winter used Klein and Riviere's analysis to explain the myth of Don Juan, "the most persistent and durable character in Western literature," an archetype involving the connection between sex and power.[10] Don Juan alternately seduced and abandoned women, going to great lengths to publicly humiliate them in the process. In his own words, "even more than seduction, the greatest pleasure is to trick women and leave them dishonored."[11] Hence, Don Juan's sexual motivation had more to do with power and a desire to humiliate a woman than it had to do with sexual pleasure. What's more, he alternates in his response, being obsessed with approach (seduction) and avoidance (abandonment). Don Juan's victims are typically involved with another man, preferably a man of high social standing. At first glance, compulsive sexuality may seem to have little to do with anger. However, if the male is in a committed relationship where conflict issues are not getting resolved or where his needs are not being met, when instead of expressing this problem to his partner he "acts out" sexually through a series of affairs, there is a strong possibility that an anger element is driving his sexuality. These "sexual tantrums" are not unknown to clinicians. Peter Trachtenberg has written an insightful analysis of what he calls the Casanova Complex, by which he refers to a variety of sexual styles men engage in with the aim of seducing a series of women. The problem faced by sexual addicts has a motivational base that transcends sex and derives from power and intimacy management. It was this issue that Winter tried to explain.

Seduction becomes a power play whereby the man evens the score. Sex, for such men, is all about power and control. When the sex is over, they can't wait to leave. Severing relations without warning or farewell, Trachtenberg points out, is a way of annihilating the partner left behind, of punishing her for failing to meet the tyrannical demands of his ego. A subsidiary objective for some men seems to be protection from getting too close to a woman emotionally. Some men maintain a long relationship but maintain at least one other sexual/emotional connection with a woman, and occasionally a series of affairs. Trachtenberg sees them as having a fear of commitment and attachment, which they deal with by discontinuing relationships when they get to a point of making plans. Typically, they search for women they can control, especially in the sense of controlling the socioemotional distance in the relationship. Usually, this means keeping the woman at a distance but available when the man wants her. Polygyny is a useful safety valve for men who fear intimacy and commitment. As Trachtenberg put it, "An abundance of sexual choice makes it possible to see women regularly for years without feeling bound to them. . . . [N]o need to worry that they will reveal too much of themselves to any one partner: they can get away with telling the same stories and same jokes a lot longer if the audience keeps changing. . . . [F]inally, polygyny greatly reduces the risk of rejection, providing jugglers with a reassuring safety net of sexual alternatives."[12]

This is also a power strategy, since demands from any one lover can be met by increased investment in her "rival." As Trachtenberg notes, this is a convenient way of diverting anger, since the women are more likely to vent their resentments on competitors than on the men they sleep with and need. Hence, the "other woman" can be turned into a scapegoat for the intimacy tensions in the relationship, as an example of what the man wants in a woman (or of what he doesn't want). The jealousy, envy, and anger that she engenders provides emotional control devices for the man. They can be used to move the woman emotionally closer or further away. Trachtenberg sums it up follows: "The struggle for dominance, with its ceaseless manipulation and testing of the beloved, is both a struggle for unconditional adoration and a defense against the threat of engulfment that is always implicit in such love."[13] The psychic costs of such arrangements include a lack of spontaneity (since the juggler is trapped by his "socioemotional position"), boredom (since women are reduced to pawns in a game), and insecurity (since the strains of the system of demands is too difficult to satisfy for long). As Sigmund Freud put it, "Where such men love they have no desire and where they desire they cannot love."[14] In this sense the split between "good girls" and "bad girls" (or Madonnas and Whores) represent male conceptual categories which themselves are emotionally based—the former representing the socialized and repressed idealized male view of mother as asexual, and the latter an emotional catchbasin for those repressed drives. In a sense the male rage demonstrated toward "bad girls" may be a form of defensive projection whereby the hated and repressed longing for the mother is projected onto the bad girl who is then punished (i.e., the victim in slasher films is always portrayed as the sexually promiscuous female). All forms of personal cost can accrue to feed this habit, which Trachtenberg sees as an addiction. He cites the case of Gary Hart, who threw away a promising political career.

Psychoanalyst Otto Rank interpreted the Don Juan legend in Oedipal terms: "The many women whom Don Juan has to replace again and again represent to him the irreplaceable mother, while his adversaries, [whom he] deceived, fought and eventually killed, represent the unconquerable mortal enemy, the father."[15] Winter rejects this interpretation, however, in favor of the pre-Oedipal analysis developed by Klein in which "Don Juan cruelly abandons women because he expects that the mother will eventually desert him. . . . These elements of the legend represent a disguised wish for reunion or fusion with the mother. . . . [R]age and aggression toward women are more important in the Don Juan figure than sexuality as such."[16] Winter then cites Klein and Riviere's section from *Love, Hate and Reparation* that deals with contempt as a defense mechanism. In their terms, contempt "can be a useful and widespread mechanism for enabling us to bear disappointments without becoming savage."[17]

Klein and Riviere saw contempt as a masked form of "turning away from what we really admire and desire" and viewed it as the main source "of all the countless varieties of faithlessness, betrayal, desertion, infidelity, and treachery so constantly manifested in life . . . especially by the Don Juans." Klein and Riviere saw this pattern as insatiable longings, leading to inevitable dissatisfaction, and then contempt and hatred for the source of the disappointment.[18] Then,

> All the evil impulses in themselves—the hate, greed and revengeful disappointment—they then expel psychologically into the person . . . from whom they had expected so much . . . and naturally feel it necessary to turn away and flee from that person. . . . [I]n fleeing from a good thing that has become bad in our eyes, we are—in our minds—preserving a vision of goodness which had almost been lost; for by discovering it elsewhere, we seem . . . to bring it to life in another place. We try to make a fantastic "reparation" by acclaiming the goodness unharmed elsewhere.[19]

Of course, one cannot always flee physically. Some men, bonded by legal marriage and a sense of commitment, flee emotionally or else stay and express their contempt in abusiveness.

This tendency in its extreme form was described by Klein and Riviere as being essentially narcissistic, the hallmark of someone who looked to others to constantly nourish them and was related to the original frustration at the breast and the turning away from the so-called bad object. The perpetual search for the Holy Grail, in the form of a better lover, was a means of maintaining the notion of the "good object."

In his brilliant Pulitzer Prize-winning work, *The Denial of Death,* Ernest Becker reprises and amplifies this theme of inevitable disappointment in the love object.[20] This disappointment was the doomed "Romantic Solution" to spiritual–existential malaise that plagued modern man deracinated from a sense of both community and spirituality. Becker pointed out how love songs deified the lover as angelic; in so doing, the lover attempted to elevate his own self to the ideal and in the process obliterate his own conflicts, contradictions, shortcomings, and sense of separation from the cosmos. The burden, obviously too much for any human relationship to bear, leads to inevitable disappointment and rage. The very problem is that the love object, being human, has imperfections—including a will of her own!

As Becker put it:

> When we look for the "perfect" human object we are looking for someone who allows us to express our will completely, without any frustration or false notes. We want an object that reflects a truly ideal image of ourselves. But no human being can do this; humans have wills and counterwills of their own, in a thousand ways they can move against us, their very appetites offend us. . . . If a woman loses her beauty, or shows that she doesn't have the strength and dependability that we once thought she did, or loses her intellectual sharpness, or falls short of our own peculiar needs in any of a thousand ways, then all the investment we have made in her is undermined. The shadow of imperfection falls over out lives. . . . This is the reason for so much bitterness, shortness of temper and recrimination in our daily lives. We get back a reflection from our loved objects that is less than the grandeur and perfection that we need to nourish ourselves. We feel diminished by their shortcomings. Our interiors feel empty or anguished, our lives valueless, when we see the inevitable pettiness of the world expressed through the human beings in it. For this reason, too, we often attack loved ones and try to bring them down to size.[21]

Becker attributes the rage of intimacy to the human partner's inability to permanently free us of the collected existential concerns of the day. Klein and Riviere attribute this rage to a "vision of goodness that has been lost," that is, a memory of perfect fusion with the breast. Whatever the source, these authors view intimacy as rage producing. Neither, however, tells us much about individual differences in intimate rage. Again we are faced with the same problem of sociobiological and feminist analyses, the problem of individual variation. Suffice it to say, however, that those men who feel more empty and anguished than others, and who feel less value or meaning in their lives, tend to place greater burdens on their intimate relationships. Those who score high on BPO feel more empty. One of the items of the Identity Diffusion subscale reads, "I feel empty inside." Anguish is a constant demon for these men. Trauma symptoms such as insomnia, depression, and anxiety are daily experiences. Usually these are blotted out by alcohol, drugs, or rage which overrides these more painful feelings. Rage is the magic elixir that restores an inner sense of power. What's more, the abuse itself can be functional: A woman convinced that she is unattractive or deficient is less likely to attempt to bond with another man. In an instant of rage the power-lessness and jealousy evaporate.

There is a way out of this perpetual process of unrealistic expectation and cyclical disappointment. That is to mourn the loss of what was never attained and attempt to integrate the good and bad aspects of what is still possible. Most people, however, rather than acknowledge the loss of what was desired and not attained, turn from it and hold it in contempt. They devalue it, dismiss it, run from it, or abuse it. The models for male grieving are few. Perhaps that's why the blues are so much more popular with men than women. They serve a socially sanctioned form of expression for this lost and unattainable process. Why introspect on personal loss when it can be done vicariously through endless songs of booze, woe and women who've caught the train and gone. When Robert Johnson sings, "I've been mistreated and I don't mind dyin'," a multitude of men feel their own unmet yearnings and nod in assent. I'm hurt and it was her fault.

Winter, too, tried to grapple with the problem of individual difference. Although as children all men probably experience the mother as a source of frustration and pleasure, all men do not resort to pathological behaviors as adults. Therefore, frustration and pleasure must be combined in some special way for men who go through approach–avoid/destroy–humiliate cycles with women in order to produce their insatiable longing and the aggressive and deprecating rage. The basis of this cyclical behavior, argues Winter, seems to be a special kind of ambivalence, or alternating behavior, in the mother: she mixes both rejection or frustration with affection and pleasure in such a complex way that the child cannot separate them, subdivide them, and distribute them elsewhere. In short, the child cannot develop a consistent and unambivalent attitude toward the mother, nor later toward women in general. For him, women will always be alluring, loving, faithless, and treacherous. For him, therefore, women are irresistible and dangerous. If the abandon-ment of the infant Don Juan was the mother's withdrawal of emotional availability, then the adult Don Juan cannot simply reject women for he is bound to them in the classic dilemma of depend-ence: fusion with the mother (i.e., with all women) is at the same time both an ultimate source of pleasure and identity and the source of frustration and threatened destruction. Don Juan is thus driven to approach women; but at the same time he is threatened by them, flees them, and is driven to an exaggerated male striving for sexual control, power, and prestige.[22]

Some contradiction and ambivalence is inevitable in maternal behavior, but why should a mother behave in an especially binding way: perhaps to control the child as an object of her own power and satisfy her own needs? Winter speculates that mothers often act ambivalently toward their sons, especially in societies where there is great sexual differentiation and women are suppressed and restricted by men. Such ambivalence arises from anger generally against men, specifically against the child's father and her own father. That anger in such special milieus infuses each woman's relationship with her sons, interspersing nurturance with rejection. Moreover, if a boy's father is rejecting and abusive, the boy is affected in several ways. He may feel hurt by the father's rejection. He may model the father's abusive behavior. Additionally the father's behavior may well impact on the boy's mother, influencing her relationship with her son. Thus the oscillating maternal behavior of the spouse of an abusive, rejecting father may be a link in the tortuous chain of a dysfunctional family. Her own ambivalence and indirect anger toward her son may stem from an intermittently abusive relationship with her husband (and/or her own father), a society that has disempowered her, or both. Winter opens a new pathway for us here. He suggests that the origin of differences in male dependency and rage may reside in early attachment relationships. We will explore this idea more in the next chapter.

Another brilliant perspective on the origin of rage was being developed at the Masters Children's Center in New York by Margaret Mahler and associates.[23] They, too, were interested in the "splitting" of internal perceptions of the mother into "all good" or "all bad" categories. They saw this as occurring during what she called the "rapprochement subphase" of separation–individuation at age 16–26 months. In their developmental model, the earliest stages are called autism (where awareness contains only physiological needs and wish fulfillment), symbiosis (where the infant becomes aware of the mothers role in need satisfaction and experiences her as a part of itself in a dual entity), and differentiation (where from months 4–10 the infant begins to differentiate the mother and itself from other external objects).

When infants become toddlers and can walk away from mother (in the practicing subphase from 10 to 14 months) some dramatic changes occur in their emotional world. They begin to exhibit frustration–anger and separation anxiety—in other words, a growing awareness of separation and of differentiation of the self from the mother. The infant boy begins to realize that he is separate and on his own. As this awareness of separation grows (in the rapprochement subphase, 15–24 months), the infant seems to have an increased need for mother to share with him every one of his new skills and experiences. His need for closeness, held in abeyance throughout the previous developmental period, becomes evident at the very time he is developing the capability of creating physical distance between himself and his mother. Mahler and associates call this the rapprochement subphase of individuation. As they put it, "One cannot emphasize too strongly the importance of optimal emotional availability of the mother during this subphase."[24] Of course, if that mother is coping with an abusive husband, she may find "optimal emotional availability" difficult to provide with constancy. This aspect of abusiveness, despite its important ramifications for the development of a rageful self, is entirely overlooked by social learning theory.

At this stage, the infant searches for or avoids body contact with the mother; voice as well as touch become prominent. The infant engages in "shadowing" (incessant watching of and following every move of the mother) and "darting away," thereby indicating his wish for reunion with the love object and fear of reengulfment by it. He has only recently achieved autonomy and experiences ambivalence. He enjoys the new freedom but doesn't want to lose the love object. He begins to learn that he is not omnipotent but small and dependent. At the same time, since this autonomy is new and exciting, the dependency must be denied or suppressed. The experiential result is vacillation between desires for reunion and merging and desires for separateness and autonomy. In his actions, he expresses this as intense demandingness and clinging, alternating with intense negativity and battling. In this sense, it is his first experience with the paradoxical demands of intimacy: to be oneself and yet be part of a relationship, with the intense ambivalence this generates. As the aforementioned authors put it, "The period was thus characterized by the rapidly alternating desire to push mother away and to cling to her—a behavioral sequence that the word 'ambitendency' describes most accurately. But already at this age there was a often a simultaneous desire in both directions; that is, the characteristic ambivalence of children in the middle of the rapprochement subphase."[25]

The toddler's ability to tolerate being apart from his mother depends on his developing "introjects" or "inner representations" of the mother. If he develops an introject of a warm nurturant base to whom he can return whenever he wants, he wanders further afield. At the same time he still needs to return to her frequently. However, when he gets there he is likely to "veer away" from her (and boys do this more than girls). The trick for the mother at this stage is to remain emotionally available while still allowing the toddler to set out on his own. If the mother becomes too unavailable, the toddler invests too much energy in "wooing her" and doesn't have enough left for developmental steps. On the other hand, if the mother is too anxious and begins her own shadowing process, the toddler is intruded upon and cannot separate. He literally forces his attention toward the outside world to avoid intrusion and cannot easily return to the mother. As Mahler et al. state, "Conceptualization of these rapprochement phenomena was made even more complicated and puzzled by the fact that this blurred identity of mother in the outside world coincided, quite frequently, with a tendency on the mother's part to react adversely to her separating, individuating toddler. The mother's reaction at that time was often tinged with feelings of annoyance at the toddlers' insistence on his autonomy."[26] Again, I wonder how an abused mother can possibly provide these crucial and sensitively tuned responses.

Thus, Mahler and colleagues view the child's developmental task as the necessity to reconcile powerful urges to develop and maintain a separate identity with equally powerful urges to reunite or fuse with the mother. The authors extended this view to the human life span by viewing life as a dance between the desire for autonomy and the desire for refusion. Put somewhat differently, relationship issues become issues of optimal distance. Too little distance carries the threat of reengulfment and identity loss; too much distance carries the threat of loss of the other. The origins of this dance occur during the "separation–individuation" phase of development when the infant has first learned to walk away from the parent.

Compare these notions of "optimal distance" with those of our earlier reports of research with wife assaulters. These men reacted with extreme anxiety and anger to scenarios of "abandonment" that seemed innocuous to other men. Males in intimate relationships react to perceived uncontrollable changes in socioemotional distance or intimacy with emotional arousal that they label as anger. An "optimal zone" for individuals was defined as that degree of emotional closeness or distance between themselves and their partners with which they feel comfortable at any given time. Departures from this comfort zone produce the most extreme rage in assaultive men. Assaultive men also have personality deficits that render them most susceptible to dependency on and anxiety about relationship loss. For assaultive males, given their typical emotional isolation and their exaggerated dependence on the female, accompanied by their often traditional sex role attitudes, the psychological result of perceived loss of the female was panic and hysterical aggression. At this point, we suggest that the roots of such emotional patterns may be found during the separation–individuation phase. My own hunch is that a by-product of an abusive father is a mother who cannot possibly balance the difficult demands of this process. In this way, the abusiveness, even if it is not physical abusiveness, has important ramifications for the boy's personality, not just his behavior. In a later chapter, we will see that the abusive personality is related to abusive behavior but the form the abuse takes can vary greatly. Some men are emotionally abusive; others, physically and emotionally abusive. Both type of men probably came from families with rejecting or abusive fathers; the physically abusive men more likely had a father who was physically abusive in addition.

At around 21 months of age, "the clamoring for omnipotent control," the extreme periods of separation anxiety, and the alternation of demands for closeness and autonomy begin to subside and each child begins to find an "optimal distance" from his mother. This is defined by Mahler et al. as "the distance at which he could function best" and represents a compromise between separation anxiety (if too far from the mother) and engulfment (if too close).[27]

As Margaret Mahler would put it, "splitting" of internal perceptions occurs because of problems in differentiating the self from the "object" (mother) during the developmental period. Since mothers are the source of universal delight and frustration in infants, rage toward the mother develops when pleasure is withheld, as it must inevitably be. The sense of one's own rage is terrifying since it carries with it the possibility of destroying (or wishing to destroy) the source of delight. Hence, infants have to defend mother against their own rage. They do this by "splitting" her into good and bad parts. The "bad mother" is initially the mother that is withholding or absent. The "good mother" is the one that is gratifying. If the child's own rage is projected onto the bad mother, then she is seen as dangerous. If this split in the young boy's psychic representations of his mother is maintained, this projection could form the basis of the view that women (or some category of women) are dangerous, evil, or both. Since males give more evidence of externalizing than do females, this splitting of the opposite gender into good and bad based on object representations would be more common for males.

Both Klein's and Mahler's analyses suggest that men may divide women into two categories that originate with splitting of the mother into good and bad parts. These categories will be colored by social values obtained later in development, but they will have their basis in this original split. For this reason, an apparently inexplicable set of rage-driven behaviors may be directed toward the "bad mother" category. This may be any woman experienced as frustrating or rejecting, more strongly so of course if she is an intimate, or it may extend to a generalized category of women seen as "Whores." The "good mother" representation is reserved for "Madonnas," who are "the kind of girl you take home to mother." The Whores become the recipients of all repressed emotions: rage, sexuality, and all blends of the two. The Madonnas are "respected" (sexuality toward them is suppressed). Both categories suffer an awful fate: the former is abused, and the latter is stifled and compared to an ideal. In the end, no full human relationship is possible with either. In between lies a continuum of ambivalence into which other relationships with women may fall. Don Juan is driven to approach women, but at the same time he is threatened by them, flees them, and is driven to an exaggerated male striving for sexual control, power, and prestige.

When in their "normal" phase, most assaultive men are unable to assert intimacy needs or dissatisfactions. As tension and feelings of being unloved and unappreciated build, the man's "rageful self" (held in abeyance and outside of consciousness) begins to emerge and his view of his wife becomes increasingly negative. He has "split off," because expressing his frustrations to the all-powerful, life-sustaining "good object" (Madonna/mother) would risk not just rejection but annihilation (just as the risk was felt to be too great in infancy). He ruminates on the concept of his wife as a Whore: unfaithful, sexually promiscuous, malevolent, and unloving. After all, doesn't society teach men that their wives are somehow responsible for making them feel good? Then if they feel bad (and men with this kind of disturbance will inevitably "feel bad" every now and then), it must be their wives' fault.

Since an uncompleted rapprochement task plagues abusive

adult males, we find certain similarities in early and later dysfunction. These include the inability to use language in a way that
generates a sense of control, or (as we call it in adults) "spouse-
specific assertiveness." Instead, these men are extreme in either of
two directions—being *unassertive*, leading to occasional explosions
(the "overcontrolled" batterer), or being *the dominator*, who uses
every form of control (financial, emotional, physical) rather than
negotiation. The development of "positive introjects" (images of a
nurturant attachment object even when that object is not present)
does not occur, so the adult abusive male cannot soothe himself or
handle stress well. As a result, adults with remnants of rapprochement conflict have a tendency to lose sight of themselves in intimate
relationships. Hence, they experience anxiety about both closeness
and separation, poor spouse-specific assertiveness, and poor tolerance of aloneness (or conversely high dependency). Assaultive males
present this very profile. Abusers search for women they can
control, especially in the sense of controlling the socioemotional
distance in the relationship, perhaps as a way of finally generating
control over the original trauma of a failed rapprochement. When
we try to control something there is usually anxiety and anger
behind the behavior. The anxiety signals a threat; the anger generates agentic or active responses to control the threat. When the
need for control is high, it is safe to assume that anxiety and anger
are also present and strong. When that control is threatened,
anxiety and anger quickly appear.

Hence, pre-Oedipal notions contain some key psychological
issues that seem relevant later in adult relationships: need satisfaction, frustration, and rage; identity and ambivalence. It is at this
pre-Oedipal age (17–24 months) that temper tantrums begin. In
other words, expressions of rage temporally coincide with the
advent of separation–individuation issues. Object relations theory,
too, describes the development of internalized representations of
self and others from a more psychoanalytical perspective. And
regardless of which theory is applicable, would these emotional
reactions persist into adulthood? My view is that they do not persist
in any evident form but become latent until another relationship
occurs that carries emotional threats in a fashion similar to the early
relationship. Intimate romantic relationships are the closest the
male comes to re-creating this early union, especially if he suffers
from identity issues that make him feel more vulnerable in the adult
relationship. The extreme, out-of-control nature of an infant's rage

is similar to the descriptions battered women make of battering incidents. In fact, this extreme violence is often referred to as "infantile rage."

Recently, David Celani developed an object relations view of battering relationships that analyses the identity problems of both the batterer and his victim. In *The Illusion of Love*, Celani describes the three basic ego processes that result in healthy development: *differentiation* of the self from the mother (sometimes referred to as separation or individuation); *introjection* of the mother's positive soothing statements into the self; and *integration* of the good and bad aspects of others. Celani sees failures in all three processes manifested in battering relationships. The lack of differentiation manifests in the extreme codependency batterers and their victims have on each other. Similarly, the lack of introjection manifests in their inner emptiness and ability to self-soothe. The lack of integration in the "splitting" we described above. But Celani traces these developmental failures in both batterers and victims back to mothers who were so involved with their own needs that they were unable to nurture the next generation. Using the fictional example of Sophie Portnoy from Philip Roth's *Portnoy's Complaint*, Celani describes the power that Sophie realizes through rejection of her son, leaving him with an "unresolved dependency": an emotional Catch-22 in which an individual cannot separate until he feels fulfilled by his parent (who cannot or will not cooperate).[28] Such individuals carry deep emotional needs into adult relationships, often choosing partners that resemble the rejecting parent or else demanding that the partner right the wrongs inflicted by the parent. When the partner fails to do the impossible, rage develops.

Object relations theory focuses on the origin of a split in the human psyche, a split that could later become the twin personality of the abusive man. The rageful personality manifests itself in the tension phase of the abuse cycle, fraught with unexpressed yearning and building negativity. The "socialized" personality becomes the contrite, repentant self who idealizes the wife who has nearly been lost through the previous abuse. Klein and Mahler focused on a narrow temporal band of child development. Soon a new approach would come to dominate research on social development. That later approach, called attachment theory (discussed in the next chapter), would focus on a broader temporal spectrum and would begin to close the gap between studies of infants and studies of the subsequent adult personality.

7

An Anger Born of Fear: Attachment Rage

The problem with the object relations approach, of course, is that it is merely a theory, based on little in the way of empirical evidence. Melanie Klein's notions were based on conjectures about the inner life of infants. Furthermore these conjectures occurred without regard for the actions of parents that may have caused those inferred thoughts and feelings. As with most psychoanalysts, Klein viewed the infant as living in a vacuum with a faceless "mother" who was little more than a role, a menu, a shopping list of responses possessing no qualities or characteristics of her own. This absence was obvious when David Winter came to apply Klein's theory to his own analysis; he was forced to use his own speculations about what kind of maternal actions might produce ambivalent men. The answer was not forthcoming from Klein's writings. Whatever happened to generate splits or primitive defenses in Klein's theory happened as part of an inevitable maturational process. The actions of the parent were not implicated, and Winter had to supply his own speculations as to what they might be. Margaret Mahler had considered the question in terms of "variations within subphases," as she put it. She wanted to determine "points of vulnerability" in development that might be influenced by "early mother–child interaction and relationship" but concluded that the process "tended to appear rather complex ... and no regular relations among the various factors could be discerned in the middle range of normalcy with our present research tools."[1]

One of Klein's own students, John Bowlby, a man psychoanalyzed by Klein, was particularly disturbed by this inattention to the context of mothering. Bowlby was about to provide a theory that would put the mother back into the equation. What's more, this theory would eventually prove testable thanks to the innovative research skills of Mary Ainsworth.

THE ANTHROPOLOGY OF ATTACHMENT

Over the course of millions of years, large skulls developed in our early ancestors (called hominids) to hold highly developed brains, probably because changes in climate forced some hominids such as *Australopithecus* to become hunters–gatherers. These larger skulls require a prolonged period of growth after birth. There was now a much longer period of developmental immaturity with human infants than with other species. Developmental immaturity required prolonged dependency on a person who could provide safety and a pervasive feeling of security and had the biological function of protecting the attached infant from physical and psychological harm. For these reasons, attachment is a sociobiologically determined cultural universal. With humans, who have a prolonged period of dependency on a caregiver (or "attachment object") providing food, shelter, and basic safety needs, this process of attachment is of paramount importance and its emotional consequences are strong. Bowlby built a bridge between sociobiology and what later came to be known as "attachment theory." There was, he argued, a strong case for sociobiological origins to infant attachment. However, what transpired between the infant and its caregiver could send that infant off along a number of individual paths each influencing its personality and emotional reactions, especially in intimate relationships. These reactions maintain "from the cradle to the grave." The anger or anxiety that someone feels in reaction to their mate leaving for a vacation or staying away too long has origins in early attachment.

The shift from forest dwellers to hunters–gatherers had two other important consequences for this issue of prolonged dependency: humankind became "specialized," with males doing the hunting and females the nurturing of infants, and "pair-bonding" developed. Hunting required great cooperation and a minimum of sexual rivalry—hence, the

> allotment of one female for one male on a semipermanent basis. In turn, this pair-bonding allowed for a great increase in hunting cooperation, in what can be termed male-bonding. Obviously, the weaker males could no longer be frustrated by stronger ones as among other primates; successful hunting required the cooperation of all males, all of whom had to be sexually satisfied. Perhaps the most important result of this pair-bonding was the birth of the nuclear monogamous family structure for the benefit of the young: one male provided for one female and her offspring. Pair-bonding was undoubtedly related to a radical change in sexual posture. The hominids personalized sex by adopting face-to-face mating, something that is of utmost importance in pair-bonding because it links the specific partners more intimately.[2]

This hunting–gathering arrangement survived for about a million years, yielding only in the last 10,000–12,000 years to agricultural ways of life.

Hence, a division of labor by gender, pair-bonding, and prolonged infant attachment to a female caregiver has been the normative family social arrangement for more than a million years. It serves the biological function of protecting the attached infant from physical and psychological harm and affords proximity to a person who can provide safety and a sense of security.

We live the first years of our lives in total dependency on another person who literally has life-and-death power over us. As attachment is necessary for survival, males learn early on that mother (and hence intimate women) has a life-and-death power over them. An enormous felt power differential exists between the male child and the apparently omnipotent mother. All socioeconomic analyses that focus on "earning power" and draw conclusions about male subjective feelings of power based on these later adult indicators miss the reality of this early power deficit vis-à-vis a woman.

Power differentials, in and of themselves, promote bonding. They are, for example, central to the bonding that occurs between victim and captor in hostage-taking situations, creating the well-known "Stockholm syndrome" where captives bond to their captors, identifying with the captors' perspective as a survival defense mechanism.[3] Hence, one reality that may differentiate males from females is that males develop a stronger bond to an opposite gender person at an earlier developmental stage. This bond contains a sense of powerlessness that may persist into adult intimate bonding.

Do feelings of this magnitude occur from the original powerlessness? And are they assuaged only by loving contact with the mother? Does sexual contact in adult life arouse these feelings of vulnerability and the attendant anxiety that calls up? Does this anxiety translate easily into anger for males? True emotional safety and security are initially associated with the physical presence of a woman. This may be why even adult males find it easier "to open up" with a woman. Conversely, when these security needs are frustrated early on by a woman, the resulting emotional reaction may be extreme and long lived. For females, these emotional lessons apply more to the same sex since women are the primary caregivers in most cultures.

THE BOWLBY ATTACHMENT THEORY

In 1939, in a paper to the British Psychoanalytic Society, Bowlby outlined his views on the type of childhood experiences that led to psychological disorders.[4] Sigmund Freud, of course, as far back as 1896 had argued that childhood trauma, of the nature of premature sexual contact with an adult, caused later psychological problems in women. The ideas in that paper, although brilliant and far ahead of their time, were subsequently abandoned by Freud, as the negative reaction to them by his colleagues appeared career threatening.[5] Victorian psychiatry could not believe that the incidence of familial sexual abuse could be as common as the incidence of "female hysteria."[6] Freud turned instead to an intrapsychic view—that these sexual contacts were, in fact, imaginary, a process called "wish fulfillment." These "wishes" rather than any actual sexual contact became the focus of psychoanalysis. Bowlby did not cross this intellectual minefield. Instead, he quietly suggested that the process of interviewing adult patients led to a neglect of the actual occurrences of childhood experience. Child health care workers of the day focused on the "home environment" in only coarse and general ways: Was the family "intact?" "Did it go to church?" "Was the house well kept?" In so doing, they missed what Bowlby considered the most important aspects of early childhood: prolonged separations from the mother, and the mothers' emotional attitude toward the child. That attitude became apparent in how she handled the feeding, weaning, toilet training, and daily aspects of maternal care. Some mothers demonstrate an unconscious hostility toward the child which shows up in small signs of dislike accompanied by an overprotective attitude designed to compensate for the hostility. This overprotection comprised "being afraid to let the child out of their sight, fussing over minor illness, worrying lest something terrible should happen to their darlings."[7] The underlying hostility emerges in "unnecessary deprivations and frustrations, in impatience over naughtiness, in odd words of bad temper, in a lack of sympathy and understanding which the usually loving mother intuitively has."[8]

In a landmark series of books entitled *Attachment and Loss,* Bowlby developed the notion that human attachment was of ultimate importance for human emotional development. It served a vital biological function indispensable for the survival of the infant. In his view, the human need for secure attachment is the result of a long-term evolutionary development that rivaled feeding and mating in importance. It had, in other words, sociobiological significance. Crawling toward mother to "attach" served an evolutionary function. Providing nourishing physical contact to one's infant did the same. Bowlby's ideas went beyond those of sociobiologists in that his views encompassed the possibility of individual differences. The individual differences came to be called "attachment styles" and referred to an entire constellations of thoughts and feelings about intimacy. These differences, he theorized, came about because of different aspects of maternal attachment behaviors. Reactions to the satisfaction or dissatisfaction of early attempts at attachment set up life-long attachment styles described as secure, fearful, or dismissing. The dismissing people tend to be wary of and stay out of relationships. The secure ones are comfortable with closeness. The fearful ones are stuck in the middle, exhibiting an ambivalence toward intimacy and to those with whom they are emotionally connected. This push–pull reaction, of course, resembles the ebb and flow of the cyclical personality we considered earlier. Could the cyclical personality have its origin in maternal intermittent unavailability?

Attachment is governed by three important principles: first, alarm of any kind, stemming from any source activates an *attachment behavioral system* of the infant. That is, whenever the infant is stressed or alarmed, it walks or crawls toward its mother and seeks soothing physical contact. Second, when this system is intensely active, only *physical contact with the attachment figure* will serve to terminate it. Nothing else will do. It has to be soothing contact with the mother. Finally, when the attachment system is activated for a long time without reaching termination, *angry behavior* is regularly observed in the infant. Hence, a fundamental conclusion of attachment theory is that anger follows unmet attachment needs. The "original anger" stems from frustrated and unsuccessful attempts to attach. When the stressed infant seeks soothing contact and it isn't available, the result is rage, followed by depression and then indifference. Thus, the original motive for anger is to reestablish soothing contact. In adults, endogenous tension cycles have an eerie resemblance to such attachment processes in children. The tension builds from within in a person who cannot self-soothe. The need for soothing is not identified or articulated. Hence, desired contact from the partner is not forthcoming. As the tension continues to build, the predominant motive is escape (with a hidden wish that the other will come to the rescue), then rage when this does not happen. The adult cycle recapitulates the early process described by Bowlby.

Bowlby defined attachment as a bond developed with "some other differentiated and preferred individual who is conceived as stronger and/or wiser."[9] Proportional to this sense of the other as having absolute and unrestricted power over the infant, threats or separations to that secure attachment should produce emotional responses that are extremely strong; like terror, grief, and rage. In males these fundamental and primitive emotions are initially connected to a woman. Since that woman has unrestricted life-and-death power over the male infant, some initial emotional tracks are laid that are extremely powerful.

Bowlby reported observations of the reactions of children (age 15–30 months) in nurseries who were separated for the first time from their parents. These reactions underwent three distinct phases which he called Protest, Despair, and Detachment. It is instructive to read Bowlby's own description of these reactions:

> [In] the initial phase [Protest], the young child appears acutely distressed at having lost his mother and seeks to recapture her by the full exercise of his limited resources. He will often cry loudly, shake his cot, throw himself about, and look eagerly towards any sight or sound which might prove to be his missing mother. All his behaviour suggests strong expectation that she will return....

> During the phase of despair, . . . his behaviour suggests increasing
> hopelessness, The active physical movements diminish or come to
> an end, and he may cry monotonously or intermittently. He is
> withdrawn and inactive . . . and appears to be in a state of deep
> mourning. . . . [In] the phase of detachment, when his mother visits
> it can be seen that all is not well, for their is a striking absence of
> the behaviour characteristic of strong attachment normal at this
> age. So far from greeting his mother, he may hardly seem to know
> her; so far from clinging to her he may seem remote and apathetic;
> instead of tears there is a listless turning away.[10]

In other words, the actions associated with the first (Protest) phase of separation can be construed as angry. They all involve actions generated agentically (outward on the world) in order to produce a result (in this case the return of the mother). Loud crying and shaking of the cot are prototypical forms of later physical acts we would call aggressive. The first and primary function of anger is to reestablish soothing contact with the attachment figure. By adulthood the male has learned and reshaped these actions over a lifetime so that crying is replaced by shouting, shaking the cot by throwing or smashing objects . Control over the woman's emotional distance becomes a preemptive strike precluding the need to display rage for her return, except when the control breaks and she leaves. At these junctures the suppressed dependency explodes in a pyro-technic display of rage and desperation. But the motive is the same even if the behaviors have changed: an attempt to regain control through physical actions. With the infant, it is only after prolonged failure to have actions lead to a successful re-creation of the mother's presence that the subsequent emotions of depression (mourning) and eventual detachment appear. With adult males, the realization that a wife or lover is leaving or has left produces deep depression and suicidal ideation (or threats/actions) after anger and violence have failed. Suicide threats are common in abusive men whose lovers are leaving them. In the more psychopathic individuals these may be purely manipulative. In the borderline cases the suicidal ideation is real.

SEPARATION AND ANGER

Anger is the typical response to separation from the mother. Bowlby cites research where observers noted significant differences in hostile play between separated and non separated children.[11] Separated children "tended to attack parent dolls." This anger toward the parent frequently is expressed intermittently and is interspersed with affection. In such cases Bowlby refers to it as ambivalence. Separated children or children who have suffered some disruption of the attachment bond respond with ambivalence toward their mother for up to 20 weeks after reunion. Such children were described as *"arching away angrily while simultaneously seeking contact"* with their mothers.[12] The ambivalence, in other words, was expressed in their conflicting bodily reactions.

Anger in these situations served two functions: it assisted in overcoming obstacles to reunion and discouraged the loved one from going away again. (Bowlby viewed dysfunctional anger after a death as occurring because the bereaved does not yet accept the death and continues to believe that the departed will return. Hence, the person is functioning emotionally like a separated child.)

As Bowlby stated:

[A]ngry coercive behaviour is not uncommon. It is seen when a mother whose child has foolishly run across the road berates and punishes him with an anger born of fear. It is seen whenever a sexual partner berates the other for being or seeming disloyal. . . . Dysfunctional anger occurs whenever a person, child or adult, becomes so intensely and/or persistently angry with his partner that the bond between them is weakened, instead of strengthened, and the partner is alienated. Anger with a partner becomes dysfunctional also whenever aggressive thoughts or acts cross the narrow boundary between being deterrent and being revengeful. . . . Separations, especially when prolonged or repeated, have a double effect. On the one hand, anger is aroused; on the other, love is attenuated. Thus not only may angry discontented behaviour alienate the attachment figure but, within the attached, a shift can occur in the balance of feeling. Instead of a strongly rooted affection laced occasionally with "hot displeasure" . . . there grows a deep running resentment, held in check only partially by anxious uncertain affection.[13]

Here Bowlby foreshadows the notion, that separation anxiety serves as a substratum for anger in adult romantic relationships. He observes that 15- to 18-year-old youths with behavioral problems seem to have been disciplined by parents who threatened to abandon them if they didn't behave. Such children are made "furiously angry" by a parent's threat to desert; on the other hand, they dare not express that anger lest the parent actually does so. "This is the main reason ... why in these cases anger at a parent usually becomes repressed and is then directed at other targets."[14]

Bowlby expands: "It seems not unlikely that a number of individuals who become literally murderous towards a parent are to be understood as having become so in reaction to threats of desertion that have been repeated relentlessly over many years."[15] Since anger (protest) is the first phase reaction to separation, and also an "*anger born of fear*," this fear must be fear of loss. The anger is designed to re-create that lost object or prevent its disappearance. It is a form both of signaling and controlling. Unfortunately, anger itself generates a subjective state of distance from others. The lack of closeness felt during anger can enhance the sense of separation which generates more anger. Also, if the fear and anger become extreme, are expressed abusively, or come to be used in a revengeful manner, they further distance the other person, and then produce even more fear and rage in response to that increased distance. For these reasons, anger in response to separation can produce an emotional spiral culminating in rage. But the "anger born of fear" constitutes an important source or origin of rage.

Bowlby saw angry expression as serving a regulatory function in attachment relationships. His description of the initial actions of separated infants conveys a sense of rage as an attempt to will the lost mother back into existence. In this sense it is a prototype for the rage adults feel at the loss of a loved one. One of the more difficult feelings for grieving clients to work through therapeutically is their rage at the deceased and their guilt over feeling that rage. As Bowlby put it:

> When a relationship to a special loved person is endangered we are not only anxious but are usually angry as well. . . . As responses to the risk of loss, anxiety and anger go hand in hand. . . . When a child or spouse behaves dangerously, an angry protest is likely to deter. When a lover's partner strays, a sharp reminder how much he or she cares may work wonders. When a child finds herself or himself relatively neglected in favour of the new baby, the child's assertion of claims may redress the balance. Thus in the right place, at the right time, and in right degree, anger is not only appropriate but may be indispensable. It serves to deter from dangerous behaviour, to drive off a rival, or to coerce a partner. In each case the aim of the angry behaviour is the same—to protect a relationship

which is of very special value to the angry person. The specific relationships, threats to which may arouse anger, are of three main types: relationships with a sexual partner–boyfriend, girlfriend or spouse, relationships with parents and relationships with offspring. . . . [W]hen these relationships are threatened, a person is anxious and perhaps angry.[16]

Maladaptive violence is the distorted and exaggerated version of potentially functional behavior.

REJECTION AND ANGER

According to Bowlby, a maternal rebuff activates the attachment systems intensely, and when they are intensely activated only physical contact with the attachment figure will serve to terminate them. If a mother rebuffs or threatens her infant but shortly thereafter permits access, no lasting conflict situation is created. But if the mother sees physical contact with their infant as distasteful (either in general, because of some acute trauma, unresolved anger, or the infant's personality), she will not permit his access thereafter. The resultant conflict within the infant must then be serious, deep, and nonverbal. A single movement on the part of the mother intended to drive her child from her at least initially brings the child toward her. Yet he cannot contact her, even though only contact would terminate the anxious activity of the attachment behavioral system. The renewed recognition of the mothers' inaccessibility should further activate the system, and conflict behaviors should be expected to appear in the infant. When the attachment behavioral system is activated without termination, angry behavior is seen in the infant.

The infant is in a state of continual activation without termination with respect to his mother. Similar to the infant who has long been separated from his mother and left in a strange environment with no substitute caregiver available, the infant cannot obtain contact, yet "must" do so. Strong anger should be expected. This conflict is self-perpetuating. Once an infant is rejected by the attachment figure, the attachment behavioral systems are activated, necessarily frustrated, and therefore still more strongly activated to meet again with more frustrations (attachment attempt → rejection → stronger attachment attempts → stronger frustration). At the same time, withdrawal tendencies conflict with approach tendencies, and the impossibility of approach arouses an anger that can probably be no more safely expressed than can attachment. Eventually, the physically rejected infant may experience anger and withdrawal in every situation that normally arouses love and attachment.

Bowlby foreshadowed the persistence of attachment into adulthood. As he put it:

> When an individual is confident that an attachment figure will be available to him whenever he desires it, that person will be much less prone to either intense or chronic fear than will an individual who for any reason has no such confidence. The second proposition concerns the sensitive period during which such confidence develops. It postulates that confidence in the availability of attachment figures, or lack of it, is built up slowly during the years of immaturity–infancy, childhood, adolescence–and that whatever expectations are developed during those years tend to persist relatively unchanged throughout the rest of life.[17]

These expectations, or as they are sometimes called "working models" or "internal representations" of self and relationship partners, are central components of personality and are "a set of conscious or unconscious rules for the organization of information relevant to attachment, attachment related experiences, feelings and ideations."[18] These "internal representations" (Klein had called them introjects) contain a model of the self as worthy or unworthy of care and love, generate unconscious expectations about the consequences of attachment, and provide a context for later social relationships. In other words, these working models are constellations of ideas about the basic lovability of the self and expectations about the trustworthiness and availability of others. Although these models can be restructured, this is difficult since once they are organized they tend to operate outside conscious awareness and resist dramatic change. Furthermore, they produce "self-fulfilling prophecies": the expectations contained in the internal representation generate behaviors that repeatedly make them come true.

ADULT ATTACHMENT STYLES

Bowlby pointed out that attachment patterns correlated with the patterns of social and play behavior with adults other than the mother. This maintained "during both the second and subsequent years of life," although research evidence available at the time of his writing already indicated continuity into the 5- to 6-year-old range. Now, of course, attachment styles have been related to adult romantic attachment styles, risk for suicide, depression, and (in our own research) adult abusiveness.[19] Before we get to the relationship of attachment to abusiveness, it is important to describe in more detail the nature of "attachment styles" and their relationship to what I would call chronic intimate anger or "an anger template."

Mary Ainsworth and her colleagues began the empirical study of the specific differences in responding to attachment and to separation from their caregiver. These responses were first noted in what has come to be called the "Strange Situation" in which a child is experimentally separated from its parent and its behavior observed. On the basis of these observations, infants were assigned to one of three categories:

The first group of infants, called "secure," greeted their mother with pleasure when she returned, stretching out their arms, and molding to her body. They were relatively easy to console and were distinguished from other groups by the frequency with which they sought emotional sharing with the caregiver, as well as this ability to seek comfort and be calmed by her when distressed. About 62–75% of a North American middle class population fits this category. They have caregivers who readily perceive their needs, accurately interpret them, and promptly and appropriately respond to them as infants. These caregivers (predominantly mothers) provided a predictable and controllable environment that promoted the infant's regulation of arousal and sense of efficacy.[20] Sometimes referred to as "attunement," the essential feature of this maternal responsiveness is that the parent matches through expression the emotional state expressed by the infant. There are vast differences in mothers' abilities to do this. The importance of attunement, however, cannot be overemphasized. In his landmark work, *Affect Regulation and the Origin of the Self,* Allan N. Schore argues persuasively that nothing less than healthy neural development depends on proper attunement during critical periods of neural maturation. The actual physical development of the neural structures that govern emotion is affected by attachment processes.[21]

The second attachment style, described by Ainsworth as "anxious–avoidant" (also called dismissing), gives the impression of independence; these infants explore a new environment without using their mother as a base, and they don't turn around to be certain of their mother's presence (as did the above securely attached group). When separations occur, anxious–avoidant infants do not seem affected, and when mothers return they are snubbed or avoided. Infants who exhibit avoidant attachment communicate with their caregiver only when they are feeling well. When distressed, these infants do not signal the primary caregiver nor seek bodily contact. At 6 years of age, many of these behaviors are still evident. Anxious–avoidant children direct attention away from their mother upon reunion, move away from her physically, seem ill at ease discussing separation, and turn away from family photographs.[22] This set of responses then defines the anxious–avoidant style: minimal displays of affect or distress in the presence of the caregiver, and an avoidance of the attachment figure under conditions that usually (i.e., with the securely attached group) elicit proximity seeking and interaction. They attend to the environment while actively directing attention away from the parent. Robert Karen describes this group as follows:

> The avoidant child takes the opposite tack [to the ambivalent child]. He becomes angry and distant (even though he becomes no less attached). His pleas for attention have been painfully rejected, and reaching out seems impossible. The child seems to say, "Who needs you—I can do it on my own." Often in conjunction with this attitude, grandiose ideas about the self develop: I am great, I don't need anybody. . . . Bowlby believes that avoidant attachment lies at the heart of narcissistic personality traits, one of the predominant psychiatric concerns of our time.[23]

About 32% of Ainsworth's sample fit this category. Mothers of anxious–avoidant children are insensitive, unresponsive, and understimulating, and they have an aversion to physical contact.[24] Dismissing mothers are rejecting of babies' bids for comfort and reassurance, using comments to override the baby's emotional displays. If these don't succeed in quelling the baby's affect display, they are followed by "sadistic misattunement" (i.e., the expression of misaligned feelings). Such mothers tend to be unable to remember details of their own childhoods or to idealize their relationship with their parents, even though they can remember contradictory rejecting memories.[25] Psychologist Kim Bartholomew has observed that although avoidant children's behavior could be interpreted as reflecting a lack of need or desire for contact, there is compelling evidence to the contrary. For example, avoidant children exhibited cardiac acceleration in response to separation in spite of a lack of overt distress.[26] Bartholomew concludes that their apparently innocuous focus on inanimate objects may be a form of displacement behavior. Furthermore, although avoidant children show little aggression in the so-called Strange Situation, they show considerable anger directed toward their mother at home.[27] Also, the greater the avoidance upon reunion with the mother, the greater the display of anger and dependent behavior towards her over the ensuing weeks, again underscoring Bowlby's argument that anger is a protest behavior aimed at increasing proximity with a caregiver. Hence, the anger that avoidant children express toward their mother in less stressful circumstances (presumably in response to her rejecting or unresponsive treatment) can be taken as evidence of their lack of indifference. In response to separation, avoidant infants feel angry with their mother, but the expression of anger in this situation risks decreased proximity, so angry impulses are suppressed and replaced with "cool" detached avoidance.[28] They are expressed when conditions are less stressful or safer. Chronically rejected infants experience particularly strong angry impulses with high avoidance of anger display. Again, in less stressful circumstances the anger is expressed indirectly. Kim Bartholomew argues that strong and unresolvable approach–avoidance may underlie the behavior of chronically avoidant people: threats lead to tendencies to approach the attachment figure, who rejects physical contact, thus generating withdrawal accompanied by an even stronger need for attachment. A self-perpetuating feedback loop ensues that leads to chronic avoidance (presumably accompanied by chronic unfulfilled attachment needs). Hence, anger is central to the anxious–avoidant attachment style. This description makes one wonder whether this particular pattern represents the emotional origin of later withdrawal styles where anger is suppressed. Gayla Margolin found similarities between physically abusive and withdrawn couples in their communication styles.[29] Both were characterized by low assertiveness and conflict avoidance.

The third group of infants, called "anxious–ambivalent" (or preoccupied), tended to be clingy to their mother and resisted exploring the room on their own. They became extremely agitated on separation, often crying profusely. This group typically sought contact with their mothers when she returned but simultaneously arched away from her angrily and resisted all efforts to be soothed. The implication is that these infants somehow incorporate anger into their terror at being "abandoned by the mother." The mothers of these infants tended to be inconsistent and least confident at coping with early caregiving tasks.[30] Later this category was split in two: (1) anxious or preoccupied and (2) ambivalent or fearful. The former subgroup is consistently anxious in intimate relationships, the latter exhibits the push–pull of ambivalence.

Karen describes the resulting behavioral style as follows: "The ambivalent child [such children represent some 10% of youngsters from middle class U.S. homes] is desperately trying to influence her. He is hooked by the fact that she does come through on occasion. He picks up that she will respond—sometimes out of guilt—if he pleads and makes a big enough fuss. And so he is constantly trying to hold onto her or to punish her for being unavailable. He is wildly addicted to her and to his efforts to make her change."[31] These styles of attachment are represented in Figure 7.1.

These ambivalent children sound similar to physically abusive men.[32] The intensity and the need for impact on the woman are reminiscent of the descriptions of the "abusive personality" and of Winter's description of the power motive, which he sees as driving the Don Juan—the sexually promiscuous male who is addicted to a successive pattern of sexual conquest–abandonment.[33]

In a longitudinal study, Allen Sroufe found that third-grade children with anxious attachment had the poorest social skills and

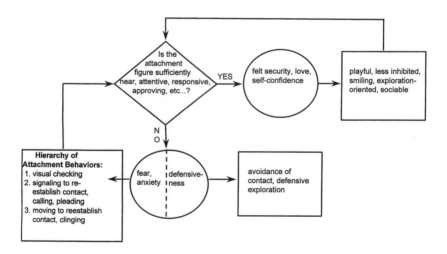

FIGURE 7.1. A flowchart model of the dynamics of attachment and exploration.

clear psychiatric disturbances.[34] Anxiously attached individuals seem to have diminished capacity to form bases of social support and seek it when needed. Hence, a lifelong pattern of isolation may derive from early lessons that support from others is unreliable. Assaultive males are characteristically isolated individuals. Also, gender specific expectations develop. For example, with an absent father and a demanding (but unavailable) mother, a boy learns that males are not available for emotional support and that women appear to be supportive but are ultimately demanding and can't be trusted. As a result, he isolates and withdraws inside himself, while feeling a gnawing anger.

FAULTY ATTACHMENT: DEVELOPMENTAL PSYCHOPATHOLOGY

Intuition tells us that an infant who is intermittently abused by a parent may not form an attachment to that person. However, there is evidence that strong bonds do form under such circumstances that are characterized both by closeness and by repressed anger. As Bowlby put it, "We may presume that an attack from any source arouses some fear and withdrawal tendencies. What is peculiar to the situation in which the attack comes from the haven of safety is, of course, the arousal of conflicting tendencies. From this single threat or signal at least two conflicting messages are received: to go away from and to come toward the haven safety."[35]

In a now classic study by H. F. Harlow and M. Harlow, "evil surrogate mothers" exude noxious air blasts to baby rhesus monkeys.[36] They also extrude brass spikes, hurl the infant monkey to the floor, or vibrate so violently as to make the infant's teeth chatter. None of the above disrupted the bonding behavior of the infant monkeys, leading the authors to conclude that "instead of producing experimental neurosis, we have achieved a technique for enhancing maternal attachment."[37] In effect, the Harlows had produced an experimental analogue of child abuse where contact comfort was intermittently disrupted by noxious behaviors. To their surprise the attachment process was strengthened, not weakened, by this process.

More recently, the effects of maltreatment on human infants' attachment systems has been examined by researchers such as Patricia M. Crittenden and Dante Cicchetti.[38] Most of this research has been established by studying maltreating families who have come to the attention of local social service agencies. In examining abused children's attachments it is again apparent that they are characterized by both avoidance–ambivalence and anger, as well as by excessive closeness, which appears as "compulsive compliance." The authors see this closeness–protective behavior in abused children as a way of both maintaining close attachment and denying pervasive anger with the abusive "caretaker." They could, in other words, be the overcontrolled wife assaulters of the future, while the avoidant–ambivalent could be the cyclical personality of the future. Filled with rage, unable to express it, possessing negative representations of himself and women but still cyclically drawn in a repetitive push–pull pattern, the avoidant–ambivalent child is a prototype for an abusive adult.

With abusive parents, the child is in a situation where he is locked into forming an attachment to his primary caregiver, who is also a source of pain and injury. The rage that is experienced with such a parent is repressed. It will not be expressed until a similar intimate attachment is formed later in life. In the meantime, the child will pass into adolescence consumed by developing his public persona. The underlying personality will remain dormant until an intimate attachment, later in life, triggers the emotional template developed in the original attachment experience.[39] Abusive males who experienced physical violence in their family of origin, often a dysfunctional, unstable family, were also at risk for ambivalent attachment. Although study of this "intergenerational transmission" of violence was initially focused on behavior modeling, attachment theory and research suggests that something more is going on. That something more involves the development of faulty internal schemata, particularly self-concepts and expectations of attachment to others fraught with fear and rage. The groundwork for abusiveness is set. In other words, abusive childhood experiences produce something more than just learned behavior patterns. They produce avoidant–ambivalent bonding styles that generate tendencies to be both overly demanding and angry in adult romantic attachments, a profile often reported by battered women about their husbands and again consistent with the descriptors of borderline males' pathology.

ADULT ATTACHMENT AND PROBLEM BEHAVIOR

One intriguing bit of evidence for the longevity of attachment longings is the research reported by psychologists L. H. Silverman and J. Weinberger. Claiming that there are "powerful unconscious wishes for a state of oneness with 'the good mother of early childhood' and that gratification of these wishes can enhance adaptation," the authors and various colleagues have presented subliminal stimuli (4 milliseconds in duration) that read MOMMY AND I ARE ONE. These presentations have produced ameliorative effects on a variety of problem behaviors ranging from schizophrenia to smoking. Silverman and Weinberger refer to this as "activating symbiotic-like" (oneness) fantasies whereby "representations of self and other are fused and merged" that originate when the mother is experienced very early in life as comforting, protective, and nurturing.[40] Gender differences appeared in their research, with males showing the ameliorative effect more than females. The authors have speculated that this may be so because daughters have less of a basis for differentiating themselves from their mothers that do sons. Studies in which "Daddy and I Are One" or "My Lover and I Are One" produced ameliorative effects on schizophrenia and anxiety in women subjects. The authors also theorize that the activation of oneness fantasies alleviates anxiety and gratifies dependency-related needs, providing empirical results to support these notions. Although Silverman and his colleagues reported studies on 40 groups of subjects with a variety of adult problems, they did not report tests that varied attachment style. Given that insecurely attached infants experienced less of the ideal nurturing mother than did securely attached adults, one might expect a difference in the ameliorative effect of the subliminal stimulation in these two groups.

The bridge from infant to adult attachment was finally built in a landmark study by social psychologists C. Hazan and P. Shaver, who made the empirical leap from infant attachment to adult attachment styles in an influential paper, "Romantic Love Conceptualized as an Attachment Process."[41] These authors made the argument that adult romantic love had attachment properties which may derive from its' infantile forms. In another paper, Shaver and his colleagues state:

> [P]ersonal continuity, in fact, is primarily due to the persistence of mental models, which are themselves sustained by a fairly stable family setting. . . . [W]e are ready to suggest more explicitly that all important love relationships—especially the ones with parents and later ones with lovers and spouses—are attachments in Bowlby's sense. For every documented feature of attachment there is a

parallel feature of love, and for most documented features of love there is either a documented or a plausible feature of attachment.[42]

Using an item descriptive of one's own attachment style, the authors found that in an adult population of more than 700, attachment styles fell into approximately the same proportions as Ainsworth had found for infant populations: 56% self-described as securely attached; 25%, as avoidant; and 20%, as anxious–ambivalent. The anxious–ambivalent lovers experienced love as involving obsession, desire for reciprocation and union, emotional highs and lows, and extreme sexual attraction and jealousy. Anxious–ambivalent respondents claimed that it was easy to fall in love and said that they frequently feel themselves beginning to do so, although they rarely find what they would call "real" love. They had more self-doubts and felt more misunderstood by others.

Attachment history was assessed by the aforementioned authors, asking respondents to describe how both parents had generally behaved toward them (and toward each other) during childhood. Anxious–ambivalent respondents described their mothers as more intrusive and unfair than secure respondents did, and described their fathers as unfair and threatening. The term "intrusive" was the main one used by Ainsworth et al. in their description of mothers of anxious–ambivalent infants. The respondents' descriptions of their mothers paralleled Ainsworth's characterization of the mothers of avoidant infants as more thoroughly negative than the (more inconsistent) mothers of anxious–ambivalent infants. Hazan and Shaver's research was an important first step in relating early attachment to adult relationship functioning.

Since this seminal research, attachment in adults has exploded as a research topic. Although debate continues, it is generally accepted that four distinct adult attachment styles exist called secure, dismissing, preoccupied, and fearful.[43] The names are pretty self-explanatory. The secure people had positive self-schemata and positive expectations about intimate relationships: they expected the best would happen and were untroubled by closeness. The dismissing people, as Hazan and Shaver described them, had "signed off" from close relationships. They were independent to a fault. They didn't need anybody.

The preoccupied individuals were the clingy types—the ones who worried a lot about being rejected by the other person and were falling over themselves to please and gain approval. The fearful group were, from my perspective, the most interesting because they seemed simultaneously drawn and repelled by intimacy. As Kim Bartholomew put it, the fearful people "desire social contact and intimacy but experience pervasive interpersonal distrust and fear of rejection."[44]

The connection of attachment style to abusiveness is made through the chronic feelings generated by insecure attachment and the way those feelings might translate into behavior for men who had a double dose of abusive role models in their early life and social conditioning into the "male role" later on. Men with early attachment problems are more likely to experience anxiety about intimacy regulation. The arousal, anxiety, and anger these men experience originates in deep-seated anxiety about the original attachment object.

Abusive males have exaggerated needs for control in intimate relationships because their need corresponds to a felt anxiety and that control represents behaviors designed to lower the anxiety/anger. These men try to diminish their anxiety about being abandoned by exaggerated control of their female partner.

As developmental psychologist Patricia M. Crittenden puts it, "[A]nxious attachments may occur at any age. Some of the indications of anxious attachment in older children and adults resemble the indications of anxious attachment in infancy: undue preoccupation with the whereabouts of the attachment figure and undue difficulty in separating from him or her, lack of trust in the attachment figure, chronic anger and resentment toward him or her, inability to seek or use support from the attachment figure when such support is needed, or absence of feeling toward him or her." Crittenden goes on to suggest that other attachment disorders are less frequent but seem to be generated by "traumatic or depriving separation from the attachment figure."[45]

THE ATTACHMENT–ABUSE CONNECTION

Although a rapid expansion of attachment research occurred after the Hazan and Shaver paper of 1987, none of it focused specifically on abusiveness. Along with some graduate students, developmental psychologist, Kim Bartholomew, and I set out to empirically test the connection between insecure attachment and abusiveness.[46] She was experienced with a variety of ways of measuring attachment from structured interviews to self-report scales. I was experienced with assessing abusiveness using self-report scales like the Conflict Tactics

Scale (CTS) and the Psychological Maltreatment of Women Inventory (PMWI).

Kim Bartholomew had developed a brief self-report scale to assess attachment style called the Relationships Style Questionnaire (RSQ; see Figure 7.2). As you can see, the questionnaire asks people to indicate the extent of their agreement with 30 statements describing their reactions to attachment. The questionnaire was tested to ensure that it agreed with attachment ratings of respondents de-

Please read each of the following statements and rate the extent to which it describes your feelings about *romantic relationships* by circling the appropriate number. Think about all of your romantic relationships, past and present, and respond in terms of how you generally feel in these relationships.

Not at all like me		Somewhat like me		Very much like me
1	2	3	4	5

1. I find it difficult to depend on other people.   1 2 3 4 5
2. It is very important to me to feel independent.   1 2 3 4 5
3. I find it easy to get emotionally close to others.   1 2 3 4 5
4. I want to merge completely with another person.   1 2 3 4 5
5. I worry that I will be hurt if I allow myself to become too close   1 2 3 4 5
   to others.
6. I am comfortable without close emotional relationships.   1 2 3 4 5
7. I am not sure that I can always depend on others to be there   1 2 3 4 5
   when I need them.
8. I want to be completely emotionally intimate with others.   1 2 3 4 5
9. I worry about being alone.   1 2 3 4 5
10. I am comfortable depending on other people.   1 2 3 4 5
11. I often worry that romantic partners don't really love me.   1 2 3 4 5
12. I find it difficult to trust others completely.   1 2 3 4 5
13. I worry about others getting too close to me.   1 2 3 4 5
14. I want emotionally close relationships.   1 2 3 4 5
15. I am comfortable having other people depend on me.   1 2 3 4 5
16. I worry that others don't value me as much as I value them.   1 2 3 4 5
17. People are never there when you need them.   1 2 3 4 5
18. My desire to merge completely sometimes scares people away. 1 2 3 4 5
19. It is very important to me to feel self-sufficient.   1 2 3 4 5
20. I am nervous when anyone gets too close to me.   1 2 3 4 5
21. I often worry that romantic partners won't want to stay with me. 1 2 3 4 5
22. I prefer not to have other people depend on me.   1 2 3 4 5
23. I worry about being abandoned.   1 2 3 4 5
24. I am somewhat uncomfortable being close to others.   1 2 3 4 5
25. I find that others are reluctant to get as close as I would like. 1 2 3 4 5
26. I prefer not to depend on others.   1 2 3 4 5
27. I know that others will be there when I need them.   1 2 3 4 5
28. I worry about having others not accept me.   1 2 3 4 5
29. Romantic partners often want me to be closer than I feel   1 2 3 4 5
   comfortable being.
30. I find it relatively easy to get close to others.   1 2 3 4 5

FIGURE 7.2. Relationship Style Questionnaire (RSQ). From Griffin and Bartholomew (1994). Copyright 1994 by Jessica Kingsley. Reprinted by permission.

rived through more elaborate interview techniques. If someone showed up as dismissing on the interview, they also showed up as dismissing on the self-report scale. The RSQ scale generated scores on the four main attachment styles: secure, dismissing, preoccupied, and fearful (see Figure 7.3).

It was really those respondents the scalp identified as fearful that I was most interested in because they experienced strong and unresolvable push–pulls in intimacy and were hypersensitive to rejection. They had negative "internal representations" of themselves, which meant they would find it difficult to self-soothe. They also had negative expectations of others, meaning that they might expect the worst (abandonment) from their female partner and be hypervigilant and controlling. Bartholomew had worked mainly with women and with college student males in her previous research. When these people perceived threats of abandonment, they withdrew in an angry distanced pose. My knowledge of abusive men suggested we would find another response to threat of abandonment: rage and abusive control.

The "fearful" men were the ones I thought would be most abusive, only I thought it was a bit of a misnomer to call them "fearful." While fear might have been at the core of their reaction to anticipated rejection, anger was the prominent feature of their emotional and behavioral expression. Whether this anger was a male cover-up for underlying fear or a vestige of what Bowlby called "the anger born of fear" didn't really matter. These men were

| | | Model of Self (Dependence) | |
		Positive (Low)	Negative (High)
Model of Other (Avoidance)	Positive (Low)	**SECURE** Comfortable with intimacy and autonomy	**PREOCCUPIED** Preoccupied (Main) Ambivalent (Hazan) Overly dependent
	Negative (High)	**DISMISSING** Denial of attachment Dismissing (Main) Counter-dependent	**FEARFUL** Fear of attachment Avoidant (Hazan) Socially avoidant

FIGURE 7.3. Bartholomew's (1990) model of attachment. Copyright 1990 by Sage Publications. Reprinted by permission.

"angrily attached." Bowlby himself recognized this in his early writings, and our research bears it out. Fearfully attached infants simultaneously *"seek proximity [to mother] and simultaneously arch angrily away."*[47]

First the data: The men's attachment reports were correlated with their female partners' reports of each man's abusiveness. The results are summarized in Table 7.1, which lists correlations between each man's attachment style, BPO, and self-reports of anger and jealousy. Finally, attachment styles are correlated with the female partners' reports of each man's abusiveness. As I suspected, men with high "fearful" attachment scores were also high in BPO and high in chronic anger, jealousy, and trauma symptoms. They didn't sleep well, got depressed a lot, and experienced dissociative states. Their attachment scores were more highly associated with reports of abuse by their female partners than any other attachment style. In fact, we put a "profile" formula of scores together that accurately predicted abusiveness reports with 88% accuracy. The ingredients of this formula were BPO scores, anger scores, and fearful attachment scores. If you combine the three you have a profile of the core of the abusive personality.

Recall that in our earlier videotape studies we had found that physically abusive males demonstrated greater arousal, anxiety, and anger while viewing video conflicts where a woman expresses her need for greater independence from the man in the scenario. At the time I referred to this as "abandonment" anxiety; however, no attempt was made to find out if some assaultive males showed this pattern of responding more than others. Now, in retrospect, I believe that "fearful (angry) attached" males would have shown it the most.

TABLE 7.1. Correlations of RSQ with Total Scores on Other Measures for the Entire Sample ($N = 160$)

	Secure	Fearful	Preoccupied	Dismissing
BPO	−.35***	.58***	.42***	−.04
Trauma symptoms	−.28***	.50***	.34***	−.03
Anger	−.36***	.49***	.20	.02
Jealousy	−.16*	.34***	.18*	−.015
Verbal abuse (PMWI)				
Dominance/isolation	−.30*	.46**	.27*	.06
Emotional abuse	−.09*	.52***	.26*	−.20

Note. From Dutton, Saunders, Starzomski, and Bartholomew (1994). Copyright 1994 by V. H. Winston & Son, Inc., 360 South Ocean Boulevard, Palm Beach, FL 33480. All rights reserved. Reprinted by permission.

*$p < .05$; **$p < .01$; ***$p < .001$.

ATTACHMENT AND THINKING ABOUT THE CAUSES OF CONFLICT

My graduate student Andrew J. Starzomski unearthed some interesting data to support this idea in his master's thesis. He found that
college undergraduates who were fearfully attached (and also high
on BPO) reacted with more arousal and anger to audiotapes of
family conflicts. He also found something else about fearfully
attached men. They attribute cause for negative events in a way that
they are constantly blaming their partner for whatever happened.[48]
Using an instrument called the Relationship Attribution Measure
(RAM), he was able to assess correlations between a man's attachment style and his way of assessing responsibility and causality for
negative actions occurring in an intimate relationship (see Figure
7.4).[49]

A "Her Fault" scale measures how much responsibility the man
places on his partner for causing the negative event. A "Stable in
Future" scale reveals the extent to which he believes his partners
negative behavior (which caused the event) is unlikely to remain
unchanged in the future. A "Generalizes" measure taps the man's
perceptions about how a particular negative event is likely to cause
difficulties in other areas of the relationship. The "Intentional" scale
is a gauge of the extent to which the negative behavior was seen to
be planned and executed by the partner. The "Selfish Motives" scale
reveals participants' evaluation of their partners' tendency to be
driven by uncaring or disrespectful motivations. The "Blameworthy"
scale taps how much fault participants find with their partner for
negative events.

From Table 7.2, it is clear that attachment style has an impact
on the attribution of cause for negative relationship events. Fearfully
attached men saw their partners as more blameworthy and saw this
trait as maintaining in the future. In other words, they externalized
blame more and saw the blameworthy features as immutable. They
also saw the action as intended and selfish. In other words, the same
action by the female was perceived differently by fearfully attached
men than by securely attached men.

Fearfully attached men were also high on BPO scores. One
aspect of BPO is "Primitive Defenses," the tendency to project
blame onto another person for intimate problems. The fearful
(angry, BPO) men did just this. Using a measure which asked men
to assign a cause for a variety of actions they witnessed on taped
scenarios, Starzomski found that the fearfully attached men blamed

This questionnaire describes several things that your spouse might do. Imagine your spouse performing each behavior, and then read the statements that follow it. Please circle the number that indicates how much you agree or disagree with each statement, using the rating scale below:

1	2	3	4	5	6
Disagree strongly	Disagree	Disagree somewhat	Agree somewhat	Agree	Agree strongly

Your spouse criticizes something you say:

1. 1 2 3 4 5 6   My spouse's behavior was due to something about him/her (e.g., the type of person he/she is, the mood he/she was in).
2. 1 2 3 4 5 6   The reason my spouse criticized me is *not* likely to change.
3. 1 2 3 4 5 6   The reason my spouse criticized me is something that affects other areas of our marriage.
4. 1 2 3 4 5 6   My spouse criticized me on purpose rather than unintentionally.
5. 1 2 3 4 5 6   My spouse's behavior was motivated by selfish rather than *un*selfish concerns.
6. 1 2 3 4 5 6   My spouse deserves to be blamed for criticizing me.

Your spouse begins to spend less time with you:

7. 1 2 3 4 5 6   My spouse's behavior was due to something about him/her (e.g., the type of person he/she is, the mood he/she was in).
8. 1 2 3 4 5 6   The reason my spouse is spending less time with me is not likely to change.
9. 1 2 3 4 5 6   The reason my spouse is spending less time with me is something that affects other areas of our marriage.
10. 1 2 3 4 5 6   My spouse spends less time with me on purpose rather than unintentionally.
11. 1 2 3 4 5 6   My spouse's behavior was motivated by selfish rather than *un*selfish concerns.
12. 1 2 3 4 5 6   My spouse deserves to be blamed for spending less time with me.

Your spouse does not pay attention to what you are saying:

13. 1 2 3 4 5 6   My spouse's behavior was due to something about him/her (e.g., the type of person he/she is, the mood he/she was in).
14. 1 2 3 4 5 6   The reason my spouse was not paying attention to what I was saying is *not* likely to change.
15. 1 2 3 4 5 6   The reason my spouse didn't pay attention to what I was saying is something that affects other areas of our marriage.
16. 1 2 3 4 5 6   My spouse didn't pay attention to what I was saying on purpose rather than unintentionally.

(Figure 7.4 continued on next page)

FIGURE 7.4. Relationship Attribution Measure (RAM). Adapted from Fincham and Bradbury (1992). Copyright 1992 by the Amercian Psychological Association. Adapted by permission.

17. 1 2 3 4 5 6   My spouse's behavior was motivated by selfish rather than *un*selfish concerns.
18. 1 2 3 4 5 6   My spouse deserves to be blamed for not paying attention to what I was saying.

Your spouse is cool and distant:

19. 1 2 3 4 5 6   My spouse's behavior was due to something about him/her (e.g., the type of person he/she is, the mood he/she was in).
20. 1 2 3 4 5 6   The reason my spouse was cool and distant is *not* likely to change.
21. 1 2 3 4 5 6   The reason my spouse was cool and distant is something that affects other areas of our marriage.
22. 1 2 3 4 5 6   My spouse was cool and distant on purpose rather than unintentionally.
23. 1 2 3 4 5 6   My spouse's behavior was motivated by selfish rather than *un*selfish concerns.
24. 1 2 3 4 5 6   My spouse deserves to be blamed for being cool and distant.

FIGURE 7.4 (*continued*)

the women. Their way of viewing the cause for relationship problems kept their anger level very high. It was always her fault, and their expectation was that she would do it again.

ATTACHMENT AND TRAUMA SYMPTOMS

As we are about to see in the next chapter, assaultive men have psychological profiles on the Millon Clinical Multiaxial Inventory (MCMI) that closely match men diagnosed with posttraumatic stress

TABLE 7.2. Correlations of Attachment Dimensions with Distress-Maintaining Attributions from Actual Relationships

Negative attributions about partner behavior	Attachment dimensions			
	Secure	Fearful	Preoccupied	Dismissing
Her fault	−.05	.20	.20	.23*
Stable in future	−.30**	.48***	.07	.36**
Generalizes	−.12	.19	.03	.14
Intentional	−.17	.26*	.11	.25*
Selfish motives	−.05	.30*	.27*	.14
Blameworthy	−.13	.43***	.31**	.17

Note. From Starzomski and Dutton (1994). $N = 72$.

$*p < .05$; $**p < .01$; $***p < .001$ (two-tailed).

disorder. This occurs despite the absence of identifiable stressors in their adult lives. Furthermore, fearfully attached men fit this profile the most. They have the highest scores on BPO measures and the highest chronic levels of stress symptoms.

Fearfully attached men have the highest levels of depression, anxiety, dissociative states (sometimes accompanied by rageful acting out), and sleep disturbances. Such men appear to have been traumatized somehow, probably by extreme attachment disruptions, and react chronically with rage whenever they are in intimate relationships. They cannot self-soothe, cannot make these symptoms go away. They expect their wives to magically do so, and when the symptoms don't disappear, the woman is blamed for her "failure." Such men have little insight into the causes of this constellation of problems and avoid seeking help, believing "it will only make things worse." Fearfully attached men experience extreme chronic anger as an inevitable by-product of attachment yet have extreme difficulty living alone (without a woman). They blame this anger, especially during their dysphoric phases, on their wives. They cannot conceive and do not understand the anger in attachment terms. Our thinking, the way we attribute causes for events including our feelings, is individualistic. In short, we blame bad feelings on an individual, usually someone close to us. Fearfully attached men also have cognitive styles that blame their wives for negative events including their dysphoric moods. If they feel "dysphoric," which they frequently do, they believe it's her fault. They attribute their bad feelings to something she does. In reality, it stems from attachment and the emotional consequences of attachment for fearfully attached people. What we still need to clarify, though, is exactly what happened to these men to make them this way.

8

The Early Antecedents Studies

Many of the subtle processes that determine successful attachment such as "attunement" cannot be studied retrospectively in adults. They are more properly the subject matter for developmental psychopathology and research on infants. We were restricted to studying the memory traces of early upbringing in our sample of abusive men. Some have argued that abusive men will report abusive childhoods in order to excuse their own use of violence. Our research found just the opposite: men sent to us by the courts for wife assault would idealize their parents' treatment of them. It wasn't until we cleansed their reports for "socially desirable responding" that a closer approximation of the truth came out: things at home had been terrible. Most clinicians who ask these questions report a similar experience. Early in the group treatment process, men will describe their father as "stern" or "strict." Later on, when you ask them specifically what each parent did to express their anger, a fuller and more horrifying story emerges. In his book on abused children who kill their parents, lawyer Paul Mones recounts a startling story in his book *When a Child Kills.*[1] The most difficult cases for him to defend were boys who had killed fathers or stepfathers. They were reluctant to talk about the abuse they had suffered and instead frequently defended the parent. As noted earlier, this strange loyalty resembles the paradoxical bonds that are forged between hostage takers and their victims in what is known as the Stockholm syndrome (so called because a hostage bank teller in that city reportedly became enamored of her male captor).[2] Anna Freud coined the term "identification with the aggressor" to describe this sort of process.[3] When someone in a life-threatening situation is entirely under the control of a stronger and potentially dangerous person, the weaker individual comes to identify with that powerful person as a way of warding off the danger. According to Anna Freud, in an attempt to fend off violence against themselves; potential victims try to see the world as the aggressor sees it. Bruno Bettelheim described such a process that took place in Nazi concentration camps: some inmates emulated their captors in desperate attempts to avoid brutal random punishment.[4] This haphazard brutality was explicitly displayed in the film *Schindler's List*, where a sadistic Nazi officer, played by Ralph Fiennes, entertains himself by randomly shooting inmates as the walk in the prison yard below his balcony. The essential features that generate this attachment are the severity and random nature of the punishment. Humans have a deep-seated need to restore some predictability and sense of control in their lives. Adopting the worldview of those in power (who have life-and-death control) is an attempt to do this.

A process like this occurs with battered women. In the early 1980s, Susan L. Painter and I studied it and called it "traumatic bonding."[5] Some ten years later we finally had the data to support this view.[6] From the beginning, we argued that there was no special deficit in a battered women that made her susceptible to getting trapped in an abusive relationship. To the contrary, the features of the relationship itself were sufficient to account for the trapping. The same can be said of abused boys. There is little they can do to extricate themselves from an abusive home.

The boys are aided in their ensuing emotional cover-up by a socializing culture that for centuries has taught males not to be emotionally expressive. The double whammy of personal shame and cultural conditioning makes the abused boy retreat inside. Safely ensconced there, he begins the task of expunging every possible source of shame from his identity. Anything that he associated with the feeling of shame during this developmental stage will be altered or eliminated.

The shame is caused, I believe, by early family dynamics; the social labels that are potential shame sources are learned later through school classmates. Again, the way in which shame operates suggests that the psychological precedes the social. There is a pool of rage and shame in these males that can find no expression—that is, not until later when an intimate relationship occurs, and with it the emotional vulnerability that threatens their equilibrium. The vulnerability and dysphoria are frequently accompanied by flashes of shame. The feelings of shame are intolerable, so they are converted immediately (and without awareness) to anger. So they blame their partner for their feelings. If it happens repeatedly with more than one woman, they go from blaming "her" to blaming "them." Their personal shortcomings become rationalized by an evolving misogyny. This misogyny then feeds on itself, contributing further to their rage with women. At this point the abusiveness is hardwired into the system. They are programmed for intimate violence. No woman on earth can save them, although some will try.

When I started running treatment groups, I was struck by this same aspect of the men's descriptions. The emotional poverty of their thought and speech, the flat affect, the noncommittal responses about their parents. They described actions that people performed, but those descriptions rarely entered the inner realm. My colleagues and I would talk facetiously of the men being in "emotional kindergarten," but it was not really a joke. Part of the treatment involved describing and defining the emotions.

The other aspect was the descriptions of growing up. These were typically euphemized. Dad had a "bad temper sometimes" or "wasn't around much." He "didn't think much of me. I guess he liked fishing more." The folks "did their best they could under the circumstances." It wasn't until we started asking specific questions and probing extensively that the real stories would come out. We would ask questions such as the following: "What did your dad (or mom) do when he (or she) was angry?" "How did your father show you that he loved you? Can you remember any specific time that he did this?"

It is not unusual for an abusive man to have difficulty recalling his childhood. Both as therapists and as researchers, we had to piece it together from probing questions to him, from interviews with his wife (who usually knows the most), and occasionally from interviews with his mother (who may or may not want to disclose her own history of victimization or her guilt about not protecting her son). Furthermore, when we started to collect research data on abusive men we found the same problem exists with fuzzy memories. From the beginning of the research, however, I had a notion that something more than the modeling or copying of abusive behaviors was occurring. I wanted to get beyond merely counting hits between family members and assess the emotional climate of the household. The "hit count" could be done with the Conflict Tactics Scale (CTS) adapted for the family of origin. To get at the emotional climate, however, we turned to a self-report instrument called (in Swedish) the Egna Minnen Beträffande Uppfostran (EMBU). The English translation is "Memories of My Upbringing." To literary fans of Marcel Proust, this may sound rather similar to his great work *Remembrance of Things Past (À la Recherche du Temps Perdu)*. The similarity goes beyond the title. Just as Proust was attempting to systematically connect all adult sensations to their origins, the EMBU can provide, for those of us less reflective than Proust, a type of retrospective lens back into our childhood. By asking questions that we may not have pondered for years, the EMBU opens up feelings and memories. Of course, these memories are colored by time and current circumstance. They do not necessarily represent veridical recordings of past events. But the memories or interpretations themselves can be illuminating. We will say more about this below.

The English translation of the EMBU[7] has been widely used in research on other clinical populations such as depressed men. It assesses recollections of parental treatment separately for the mother and the father. The main aspects we were interested in were memories of parental warmth and rejection. Both seemed to be broader aspects of parenting than actual incidence of violence. The EMBU has 43 items or statements bearing on these particular aspects of parental treatment (see Figure 8.1).

First, we wanted to know if wife assaulters scored differently on these scales than men in the control group. Referring to Table 8.1, we can readily see that the answer was yes. The recollections of assaultive males was characterized by memories of fathers who were rejecting and cold. This difference between the two groups was the largest and most salient difference of all. The second difference was that the fathers of assaultive men were more violent. But it was more than violence that helped create the difference. EMBU scales measuring rejection came out as more important than CTS scores measuring physical abuse in influencing abusiveness, and paternal treatment came out as more important than maternal treatment. It seemed that the emotional aspect of paternal treatment was para-

Did your parents remain together during your childhood? Yes___ No___.
If "no," please indicate your age at the time of separation: ___ years old. Whom did you
then live with? Mother___ Father___ Other (specify) _____.
Beside each statement, please write in the number of the response listed below (1–4)
that best describes how often the experience happened to you with your mother (or
female guardian) and father (or male guardian) when you were growing up. If you had
more than one mother/father figure, please answer for the persons who you feel played
the most important role in your upbringing.

1	2	3	4
never occurred	occasionally occurred	often occurred	always occurred

	Father or guardian	Mother or guardian
1. My parent showed with words and gestures that he/she liked me.	1 2 3 4	1 2 3 4
2. My parent refused to speak to me for a long time if I had done anything silly (stupid).	1 2 3 4	1 2 3 4
3. My parent punished me even for small offenses.	1 2 3 4	1 2 3 4
4. I think that my parent wished I had been different in some way.	1 2 3 4	1 2 3 4
5. If I had done something foolish, I could go to my parent and make everything right by asking for his/her forgiveness (apologize).	1 2 3 4	1 2 3 4
6. I felt that my parents liked my brother(s) and/or sister(s) more than he/she liked me.	1 2 3 4	1 2 3 4
7. My parent treated me unjustly (badly) compared with how he/she treated my sister(s) and/or brother(s).	1 2 3 4	1 2 3 4
8. As a child I was physically punished or scolded in the presence of others.	1 2 3 4	1 2 3 4
9. If things went badly for me, I felt my parent tried to comfort and encourage me.	1 2 3 4	1 2 3 4
10. My parent gave me more corporal (physical) punishment than I deserved.	1 2 3 4	1 2 3 4
11. My parent would get angry if I didn't help at home when I was asked to.	1 2 3 4	1 2 3 4
12. I felt that it was difficult to approach my parent.	1 2 3 4	1 2 3 4
13. My parent would narrate or say something about what I had said or done in front of others so that I felt ashamed.	1 2 3 4	1 2 3 4
14. My parent showed he/she was interested in my getting good marks.	1 2 3 4	1 2 3 4
15. If I had a difficult task in front of me, I felt support from my parent.	1 2 3 4	1 2 3 4
16. I was treated as a the "black sheep" or "scapegoat" of the family.	1 2 3 4	1 2 3 4
17. My parent wished I had been like somebody else.	1 2 3 4	1 2 3 4
18. I felt my parent thought it was my fault when he/she was unhappy.	1 2 3 4	1 2 3 4
19. My parent showed me that he/she was fond of me.	1 2 3 4	1 2 3 4

(Figure 8.1 continued on next page)

FIGURE 8.1. Selected items from Egna Minnen Beträffande Uppfostran (EMBU). Adapted from Ross, Campbell, and Clayer (1982). Copyright 1982 by Munksgaard International Publishers Ltd. Copenhagen, Denmark. Adapted by permission.

20. I think my parent respected my opinions.	1 2 3 4	1 2 3 4
21. I felt that my parent wanted to be with me.	1 2 3 4	1 2 3 4
22. I think my parent was mean and grudging toward me.	1 2 3 4	1 2 3 4
23. I think my parent tried to make my adolescence stimulating, interesting, and instructive (for instance, by giving me good books, arranging for me to go to camp, taking me to clubs).	1 2 3 4	1 2 3 4
24. My parent praised me.	1 2 3 4	1 2 3 4
25. I could seek comfort from my parent if I was sad.	1 2 3 4	1 2 3 4
26. I was punished by my parent without having done anything.	1 2 3 4	1 2 3 4
27. My parent allowed me to do the same things my friends did.	1 2 3 4	1 2 3 4
28. My parent said he/she did not approve of my behavior at home.	1 2 3 4	1 2 3 4
29. My parent criticized me and told me how lazy and useless I was in front of others.	1 2 3 4	1 2 3 4
30. Of my sister(s) and brother(s), I was the one my parent blamed if anything happened.	1 2 3 4	1 2 3 4
31. My parent was abrupt with me.	1 2 3 4	1 2 3 4
32. My parent would punish me hard, even for trifles (little things).	1 2 3 4	1 2 3 4
33. My parent beat me for no reason.	1 2 3 4	1 2 3 4
34. My parent showed an interest in my own interests and hobbies.	1 2 3 4	1 2 3 4
35. My parent treated me in such a way that I felt ashamed.	1 2 3 4	1 2 3 4
36. My parent let my sister(s) and brother(s) have things that I was not allowed to have.	1 2 3 4	1 2 3 4
37. I was beaten by my parent.	1 2 3 4	1 2 3 4
38. I felt that warmth and tenderness existed between me and my parent.	1 2 3 4	1 2 3 4
39. My parent respected the fact that I had other opinions than he/she had.	1 2 3 4	1 2 3 4
40. My parent would be angry with me without letting me know why.	1 2 3 4	1 2 3 4
41. My parent let me go to bed without food.	1 2 3 4	1 2 3 4
42. I felt that my parent was proud when I succeeded in something I had undertaken.	1 2 3 4	1 2 3 4
43. My parent hugged me.	1 2 3 4	1 2 3 4

FIGURE 8.1 (*continued*)

mount. Being punished in a rejecting way by your father was the worst thing that could happen, far worse than simply being punished.[8]

FATHERS AND SONS

To our surprise, we found that the biggest childhood contributors to adult abusiveness were (in order of importance) feeling rejected by one's father, feeling a lack of warmth from one's father, being physically abused by one's father, being verbally abused by one's

**TABLE 8.1. Correlations of Early Experience Factors
with Discriminant Function for Abusive Personality**

	Discriminant function
EMBU	
Paternal rejection	.89
Paternal warmth	−.63
Maternal rejection	.39
Maternal warmth	−.39
Conflict Tactics Scale (CTS: FOO)	
Physical abuse (father to you)	.64
Verbal abuse (father to you)	.41
Physical abuse (mother to you)	.34
Verbal abuse (mother to you)	.34
Physical abuse (father to mother)	.24
Verbal abuse (father to mother)	.36
Physical abuse (mother to father)	.27
Verbal abuse (mother to father)	.38

Note. FOO, Family of Origin. From Dutton, Starzomski, and Ryan (1996). Copyright 1996 by Plenum Publishing Corporation. Reprinted by permission.

father, and feeling rejected by one's mother. We had expected that the relationship with the mother would have been the more important. That wasn't what the data told us. The picture that emerged from the data was of a cold, rejecting, and intermittently abusive father. The impact of such fathering was to produce a boy with a poor sense of identity (identity diffusion)!

In his classic *The Art of Loving*, Erich Fromm describes mother love as "the home we come from, nature, soil, the ocean."[9] All yearning for connection is yearning to return to that perfect, all-embracing love. Paternal love, on the other hand, comes with conditions attached. Fromm characterizes it as earned or deserved love carrying an unspoken message: "I love you because you fulfill my expectations, because you do your duty, because you are like me." Fatherly love sets limits, punishes and rewards, and judges. When this type of love is generated by an abusive or rejecting father, a boy is doomed to live in darkness. He cannot please, nothing is ever good enough for father, and so the boy feels unlovable to the main source of his male identity. Figure 8.2 summarizes these relationships.

Men who initially balk at filling out CTS reports for their family of origin would subsequently turn out to be the ones most abused. They had blanked out or fuzzed over the memories. They would complain to the researcher that they couldn't remember. Those that

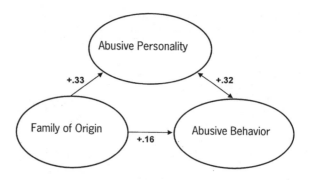

FIGURE 8.2. Model of family-of-origin effects on abusive personality and behavior corrected for social desirability.

scored highest on impression management scales or social desirability also described their parents as warm and accepting people. It wasn't until the scores were corrected for socially desirable responding that a truer, less flattering picture emerged: their fathers were either absent, rejecting, or downright punitive. The men were generally more positive about their mothers, although a sense of alternating warm and cold currents was revealed. Mother was available at some times; at others she was cold or angry. (I suspect, although I cannot prove it from my data, that these women were frequently trying to provide maternal support while coping with an abusive husband. Unfortunately for their sons, the result was an alternation between warm "availability" and cold "frustration." I think it's important to state that this appears to be a reasonable reading from the aggregate scores. Its also important to note that this uneven quality is generated by the abusive situation created by the father's personality; it is not necessarily inherent to the woman's mothering style.)

When we started to focus on these aspects of their upbringing, the picture that emerged showed that three parallel learning processes occurred for these men. One was an emotional process instrumental in forming their abusive personalities. It was based largely on the emotional attacks and shaming experiences by parents and left them with—as the borderline personality organization (BPO) scale called it—"identity diffusion," a wounded and vulnerable self that they shored up by going on the offensive. The second process was based on physical abuse either directed at them or at their mothers. It gave them the opportunity to witness how to be abusive, the model for behavior through which to express their personality style. Usually, these two processes occurred together. Emotionally abusive parents were typically physically abusive as well, and faulty attachment was often a result of this poisonous home atmosphere. This combination of processes most commonly led to physical abusiveness. Occasionally our research uncovered cases where the emotional abuse occurred without the physical, although these were rare. In these cases, the adult men who had experienced only emotional abuse were more likely to be emotionally abusive to their partners. We found these cases, to our initial surprise, in our control group samples: blue-collar workers, college students, and psychiatric outpatients. The third process, insecure attachment, we have described in Chapter 7. The fearful attachment of the men in our sample ensured that their anger and rage would be played out in the context of an intimate relationship. It was the combination of these three processes that generated the abusive personality. This combination generated, in vulnerable boys, a type of traumatic experience.

TRAUMA SYMPTOMS

Although previous studies had found an effect of witnessing violence in the family of origin on adult abusiveness, our studies revealed that something far more profound than copying actions was going on. Our first clue that something darker had transpired in the childhood of these men was the unexpected finding that they experienced high chronic levels of trauma symptoms and that these were strongly related to their memories of parental rejection, shaming, and abusiveness. The memories alone might not have clued us to the extent of the mistreatment. It is one thing to rate your father as cold and rejecting; but the combination of memories and trauma symptoms was telling. When that rejection related to present experiences with depression, suicidal thoughts, anxiety, and sleep disorder, the larger impact of the rejection was revealed.

We used a measure called the Trauma Symptom Checklist (TSC), which assessed depression, dissociative states, sleep disorders, and anxiety.[10] Respondents indicate how frequently they experience a variety of trauma symptoms. Trauma symptoms are highly associated with borderline personality organization (BPO) scores—to the point where we came to view them as a by-product of what we called the abusive personality.

Further analysis took us a step further and revealed the greater significance of the trauma symptoms: that they were related to experiences in upbringing.[11] What we found was that men who reported cold, rejecting parents also reported experiencing more severe, extensive, and frequent trauma symptoms. Also, as we described at the end of Chapter 7, men who were fearfully attached experienced more trauma symptoms. We also developed a scale of shaming actions that parents had used against the boy (described below). The shaming scale, too, was strongly related to adult trauma symptoms. This suggested that these adult levels of chronic trauma symptoms might originate in childhood experiences. This idea, of course, is not new. Sigmund Freud long ago suggested it for women's "hysteria" in his controversial 1896 paper on sexual abuse.[12] Psychiatrist Bessel van der Kolk described rage reactions and difficulties in modulating aggression in traumatized children.[13] His research also implicated trauma as the basis for borderline personality. Our data point toward a combination of shaming, emotional and physical abuse by the father, and insecure attachment to the mother as a source of this trauma. The trauma symptoms that the respondents reported as adults were strongly related to their chronic anger level and to their adult abusiveness.

Some other studies had developed psychological profiles of men diagnosed with posttraumatic stress disorder (PTSD).[14] Using the Millon Clinical Multiaxial Inventory (MCMI; version II), a measure of psychopathology, the authors of these studies found what is called an "82C" profile for men suffering from PTSD. This profile means that these men score extremely high on three scales of the MCMI called negativity (8), avoidant (2), and borderline (C). When we sketched out the profile for assaultive men on this same inventory we were startled. The same 82C profile emerged. Assaultive men closely match psychological profiles for groups diagnosed with PTSD (see Figure 8.3). On almost all psychological measures, assaultive males are indistinguishable from men diagnosed with PTSD. The only differences are that PTSD men feel worse and assaultive men release more aggression. This aggression may release the anxiety and bad feelings in the manner described in Chapter 7.

In addition, we found that trauma experiences appear closely related to attachment style. Fearfully attached men had the highest trauma scores and an overall correlation of their RSQ scores on

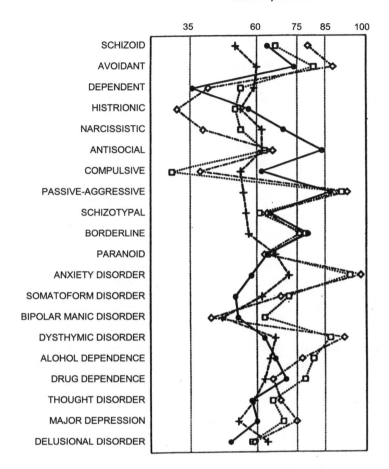

FIGURE 8.3. MCMI profiles of PTSD, wife assault, and control groups. ··□··, PTSD (Roberts et al., 1985); –◇–, PTSD (Hyer et al., 1989); –●–, wife assaulters; –+–, non-PTSD (Roberts et al., 1985).

fearful attachment and trauma scores of +.51. They experienced depression, anxiety, sleep disorders, and dissociative states more than men with other attachment styles.

Trauma victims have exaggerated separation anxiety, anger, and a clinical description that is similar to that of persons diagnosed as having a borderline personality disorder. This profile also includes problems with regulation of affect and impulse control, an intense dependency on primary interpersonal relationships, and an inability to tolerate being alone. Van der Kolk hypothesizes that childhood trauma may play a significant role in the development of borderline personality disorder. Childhood trauma, of course, almost always involves attachment disruptions for the child.

As Table 8.2 shows, the man's experiencing chronic trauma symptoms is significantly related to both his anger and abusiveness. Now another dimension was emerging in the overall picture of abusiveness. BPO scores were now highly associated with both trauma symptoms and fearful attachment. The profile of the abusive personality now contained high BPO, fearful attachment, frequent anger, a blaming style, and frequent trauma symptoms. There were two strong clues that the trauma symptoms were related to something in the man's early upbringing: the relationship to his reports on the EMBU and the relationship to his attachment style. Both were strong statistical relationships and suggested that cold, rejecting, or shaming parents and fearful attachment generated frequent adult trauma symptoms. Of course, the data were only correlational, so other interpretations were possible. But what it looked like was that fearfully attached men had been traumatized in some way by their early upbringing. They had fearful/angry attachment styles consistent with this interpretation. As adults, they experience high chronic levels of trauma symptoms. They had little insight into the causes of this constellation of problems and avoided seeking help, believing "it will only make things worse."

TABLE 8.2. Pearson Correlations of TSC-33 and Measures of Wife Abuse in Wife Assaulters (N = 132)

	TSC-33 total	Depression	PSAT	Anxiety	Sleep disturbance	Dissociation
Self-reports						
Anger (MAI)	.55***	.54***	.47***	.46***	.43***	.44***
Physical violence to wife (CTS)	.28**	.18	.29**	.03	.23*	.29**
Verbal abuse to wife (CTS)	.27**	.26**	.27**	.14	.23*	.29**
Wives' reports						
Dominance/ isolation (PMWI) by husband	.43***	.30**	.36**	.55***	.37***	.33***
Emotional/verbal abuse by husband (PMWI)	.41**	.30**	.36**	.41***	.16*	.18*

Note. MAI, Multidimensional Anger Inventory; CTS, Conflict Tactics Scale; PMWI, Psychological Maltreatment of Women Inventory. From Dutton (1995b). Copyright 1995 by Plenum Publishing Corporation. Reprinted by permission.

*p < .05; **p < .01; ***p < .001.

In any event, several signposts pointed toward the men's childhood as the initial problem. Assaultive men have high BPO scores; BPO has its origins in early trauma.[15] They also have high levels of trauma symptoms, and these are related to their memories of unpleasant childhoods. We couldn't prove that these experiences really happened, of course, but the men seemed to remember them and this memory was not presented in an self-exonerating way. Furthermore, they experienced trauma symptoms consistent with these recollections.

SHAMING AND THE ABUSIVE PERSONALITY

Another clue to the nature of these early traumatic experiences came through the work of social psychologist June Tangney and her colleagues.[16] Drawing on earlier work by Helen Block Lewis on "humiliated fury" and "the shame–rage spiral," Tangney et al. developed a measure called the Test of Self-Conscious Affect (TOSCA). Respondents described which of several reactions they would have to a variety of everyday mishaps. Tangney et al. differentiated between what she called a "shame-prone" and a "guilt-prone" style. The latter was characterized by someone accepting blame for the mishap but seeing it as a specific mistake. The shame-prone respondents, on the other hand, see every mishap as indicative of a general flaw in themselves. They cannot make the distinction between the specific mistake and the general flaw. Such shame-prone people were described as having an emotional style marked by "hostility, anger arousal and tendencies to blame others for negative events."

I went back to the EMBU to look specifically for descriptions of events that could be shame inducing. The guideline was that the recalled action by the parent could induce a felt attack on the whole self. For example, being told "You're a bad boy" or "You'll never amount to anything" attacks the whole self; being told "I don't like what you did" does not. In addition to direct verbal global attacks, we found two other categories that were potentially shame inducing: being publicly humiliated or punished in front of others and being punished at random. The latter, as noted above, makes it impossible to know what specific act you did that was wrong. The effect is to generalize the "wrongness" to the whole self.

We came up with a 22-item (11 items from each parent) "shame

1	2	3	4
never occurred	occasionally occurred	often occurred	always occurred

1. I think that my parent wished I had been different in some way.
2. As a child I was physically punished or scolded in the presence of others.
3. My parent would narrate or say something about what I had said or done in front of others so that I felt ashamed.
4. I was treated as the "black sheep" or "scapegoat" of the family.
5. I felt my parent thought it was my fault when he/she was unhappy.
6. I think my parent was mean and grudging toward me.
7. I was punished by my parent without having done anything.
8. My parent criticized me and told me how lazy and useless I was in front of others.
9. My parent beat me for no reason.
10. My parent treated me in such a way that I felt ashamed.
11. My parent would be angry with me without letting me know why.

FIGURE 8.4. EMBU shame scale items.

scale" from the EMBU that we related to the measures of abusive personality and abusiveness already described (see Figure 8.4). After the socially desirable response styles were "cleansed," the reports of shaming started to come out of the data loud and clear: the experience of having the global self attacked, of being humiliated, embarrassed, shamed. The respondents' parents would often publicly humiliate them or punish them at random. Often parents would verbalize this, saying "You're no good, you'll never amount to anything." The global sense of who the kid was, his self-integrity, became the object of attack. The results were very powerful. Shaming experiences, again primarily by the father, were strongly related to BPO, anger, trauma symptoms and to the man's partner's reports of his abusiveness. The results were so strong that, if I had to pick one single action by the parent that generated abusiveness in men, I would pick being shamed by their father. Of course, fathers who shame their sons also tend to be physically abusive, so again the boy is getting the "double whammy" of both attack on the self and abuse modeling. But it is possible to separate being physically abused from being shamed through a statistical technique called partial correlation. This enables the researcher to look at the direct effects of shame on abusiveness as though physical abuse by the father had not happened. When we did this we found that shaming experiences were still strongly related to both BPO and anger scores. The opposite was not true, however. With shame removed from the equation, paternal physical abuse by itself did not predict BPO, anger, or even abusiveness. A lethal combination of shaming and physical abuse was required to generate the kind of abusiveness we have described above. Unfortunately, that lethal combination was the rule rather than the exception: shaming experiences were strongly related to having a father who also physically abused the boy.

What shaming does is to create a vulnerable sense of self, one that can be easily attacked. The shame-prone person feels the first flashes of humiliation at the slightest affront and responds quickly with open rage, what Helen Block Lewis called "humiliated fury." This rage appears so out of proportion precisely because it is being used to prevent idiocide, a felt death of the self, a self weakened through early attacks. As psychiatrist Leon Wurmser put it in expressing the feelings of one of his patients, "I have never been myself except in anger."[17] The title of his book *The Mask of Shame* conveys that the exposed, vulnerable self forces one to hide behind a mask. The word shame comes from the Old High German root *scama*, meaning "to cover oneself." Anger provides such a mask, and through externalizing blame prevents shame from being reexperienced. Both are essential criteria of the abusive personality.

The EMBU contained several items that assessed parental shaming actions. Shame could be generated through three sets of actions that attacked the global nascent self. This included public humiliation, random punishment, and direct verbal "global attacks." With random punishment (as with the terrible trauma of random violence in Nazi concentration camps described by Bruno Bettelheim above), the specific act that "caused" the punishment cannot be ascertained. Hence, the punishment generalizes to the entire self, which comes to be experienced as bad or unlovable. By blurring the connection between any specific action that the boy had done and its ensuing punishment, shaming parents created a generalized corrosive attack on the boy's sense of self. The punishment was seen as punishment of the self rather than punishment of the act.

Table 8.3 shows the direct correlations of shaming actions by the parent with the man's abusive personality (BPO, anger, trauma symptoms) and abusiveness (reported by his female partner). Shaming actions by the father are significantly more highly correlated with adult abusiveness than shaming actions by the mother. Shaming and guilt-inducing words and actions by the parents were highly intercorrelated with physical abuse. The physically abusive parent was also the one who shamed and guilt-induced their child. As described above, when we performed partial correlations on the

TABLE 8.3. Correlations of Shame, Guilt, and Unloved Experiences to Associated Features of Abusiveness (Anger, Trauma Symptoms, and Borderline Scales) and to Abusiveness in a Population of Assaultive Men ($N = 140$)

	Shame		Guilt		Unloved	
	Mother	Father	Mother	Father	Mother	Father
BPO						
Total	.37**	.55***	.31*	.38***	.27**	.23***
Identity diffusion	.29*	.58***	.27*	.46***	.25*	.27***
Primitive defenses	.31*	.45***	.29*	.44***	.23*	.26**
Reality testing	.27*	.55***	.17	.49***	.22*	.17***
Anger (MAI)	.43***	.43***	.28*	.30**	.28*	.23**
In	.38**	.46***	.19	.25**	.23*	.20*
Out	.25*	.62***	.28*	.34***	.05	.29**
Magnitude	.35**	.29*	.25*	.26*	.11	.18*
Frequency	.41***	.35**	.32**	.19*	.27**	.17*
Hostility	.41***	.42***	.32**	.30**	.27**	.21*
TSC						
Total	.27*	.38***	.26*	.37***	.25*	.19*
Sleep deprivation	.26*	.29*	.23*	.21*	.18	.20*
Depression	.29*	.41***	.28*	.33**	.19	.34**
Anxiety	.28*	.36***	.26*	.30**	.19	.34**
Dissociation	.21*	.27**	.20*	.24*	.21*	.31**
PSAT	.18	.24*	.14	.20*	.22*	.30**
PMWI 1	.39***	.35***	.33**	.31**	.29***	.27**
PMWI 2	.34***	.33***	.32**	.30**	.10	.08
CTS Physical						
Man's self-report	.38**	.31*	.12	.09	.41***	.35***
Wife's self-report	.24*	.26*	.18	.17	.55***	.50***
CTS: FOO						
Phys. DY	.66***		.41***		.36**	
Phys. MY	.59***		.50***		.11	

Note. MAI, Multidimensional Anger Inventory; TSC, Trauma Symptom Checklist; BPO, Borderline Personality Organization Scale; PMWI 1, Factor 1 of the Psychological Maltreatment of Women Inventory (Dominance/Isolation); PMWI 2, Factor 2 of the Psychological Maltreatment of Women Inventory (Emotional Abuse); CTS, Conflict Tactics Scale; FOO, Family of Origin; Phys. DY, Physical violence by Dad to you; Phys. MY, Physical violence by Mom to you. From Dutton, Starzomski, and van Ginkel (1995). Copyright 1995 by Springer Publishing Company, Inc. Reprinted by permission.
*$p < .05$; **$p < .01$; ***$p < .001$.

relationship between parental actions and the man's current abusiveness toward his partner, we found that physical punishment by the parents was no longer significantly correlated with the man's abusiveness once shame was partialled out. The same effect occurred for guilt. Similarly, when we partialled out physical abuse, shame and guilt lost their significant relationship with current abusiveness. In other words, it is the combination of physical punishment and psychological abuse that is so toxic. The abusiveness these men exhibit in their adult intimate relationships is produced by a combination of physical and psychological maltreatment they experience as a child. This combination not only models abusive actions, it attacks the boys' sense of self.

HUMILIATION AND SHAME

As Lenore Terr puts it in her excellent book *Too Scared to Cry*, shame comes from

> public exposure of one's own vulnerability. Guilt, on the other hand, is private. It follows from a sense of failing to measure up to private, internal standards. . . . Exchanges of guilt for shame begin to occur very early in life, too early . . . for a child to possess a fully formed conscience. But if the child has just finished passing through infancy, the most vulnerable period of life, the youngster will hate having this vulnerability exposed. Rather than risking shame, the toddler will be able to create some guilt to cover over this humiliation. The new 'convert' to autonomy, in other words, is the most adamant of converts. No person is more mortified by the loss of autonomy and personal control than is a traumatized three year old. And so, even the relatively young pre-schooler will make this trade-off—guilt for shame.[18]

Shame gets converted to guilt to spare the infant the uncontrollable attacks from without—the *public* condemnation. If we learn to blame ourselves, these can be avoided and we can feel a sense of control in the ability to avoid future instances of "bad behavior." Shame and humiliation are strong and common for toddlers precisely because at this age the sense of self is still quite tenuous and hence easily subject to a sense of public attack.

In *The Seductions of Crime*, Jack Katz defines humiliation as a loss of control over one's identity.[19] Wouldn't it seem that one who had a shaky sense of self would be more prone to humiliation? And wouldn't men who suffered from faulty mothering during the separation–individuation phase have a more shaky sense of self? Interestingly, Katz sees a common underpinning to rage and humiliation that accounts, in his view, for the rapid transformation of humiliation to rage. In both, for example, the individual experiences himself as an object compelled by forces beyond his control. His control of his identity is lost when he is humiliated. He becomes "an object of ridicule." As Katz puts it, "Thus, a husband knows that others know he is a cuckhold, and he senses that they always will see him that way. Suddenly, he realizes that his identity has been transformed by forces outside his control some fundamental way. He has become morally impotent, unable to govern the evolution of his identity."[20] Similarly with anger, the perpetrator says, "I got carried away, I didn't know what I was doing," and expresses the rage as somehow external and taking him over.

Both are holistic feelings experienced as transcending bodily limitations. In humiliation, the person is overcome with an intolerable discomfort: one's very being is humiliated. Rage, too, "draws the whole body to its service." The conversion of humiliation to rage is a swift transition, according to Katz, because one is the perfect opposite of the other: humiliation is defined as the experience of being reduced to a lower position. "To disparage someone, [we] might say that he 'sucks' . . . as a reference to the infancy's sucking at the breast. . . . [I]n its sensuality humiliation makes one feel small. In humiliation, one feels incompetent and powerless as if one's stature has been reduced to that of a baby."[21] Humiliation works from the top of the head down; rage surges in the opposite direction, starting in the belly and working up until we "blow our top" or "rise up" in anger. The question that is raised but left unanswered in Katz's analysis is how men who feel humiliation at, say, their wife's infidelity have so much of their identity riding on their ability to generate her sexual loyalty. Sociobiologists like Martin Daly and Margo Wilson believe that aggression towards unfaithful wives indicates that they cannot guarantee their husbands contribution to the gene pool.[22] This does not speak, of course, to the problem of humiliation. In order to do so we have to examine the construction of the male social identity and why so much of that identity requires sexual control on one's woman/wife/partner.

Early upbringing plays a major part in formation of the self. At young vulnerable ages, children are open and susceptible to the vicissitudes of family function and dysfunction. The impact of such experiences as violence between parents, angry divorce, rejection and shaming can take a toll on everything from the self-concept, the ability to self-soothe or to tolerate aloneness, the ability to modulate anger and anxiety, up to the ability to elaborate opiate receptors in the brain, *and even affecting the development of neural structure.*[23] At every level from the physiological–neurological to the psychological, the abused/rejected/shamed boy is primed to use violence. It is not merely the learning of an action that occurs in violent families, it is the configuration of an entire personality. Table 8.4 summarizes the psychological and behavioral sequelae of each antecedent described

TABLE 8.4. Disentangled Antecedents of Abusiveness

	Antecedent	Psychological sequelae	Behavioral sequelae
I	Rejection, shaming	• Inflated self-esteem, anger • Affect regulation dysfunction • Anger/rage • Externalizing blaming attributions	• Frequent rage proneness • Emotional abuse: PMWI
II	Insecure attachment	• Jealousy/attachment anger	• Control: PMWI • Intimate focus to rage
III	Victim of physical abuse Witnessed physical abuse	• Decreased empathy for victim of violence • Violence patterns in memory • Absence of positive resolution strategies	• Abuse: CTS
I and II	Rejection, shaming, insecure attachment	• Anger focused on intimate relationship	• Intimate rage
I, II, and III	Rejection, shaming, insecure attachment Victim of physical abuse Witnessed physical abuse	• Reliance on relationship for ego integrity	• Control/abuse/stalking

in the above chapters. Here we have teased out or disentangled the antecedents into discrete processes. In real life, of course, they are confounded.

That configuration lays the groundwork, the foundation for the abusive personality. It creates certain pathways, ways of responding, that will lead to further reinforcement for abuse: rage with girlfriends; possessiveness; selection of male friends who tolerate or even envy the violent streak. As the "preabusive" boy enters his teen years, he passes from a latency period when girls were irrelevant to a new phase of life with peer groups and messages from the culture and his subculture about what it means to be a man. I believe that abused/rejected boys interpret and accept this information differently, even seek out different information. The message they want to hear is the one that tells them they're all right, that their anger is justified, that women are the problem.

One of the criticisms of retrospective research is that, by focusing, on a "problem" group (such as abusive men) and searching for background causes, the problems found may be overesti-

TABLE 8.5. Trauma Effect on Children and the Observed Deficit in Batterers

Trauma effect on children	Observed deficit in batterers
• Restricted affect (van der Kolk, 1987)	• Restricted affect (Dutton, 1984)
• Limited cognitive problem-solving skills (Dodge et al., 1995)	• Blaming orientations (Dutton & Starzomski, 1994)
• Arousal dyscontrol problems (van der Kolk, 1987)	• Extreme arousal patterns (Gottman et al., 1995)
• Insecure attachment (Cicchetti & Barnett, 1991)	• Insecure attachment (Dutton et al., 1994)

Note. From Dutton and Holtzworth-Munroe (1997). Copyright 1997 by University of Rochester Press. Reprinted here with permission of the publisher.

mated. We have tried to answer this in part by using nonabusive controls. Another approach is to turn to a different research paradigm and ascertain the fit between the findings of the two approaches. Amy Holtzworth-Munroe and I did this, comparing the developmental factors found in the backgrounds of adult abusive males with the results of studies in "developmental psychopathology."[24] These latter studies were prospective in nature, ascertaining that abuse of a child had occurred and then monitoring or assessing that child-victim at a later point in time. Comparison of these two sets of research findings are displayed in Table 8.5. The two sets of research findings mutually reinforced each other. Longitudinal studies of abused children found problems in regulating emotion, insecure attachment, and ability to constructively problem solve.[25] Our retrospective results on adult abusers found the same. I believe it is just a matter of time until these two research paradigms close

TABLE 8.6. Trauma Model of Abusiveness

Family of origin	Adult deficits

Physical abuse
  Between parents
  Directed at child
	Cognitive problem resolution deficits
	Violent response repertoire

Parental rejection/shaming
  Public punishment
  Random punishment
  Global criticism
	Externalizing/blaming attributional style
	High chronic anger

Insecure attachment	Rejection sensitivity
	Ambivalent attachment style
	Disturbed self-schema
	  Inability to self-soothe
	  Anxiety depression

the age gap and present a comprehensive life span developmental portrait of the long-term consequences of early abuse experiences. Boys in violent families do not simply "witness abuse," they are traumatized by the variety of sources described above. Table 8.6 presents the trauma model of the development of intimate abusiveness.

9

The Treatment of Assaultiveness

If one conclusion stands out from the rest in the preceding chapters, it is that assaultiveness and abusiveness have a psychology. They are not merely the product of "bad attitudes," nor can they be narrowly defined as the robotic imitation of action. The actions of abusiveness are supported by ways of looking at and feeling about the world, about oneself, about intimate relationships, and about one's partner. These attitudes themselves emanate from personalities destined to destroy intimate relationships and to blame their demise on their female partner. The abusive male is easily shamed and tends therefore to externalize problems by blaming others. He experiences high levels of anxiety and depression. These dysphoric feelings become "evidence" for the partner's failures and generate substance abuse problems, which further exacerbate the marital conflicts. The man experiences but remains unaware of his "abuse cycles" comprised of collected tension, abusive "blowouts," and consequent contrition. In his mind the changes are not within himself but in external reality. Clearly, this will not represent a receptive client population. Given the tendency to shame easily, abusive men must not be confronted too quickly or too strongly. (A form of treatment for borderline personality disorder [BPD][1] provides a method to remedy this therapeutic problem. We discuss Marsha Linehan's work below, given the centrality of borderline problems to abusiveness.)

On the other hand, given abusive men's well-established denial system and tendency to minimize the consequences of their abusiveness, some confrontation must occur. Similarly, given their isolation from other men, a group treatment format will seem intimidating; yet individual treatment, the alternative treatment approach, is expensive and frequently abandoned prematurely. Accordingly, before focusing on a treatment group regimen, it is important to put treatment in context.

As cited in their article on pharmacological treatment for assaultive males, Maiuro and Avery[2] developed a three-stage program termed "biopsychosocial intervention." The biological aspect involves administering pharmacological treatment for problems such as depression, irritable temperament, hyperreactivity, emotional lability, pathological anxiety, obsessiveness, compulsiveness, and postconcussive or other related syndromes. The biological treatment results suggest that pharmacological agents such as antidepressants, anxiolytics, and serotonin reuptake moderators might aid in treating certain aspects of the abusive personality. Cocarro and Kavoukian[3] have found low levels of serotonin to be associated with aggressive behavior in animals. Other pharmacological treatments such as depakote and Prozac have been useful in treating impulsivity and obsessiveness/depression, respectively. However, as the researchers point out, this form of intervention cannot be substituted for social change or psychological (group) treatment. Recall Bandura's analysis of the effect of hypothalamic stimulation in animals of differing social status (p. 16). Delgado had found that hypothalamic stimulation produced cowering in submissive female monkeys. As these females were "promoted" by successive entry into less aggressive tribes, they became progressively more assertive and aggressive themselves. After several such promotions, the same hypothalamic implant now produced aggression. Neurobiology, by itself, was not the complete answer.

Hence, even with drug treatment several targets for psychological treatment remain. The following were listed by Maiuro and Avery as potential psychological treatment targets: defenses against acknowledgment of responsibility (e.g., denial, minimizing, blame projection), anger management (detection and control of anger responses), personal acceptance or justification of violence, assertiveness, bargaining and communication skills, attitudes toward women, family-of-origin modeling influences, relationship enhancement skills (including nonviolent conflict resolution skills), and relapse prevention skills. I agree that these appear to be reasonable targets for psychological intervention, yet both the narrower biological and psychological interventions must be set within a social context of activism concerning general cultural acceptance of violence, violence toward women, women's safety, and male sex-role conditioning.

Treatment groups for assaultive males were developed in the late 1970s by Dr. Anne Ganley, then a psychologist at the Veterans Administration Hospital in Tacoma, Washington. Ganley's treatment model was based on the notion of abusiveness as a learned behavior, that is, a social learning model.[4] We adopted her treatment model and, in line with our own experience, revised it somewhat. I outline this model here, including extended applications relating to BPD, psychopathy, attachment issues, and trauma. I then examine the outcome research on treatment effectiveness. The clinical goals of treatment are relatively simple: to get the man to recognize and to accept responsibility for his abusiveness, and to develop control over and to reduce the frequency of such behavior. The treatment program described below is simply one means of achieving these objectives.

SIXTEEN WEEKS IN A TREATMENT GROUP

Court-mandated treatment models arose in a number of locations in the early 1980s. The criminal justice system needed an effective way for judges to settle wife assault cases before them, and treatments were developed to meet that need. Many men who are sent by the courts for wife assault treatment have had no experience with psychotherapy. They imagine their worst fears and weaknesses being exposed; consequently, the experience is initially terrifying.

Robert Wallace and Anna Nosko have described the opening night ritual in such groups as a "vicarious detoxification" of shame.[5] Men who come to group, assuming they are "normally" socialized, experience high levels of shame as a result of their violent behavior. Hearing other men in group discuss their own violence allows the man to "vicariously detoxify," that is, to face his own sense of shame. This sense of shame, were it not detoxified, would maintain the man's anger at a high level and preclude his opening up to treatment. The anger is maintained to keep the shame at bay. Anger allows blame to be directed outward, preventing shame-induced internalized blame.

For this reason, we start very slowly in our groups (see Figure 9.1), simply asking men on opening night to describe "the event that led to your being here" (e.g., the assault). Their stories provide them with a sense of mutual affliction and of shame detoxification that furthers the bonding process. Moreover, these stories provide us with an initial assessment of the man's level of denial and willingness to accept responsibility for his violence.

The only other thing we try to accomplish on opening night is to review the group rules with the clients. These rules are reproduced in Figure 9.2. Apart from commonsense rules such as attending consistently in a sober condition, these rules also outline the

Week	Didactic Exercise	Group Process Goal
1	Describe the assault that led to your being there; participation agreement	Shame detoxification; group cohesiveness; assessment of denial levels; authority issues
2	Conflict issues: Emotions, actions	Group cohesiveness; shame detoxification
3	What is "abuse"? Definitions; power wheel	Hierarchy in group; authority issues
4	Explanation of confrontation; first group check-in	Attitude confrontation
5	Violence policy	Authority issues; personal responsibility
6	Anger diaries	Emotion detection
7	Stress management: Reichian breathing	Repeat of above
8	Abuse cycle	
9	DESC scripts	
10	Family of origin: How did you dad/mom show his/her anger?	
11	Continuation: How did you/your siblings feel?	
12	DESC scripts; role play	
13	Detection of other prevalent emotions (resentment, guilt, shame, etc.)	
14	Consolidation of communication skills	
15	Preparation for end: Relapse prevention	
16	What did you learn? What continues to be a problem? What other therapies are available?	

FIGURE 9.1. Treatment outline.

ALTERNATIVES TO VIOLENCE PROGRAM

Participation Agreement

I, _____, agree to join the Alternatives to Violence Program. I understand that the group will give me an opportunity to

1. Take responsibility for my behavior.
2. Learn to manage anger and express feelings in appropriate ways.
3. Learn new and constructive ways of coping with stresses and difficulties in my life.

I agree to cooperate with the following group rules.

1. I will attend every week and will be on time for all group sessions. If I miss more than two sessions, I may be expelled from the group. My probation officer will be notified of this, and I may be charged with a breach of the terms of my probation.
2. I will attend all sessions in a sober condition and not under the influence of any mood-altering drugs. If I come to a group under the influence of alcohol or drugs I will not be allowed into the group for that evening. This will count as one missed session, and my probation officer will be notified about this.
3. I will participate to the best of my ability by sharing honestly my thoughts and feelings and by completing all written assignments.
4. I am in the group to learn skills for respectful and healthy relationships. If I am violent or abusive I will report this at the next group session. Failure to do so may result in my being expelled from the group.
5. I have been given a copy of the "time-out" procedure and will use this to increase my ability to create healthy relationships in all areas of my life.
6. I understand that what is said or done in the group sessions is confidential and I should not discuss information about other group members outside the group. I am free to share my own thoughts, feelings, and experiences about being in the group with those who are close to me in my own life.
7. If I am seeing a counselor, psychologist, psychiatrist, or other professional for either individual or group counseling I understand I may be asked to sign a release to share information so that the Alternatives to Violence staff may consult with these professionals in order to coordinate the help I am receiving. Withholding my consent for this will not be grounds to expel me from the program.
8. I understand that my wife (partner) will be interviewed as part of the assessment process. The purpose will be to better understand my life situation, give her information about the program, obtain my wife's point of view, and provide information for her regarding counseling or support for herself. The program staff will not repeat information given by my partner to me, nor will they share information, given by me, with her. Her participation with this interview is voluntary and will in no way reflect upon my status.
9. I understand that if the therapists have reason to believe that I could be a physical risk to anyone they will contact the appropriate authorities and the person(s) who may be at risk.
10. I understand that I will be asked to complete brief weekly written assignments to help me understand my anger. I will not be admitted to the group without a completed assignment. This will count as one missed session.
11. If I am attending on a probation order a one-page summary of my attendance and progress will be given to my probation officer upon my completion or expulsion from the group. I can receive a copy of this report if I wish.

My signature below indicates that I have read this agreement and understand it, having had a chance to ask questions and have them answered.

Date _____

Signature _____

Name _____

Witness _____

FIGURE 9.2. Participation agreement.

confidential nature of the group and the exceptions to this rule (such as disclosures of child abuse or of direct threats toward another person). As straightforward as these rules may be, they still trigger resentment concerning the criminal justice system's handling of the man's case. Many men feel poorly treated by the system and see therapists as extensions of that system. These feelings frequently surface during discussion of the participation agreement.

At the end of the first group session we ask men how they feel at this juncture. Generally, they express relief about "surviving" the first group and about being in a group composed of men with similar problems. Their relief generally has to do with not feeling judged; this aspect proves to be particularly important given the shame feelings often experienced by abusive males, as described by Wallace and Nosko. For this reason, I would not recommend confrontation on opening night.

Immediately following the beginning of group, therapists should interview each female partner to assess her safety plans, her perception of personal risk, the man's current level of abuse, and any feedback he may have brought home from his first group experience. One danger sign, for example, is the use of the group to minimize one's abuse: "You think I'm bad, you should hear these other guys in my group." The therapist should also ascertain what information can safely be fed back to the man. If the woman isn't comfortable with direct feedback (attributed to or traceable to her), present the issue during group in general terms. Ask the men if they have any lingering reactions to what they heard the preceding week and discuss "defensive social comparison," where one uses the group to deny or to minimize one's own abuse. The point should be that each man, regardless of his level of abuse, has to take responsibility for that abuse. It is irrelevant that someone else may be more violent than he is.

The second meeting should begin with addressing residual feelings from week 1. It is useful to get the clients to focus on and to describe such feelings; this begins a weekly "check-in" exercise that will initiate the group process for each week to come. It can also lead into a simple exercise for week 2: differentiating feelings from "issues" and actions. An example is presented in Table 9.1.

We present this as an exercise; men are asked, "What do you argue about?", "How do you feel after these arguments?", and "How do you act when you are arguing?" This exercise is again deceptively simple; it outlines some apparent distinctions between feelings and

TABLE 9.1. Issues, Feelings, and Actions

Issues	Feelings	Actions
Money	Anger	Yell, scream
Disciplining the kids	Hopelessness	Walk out
In-laws	Anxiety	Pushing
Sex	Depression	Hitting
Friends		Breaking things
Drinking		

actions. At the same time, it again shows clients that other men share many of the same issues. This revelation furthers the bonding process in the group and facilitates shame detoxification. We tend not to confront men much during these initial few weeks. We describe what confrontation is and distinguish it from attack or put-downs. We explain that confrontation is a device to help someone change, whereas attack is simply done to make the attacker feel powerful. We warn men that we will later use confrontation as a part of treatment. If a group is particularly woman-blaming, however, it is important to initiate the confrontation process earlier, before a negative form of group cohesiveness develops, built on shared commiseration about how difficult women can be. Reorienting the men from an other-blaming orientation to a self-control orientation typically has to be repeated during early sessions. As the guiding philosophy, a self-control orientation emphasizes personal responsibility and control of self (along with negotiation with, rather than control over, others).

Week 3 begins with a feeling check-in again and deals with the question of what is meant by "abuse." The various forms of abuse (physical, sexual, emotional) are discussed, and the "power wheel," developed by a program in Duluth, Minnesota,[6] is explained (see Figure 9.3). A working definition of abuse also includes the motive of harming the partner's self-esteem or restricting her autonomy. Men are informed that, for the duration of the group, they will be asked to report any abuse committed that fits the aforementioned definitions. One practical issue regarding the "check-in" exercise deserves mention: it can run for an hour and a half in a 10-man group, reducing group time for other exercises. If this begins to happen, get the men to respond succinctly to three questions: Was there any abuse this week (if so describe)? Did you handle your anger well on any occasion? Do you need any group time for special problems?

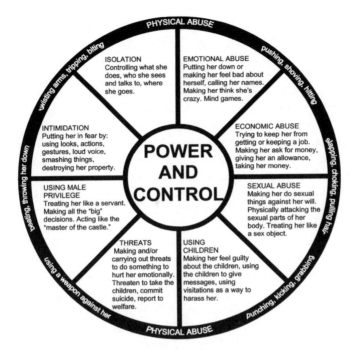

FIGURE 9.3. Power wheel. From Pence and Paymar (1986).

Week 4 examines the gains and losses each man experiences through the use of violence. This leads to asking the men to develop a personal "violence policy" for the following week. Each violence policy must be a response to this poser: "I believe it all right to be violent under the following circumstances. . . . " Each man has to develop his personal policy as a homework exercise. (Again, from a process perspective, this is a test of the man's commitment to the groupwork.) Most men will cite self-defense or protection of family, while others may cite reactions to home invasion and the like as justifying violence. Few will cite violence as acceptable during arguments with their wives. It is important that this policy come from the client. This undercuts his erroneous conviction that actions and beliefs are being imposed on him. If it is his own policy, which the therapist will hold him to, there exists a greater feeling of coauthorship between the client and therapist. Men who have a policy that is at odds with the group philosophy will need to have their attitude identified and confronted directly. The role of the "pro-violence" attitude in sustaining destructive behavior patterns must also be addressed. If the man refuses to change his attitude, the therapist must decide whether this is a "protest gesture" (against the therapist, who is seen as an extension of the criminal justice response, still angering the man) or a bona fide attitude that impedes the client's progress. This is a situation where confrontation by another group member or by a "catalyst" (a man returning from a prior group to co-facilitate and to act as a catalyst) is especially helpful. In the face of prolonged failure, however, men who refuse to change their pro-violence attitude may be asked to leave the group; their refusal to adopt a more constructive perspective is contradictory to a commitment to change.

Around this time in the group progress, friendships may begin to form. We capitalize on this by forming help triads. Men self-select into groups of three. They realize that in making this choice, they are agreeing to be on 24/7 emergency helpline for each other and that the other two will also do it for them. Help triads are to be used when a time-out has failed, anger is escalating, and an overnight cooling off is called for. All that is expected is a place to stay and some support. Alcohol and drugs are forbidden.

Week 5 introduces the anger diary or anger log (see Figure 9.4). This anger diary is the basic tool to improve the men's ability to detect and manage their anger. It requires them to specifically state what triggered their anger as objectively as possible (under the "trigger" column), to list how they knew they were angry (what physical cues told them so?), to rate their anger severity on a scale where 10 is their own personal extreme, and to describe their "talk-up" (their thoughts as their anger escalates) and "talk-down" thoughts (their thoughts as their anger diminishes). Most clients have some initial difficulty with the latter. A list of talk-down statements is provided to help them with this (see Figure 9.5). Men are instructed to select a statement that feels soothing to them personally and to use it during their anger arousal.

Comparison of the "trigger" and "talk-up" columns of the anger diary will assist the therapist in making explicit the interpretations and assumptions that color the client's perception of the trigger. Assumptions of malevolent intent (i.e., that the actions of the other person were intentional, to hurt them) are frequent with angry clients. Group discussion should clarify that other interpretations are possible and more likely. This exercise can also be used to evaluate the client's ability to empathize with the other person. As-

Date of Event	Trigger	How Anger Known	Rating (1-10)	Self Talk Talk-Up	Self Talk Talk-Down
Nov. 17	WIFE KEPT BOTHERING FRIEND OF SON BY REPEATEDLY ASKING HIM QUESTIONS ABOUT A BOOK HIS FATHER WROTE.	STARTING FEELING MORE UPTIGHT THE MORE SHE WENT ON.	4	WHY DOESN'T SHE LEAVE THE POOR KID ALONE. WHY DOESN'T SHE JUST SHUT UP AND WATCH THE MOVIE LIKE EVERYONE ELSE.	I FEEL ANGRY ABOUT THE WAY SHE'S TREATING THIS KID BUT MAKING A SCENE ABOUT IT IN FRONT OF THE KIDS WILL ONLY BRING ME TO HER LEVEL.
Nov. 18	WIFE CONTINUALLY NAGGING AT ME + POINTING HER FINGER IN MY FACE.	NECK + BACK FELT TENSE + HAD EMPTY FEELING IN GUT.	7	THIS BITCH IS PUSHING ME TO THE LIMIT ONCE AGAIN. WHY CAN'T SHE BACK OFF AND TRY TO WORK THINGS OUT QUIETLY.	I FEEL REALLY MAD BUT I WON'T LOOSE CONTROL. (YOU) BETTER GET AWAY FOR AWHILE AND HOPE THINGS COOL DOWN.
Nov. R	WIFE NOT HELPING WITH ANYTHING AROUND THE HOUSE BECAUSE SHE SAYS SHE IS SICK.	FELT UNUSUALLY NERVOUS + UPTIGHT.	3	THE ONLY REASON SHE FEELS SO SICK IS BECAUSE SHE DRANK ALL WEEKEND AND NOW I HAVE TO PAY FOR IT ONCE AGAIN MORE WORK TO DO.	I'M GETTING ANGRY AGAIN FOR THE SAME OLD REASON HER DRINKING WON'T LET IT GET TO YOU. THINGS WILL HAVE TO IMPROVE OR OUR RELATIONSHIP WON'T LAST.

Date of Event	Trigger	How Anger Known	Rating (1-10)	Self Talk Talk-Up	Self Talk Talk-Down
Nov. 30	FINDING OUT WIFE HAD GONE OUT AND NOT COME HOME ALL NIGHT.	FELT MY ADRENALIN START TO FLOW AND STARTED MOVING AROUND HOUSE AT A QUICK PACE.	4	SHE'S DONE IT AGAIN GONE OUT WITHOUT AS MUCH AS A NOTE OR PHONE CALL TO SAY WHERE SHE IS. THAT BITCH DOESN'T GIVE A SHIT ABOUT MY FEELINGS.	THIS ISN'T THE FIRST TIME OR I MIGHT REALLY GET WORRIED. I'M SURE SHE WILL SHOW UP TOMORROW SO NO SENSE TO WORRY. I MIGHT AS WELL GO BACK TO BED. ACTUALLY I FEEL RELIEVED THAT SHE ISN'T HURT HERE.
Dec. 1	WIFE STARTED YELLING AT ME—WHY DIDN'T YOU LEAVE ME ALONE TO SAY WHAT YOU WANT (NAMES ETC.) THEN TOLD ME NOT TO TOUCH THE FRYING PAN BECAUSE EVERYTIME I BEGAN TO HANG DINNER SHE SAW (SAW) BOTTLE OF RUM ON COUNTER.	ENTIRE BODY BECAME TENSE AND STOMACH GOT VERY UPSET.	9	THAT FUCKING BITCH. HOW DARE SHE QUESTION + TALK TO ME LIKE THIS WHEN SHE DISAPPEARED LAST NIGHT WITHOUT AN EXPLANATION SHE'S DRUNK AND I'M FEELING WEATHER-BEATEN.	TIME OUT! GET OUT OF HERE NOW SHE'S PUSHING ME BEYOND MY CONTROL. GET AWAY FROM HER NOW!
Dec. 2	BARGING IN HOUSE DRUNK LATE AT NIGHT AND STARTED YELLING NOT TO COME NEAR HER. THEN SMACKED ME WITH HER HAND RIGHT IN THE LEFT EYE.	KNUCKLES BECAME TENSE+FACE BECAME HOT.	7	WHAT A FUCKING NERVE. I'VE NO INTENTION OF GOING ANYWHERE NEAR HER. JUST GOTO BED AND PASS OUT. I DON'T WANT ANYTHING TO DO WITH YOU.	I'M FURIOUS WITH HER BUT I'M NOT GOING TO RETALIATE OR I'LL BE THE ONE TO PAY FOR ALL THIS SHIT SHE'S CAUSING.

FIGURE 9.4. Anger diary. Provided by a client in the Assaultive Husbands' Project.

suming the client's perception of the event that precipitated his action is accurate (this needs checking), the therapist must assess the
extent to which the client can imagine and accept another interpretation for the other person's emotional response.

Week 6 should focus on the feelings that can be converted to
anger, such as guilt, shame, jealousy, or humiliation. A bit of theory
(e.g., how shame or fear can be converted to anger because anger is
more consistent with "agency" of the "male sex role") helps here,
but it is also important to return to the anger diary and to ensure
that each client can and is completing it weekly. We also institute a
"gut check" (see Figure 9.6) on honest participation around this
time by asking the men to describe (on a written note) who they
think has been the most and least honest in the group. They are
also asked whom it is that they feel they know the least well. When

Both research and experience show that when people with anger problems change their
self-talk, their anger deescalates and they regain control. When you notice your cues escalating or start to feel angry, take a TIME-OUT and read these statements to yourself.

- I don't need to prove myself in this situation.
- As long as I keep my cool, I'm in control of myself.
- No need to doubt myself, what other people say doesn't matter. I'm the only person
  who can make me mad or keep me calm.
- Time to relax and slow things down. Take a time out if I get uptight or start to notice my
  cues.
- My anger is a signal. Time to talk to myself and to relax.
- I don't need to feel threatened here. I can relax and stay cool.
- Nothing says I have to be competent and strong all the time. It's okay to feel unsure or
  confused. It's impossible to control other people and situations. The ONLY thing I can
  control is myself and how I express my feelings.
- It's okay to be uncertain or insecure sometimes. I don't need to be in control of every-
  thing and everybody.
- If people criticize me, I can survive that. Nothing says that I have to be perfect.
- If this person wants to go off the wall, that's her/his thing. I don't need to respond to
  her/his anger or feel threatened.
- When I get into an argument, I can use my control plan and know what to do. I can
  take a time-out.
- Most things we argue about are stupid and insignificant. I can recognize that my anger
  comes from having my old primary feelings restimulated. It's okay to walk away from
  this fight.
- It's nice to have other people's love and approval, but even without it, I can still accept
  and like MYSELF.
- People put erasers on the ends of pencils for a reason; it's okay to make mistakes.
- People are going to act the way they want to, not the way I want.
- I feel angry: that must mean I have been hurt, scared, or have some other primary
  feeling.

FIGURE 9.5. Self-talk.

1. How honest am I being in the group?
   1..10
   not at all   completely

2. How much effort am I putting into the group?
   1..10
   not much   completely

3. How much feedback am I giving to others in the group?
   1..10
   not much   completely

4. Who do I know the most/least about in the group?

5. Who is denying his violence most/least in the group?

6. How much am I getting out of the group?
   1..10
   not much   completely

FIGURE 9.6. "Gut check."

these notes are collected from each man, the therapist asks whether or not they would like feedback. At this point, a summary of the notes can be delivered either individually or collectively. The former involves telling an individual how the group rates him; the latter, tallying all of the ratings on a grid.

At this point, we introduce attachment issues to the group by examining the diaries of men who have reported jealousy as a point of entry. Dutton and Sonkin[7] have written about conjoint therapy for batterers with insecure attachment. As we have seen in earlier chapters, insecure attachment is positively correlated with wives' reports of amount of abusiveness (more about this below). The first step in the treatment of attachment issues actually begins in the first week of treatment with the establishment of a secure base (therapist–client) for each man in the group. This requires a stable, nonjudgmental, caring, and sensitive therapist who does not change from week to week. In working with abusive men, it is important to differentiate stopping abuse from generic acceptance of the man. One way of doing this is to explain confrontation as a means of stopping abuse and to remove any sense clients might have of being criticized in group. A next step is to add a didactic exercise about attachment, reviewing the importance of attachment to people in general, how it serves to reduce alarm reactions, how early alarm reactions transform into fear of abandonment and are called jealousy in the culture, how jealousy is an "early warning system" for abandonment, and how jealousy can feed on itself and magnify without evidence. Ultimately, the "solution" to such problems is a buttressing of the sense of self and more open communication with the spouse.

Open communication is synonymous with assertiveness. DESC scripts are the men's introduction to assertive communication and function to replace previously used coping mechanisms, including abuse and repression of feelings. DESC is an acronym that stands for describe, express, specify, and consequences. This term was borrowed from an excellent book on assertive communication by Gordon Bower and Sharon Bower called *Asserting Yourself.*[8] These DESC scripts take the internal work of the anger diary and transform it into an interpersonal tool for improving communication (see Figure 9.7). The key is to get the men to improve at recognizing irritations sooner, and to express them. The concept here is that relationships are "yoked outcome" situations, where what is good for one party improves the other's lot in life as well. The DESC script initiates this process. Men should be cautioned not to expect to "get their way" by using these scripts. The rules for using a DESC script are outlined in Figure 9.8.

Week 7 focuses on teaching breathing and stretching exercises to improve stress management. Wilhelm Reich described character armor as the result of storing tension in the fascia or connective tissue of the body.[9] Since many assaultive men react to a buildup of internal tension, it is important to teach them, through daily routines of breathing–stretching, how to maintain tension within acceptable levels. A variety of useful stretching programs exist that can be combined with breathing and breath-control exercises to develop useful tension self-management techniques. The therapist can demonstrate these in the group session and encourage participation. Some therapists like to teach these techniques much sooner in the schedule and to start each group with breathing–stretching. The didactic goal here is to teach effective tension management so that the reliance on abusive outbursts to diminish tension is lessened.

We include a didactic session on the "cycle of violence" in week 8. Refreshers can be used when risk of recurrence is reported. Start with the general lesson and then ask the men if any of them are currently experiencing "cyclical symptoms" (increasing anger, irritability, withdrawal, etc.). Eventually, focus on the client in question. Ask him if this has been a problem in the past. Does he consider it to be something he would like to change? How could he improve at spotting the cues? The trick here is to move him from attributing changes to external factors to attributing changes to internal states,

Your DESCRIBE lines
- Does your description clarify the situation, or does it just complicate it?
- Replace all terms that do not objectively describe the behavior or problem that bothers you. Be specific.
- Have you described a single specific behavior or problem, or a long list of grievances? Focus on one well-defined behavior or problem you want to deal with now. One grievance per script is generally the best approach.
- Have you made the mistake of describing the other person's attitudes, motives, intentions? Avoid mind reading and psychoanalyzing.
- Revise your DESCRIBE lines now, if necessary.

Your EXPRESS lines
- Have you acknowledged your feelings and opinions as your own, without blaming the other person? Avoid words that ridicule or shame the other person. Swear words and insulting labels (dumb, cruel, selfish, racist, idiotic, boring) very likely will provoke defensiveness and arguments.
- Have you expressed your feelings and thoughts in a positive, new way? Avoid your "old phonograph record" lines that your Downer is tired of hearing and automatically turns off.
- Have you kept the wording low key? Aim for emotional restraint, not dramatic impact.
- Revise your EXPRESS lines now, if necessary.

Your SPECIFY lines
- Have you proposed only one small change in behavior at this time?
- Can you reasonably expect the other person to agree to your request?
- Are you prepared to alter your own behavior if your Downer asks you to change? What are you prepared to change about your behavior?
- What counterproposals do you anticipate, and how will you answer them?
- Revise your SPECIFY lines now, if necessary.

Your CONSEQUENCES lines
- Have you stressed positive, rewarding consequences?
- Is the reward you selected really appropriate for the other person? Perhaps you should ask what you might do for the other person?
- Can you realistically carry through with these consequences?
- Revise your CONSEQUENCES lines now, if necessary.

FIGURE 9.7. Writing your own DESC script.

and to encourage him to focus on changing such states. We show Figure 4.2 (p. 56) to men in group to facilitate this learning. One problem requiring sensitive handling is that many men who go through this borderline cycle are not aware that it is they who are cycling. This is because their phenomenology changes with phases in the cycle. They believe the changes are in the outside world and in their wives' behavior. Getting feedback from the wife and checking her level of comfort with sharing this with the man is one way to begin to approach this problem. Later in this chapter, I examine how Linehan's dialectical behavior therapy (DBT) for borderlines can also be used in wife assault treatment. Figure 9.9 provides a spe-

No.	Do	Don't
DESCRIBE		
D1	Describe the other person's behavior objectively.	Describe your emotional reaction to it.
D2	Use concrete terms.	Use abstract, vague terms.
D3	Describe a specified time, place, and frequency of the action.	Generalize for "all time."
D4	Describe the action, not the "motive."	Guess at your Partner's motives or goals.
EXPRESS		
E1	Express your feelings.	Deny your feelings.
E2	Express them calmly.	Unleash emotional outbursts
E3	State feelings in a positive manner, as relating to a goal to be achieved.	State feelings negatively, making put-down or attack.
E4	Direct yourself to the specific offending behavior, not to the whole person.	Attack the entire character of the person.
SPECIFY		
S1	Ask explicitly for change in your Partner's behavior.	Merely imply that you'd like a change.
S2	Request a small change.	Ask for too large a change.
S3	Request only one or two changes at one time.	Ask for too many changes.
S4	Specify the concrete actions you want to see stopped and those you want to see performed.	Ask for changes in nebulous traits or qualities.
S5	Take account of whether your Partner can meet your request without suffering large losses.	Ignore your Partner's needs or ask only for your satisfaction.
S6	Specify (if appropriate) what behavior you are willing to change to make the agreement.	Consider that only your Partner has to change.
CONSEQUENCES		
C1	Make the consequences explicit.	Be ashamed to talk about rewards and penalties.
C2	Give a positive reward for change in the desired direction.	Give only punishments for lack of change.
C3	Select something that is desirable and reinforcing to your Partner.	Select something that only you might find rewarding.
C4	Select a reward that is big enough to maintain the behavior change.	Offer a reward you can't or won't deliver.
C5	Select a punishment of a magnitude that fits the crime of refusing to change behavior.	Make exaggerated threats.

FIGURE 9.8. Rules for writing assertive DESC scripts.

Have you done any of the following in the last week:

- Missed an appointment with a therapist
- Missed an appointment with a priest, rabbi, or minister
- Missed an AA meeting
- Made fewer phone calls to friends or family enlisting their support to get your spouse to return

Have you had any of the following thoughts in the past week (1 = occurred once; 2 = happened twice; 3 = happened 3 to 5 times; 4 = had that thought a lot):

- I think the worst with her is over now, she's back.
- Why can't she let go of things and forgive and forget?
- She is trying to punish me now.
- I'm starting to remember why she bugs me so much.
- I'm getting back into the same old rut.
- If I'm going to be lonely, I'd rather live on my own.
- She's really not able to give me what I need.
- I'm slipping down again.
- Why can't she make the pain go away?

FIGURE 9.9. Cycle management.

cific way of helping men chart shifts from the contrition phase back to the tension-building phase of cycle management.

If you have men in your group who exhibit borderline traits (extreme swings in positivity–negativity toward their spouse, yourself, and/or the groupwork), some special treatment needs should be addressed. First, you must keep in mind that your group has a limited therapeutic goal: to stop abusiveness. It is not designed for deeper work on personality disorders. Nevertheless, there are some therapeutic imperatives that may benefit borderline men in their ability to self-soothe and self-control. Notice the thinking errors common to borderlines in Table 9.2. These are issues that need to be addressed in most groups anyway—especially the issues surrounding lack of integration of the other and of personalization.

TABLE 9.2. Borderline Thinking Errors

- Dichotomous (black-and-white) thinking
  For example, splitting of intimate other; splitting of self-concept

- Personalization
  Tendency to excessively relate external occurrences to the self
  Includes self-blame

- Catastrophizing
  Inability to differentiate others' wishes from demands

Note. Data from Arntz (1994).

The latter will come up through the interpretation of anger diaries. Again, interviews with partners are an invaluable source of information about the man's mood and temper swings. These are the men who go through the "abuse cycles" of tension buildup, abuse outburst and contrition. In a tracking study of cyclical males, Dutton and Winters found that the men's wives were better at tracking their husbands' swings than were the men.[10] It is important to help these men become more aware of how they are storing tension, what cues they can use to anticipate an outburst, and what alternative tension-reduction methods are available. Borderline clients vary in the extent to which their cycles are demonstrated publicly (see Table 9.3). A strong channel of communication with the man's partner can be used effectively with men whose tension buildups are solely expressed in their intimate bond. Be sure to check with the partner as to how safe it is to confront the man based upon her report.

A cognitive-behavioral treatment for borderline clients was developed by Arnoud Arntz that is quite compatible with the Ganley model and much less labor-intensive than the Linehan approach.[11] Arntz emphasizes the importance of the therapist remaining consistent from week to week. Any changes in the borderline client's reaction to the therapist can then be more clearly attributed to the client. Some men may be so deeply personality disordered that individual therapy (such as DBT) is required in conjunction with treatment for wife assault. We discuss the integration of DBT with cognitive-behavioral treatment in more detail below.

TABLE 9.3. Borderline Treatment

- Consistency of therapist

- Direct attention to clients' fluctuations in
  1. Affect
  2. Perception of self
  3. Perception of partner
  4. Perception of others
  5. General optimism–pessimism

- Challenge fundamental assumptions
  1. Others are dangerous and malignant
  2. Client is powerless and vulnerable
  3. Client is inherently bad/unacceptable
  Differentiate problem behavior (abuse) from client's self

Note. Data from Arntz (1994).

Weeks 9 and 10 involve confronting the men's family-of-origin issues. We ask each of them the following questions: How did your father/mother express his/her anger? What did he/she do? How did this make you feel? How did others react? Did you ever talk to brothers/sisters about it? How did they feel? What message do you take from this for raising your own children? This typically produces strong emotion because many of these men will have experienced an abusive childhood. This also marks the completion of the group bonding process begun in week 1.

Weeks 11 to 14 involve consolidation of the techniques developed during the group. These sessions function to improve communication which, in turn, sets the men up for effective couple counseling. We focus on using "I" statements, on improving empathy, and on distinguishing between argument versus acknowledgment.

In week 15, we prepare the men for the end of treatment by asking them to spend the week considering what they learned, what they changed, what they still have to work on, and how they will replace the honest male-to-male communication developed in the group once they leave. We sensitize them to relapse prevention, asking them what plan they could develop for a "worst-case scenario," that is, if they were to relapse and to abuse again.

WORKING WITH BORDERLINE PERSONALITY
IN BATTERER GROUPS

Since borderline personality organization is so central to abusiveness, I feel that this form of self-disturbance should be generally treated in assaultiveness groups. Marsha Linehan's approach, dialectical behavioral therapy (DBT), has several strengths that standard treatment groups for batterers have not fully utilized. DBT takes into account the polarities in patients, for example, their own valid self and insights as well as their weaknesses such as an unstable self and acting out. As Linehan puts it, "within dysfunction there is also function."[12] She uses a lot of early group time exploring all the potential impediments to clients' completing the group, and gets all the resistances out of the way at the beginning. Batterer groups could benefit from this aspect of Linehan's work alone, since their dropout rates are notoriously high.[13]

Stage 1 in Linehan's DBT groups lasts for 1 year (note that this therapy takes much longer than batterer treatment; in California an entire batterer treatment group takes 1 year, and in other locations is much shorter). This stage focuses on therapeutic commitment and skill development. A skills training manual is available that contains many valuable skills for batterer treatment.[14] Linehan focuses on the borderline client's inability to regulate emotional arousal that interferes with the maintenance of a sense of self. Bear in mind that my own research suggests that the abuse cycle may represent a borderline form. The skills Linehan develops are "mindfulness," interpersonal effectiveness, emotional regulation, distress tolerance, and stress management. She begins by reviewing the goals of skills training and the participants' agreement to adhere to the rules. For example, mindfulness is the ability to go within to find oneself and learning to observe oneself. Participants are given homework practice in taking control of their own thought processes: attending to events, emotions, and other behavioral responses, describing them in words, and participating without self-consciousness—in other words, developing the quality of awareness that individuals bring to activities. Linehan's training manual outlines step-by-step goals, discussion points, and practice exercises for this and other skills. With mindfulness, participants practice observing thoughts, labeling them as thoughts, and putting them into categories (e.g., thoughts about myself, thoughts about my partner), and learn how to describe these thoughts without judging them. There is some similarity here to the "talk-up" exercise on anger diaries, but the process is more elaborated and standardized.

Linehan's interpersonal effectiveness skills training is similar to the assertiveness exercises in batterer groups, but has different emphases than simply assertive communication. It stresses attending to relationships and balancing priorities versus demands from life and relationships. In object relations terms, this may also be thought of as developing "differentiation." Linehan also reviews balancing "wants and shoulds" ratios in relationships. An imbalance in the direction of "wants" is impulsive behavior, whereas an imbalance in the direction of "shoulds" leads to depression, frustration, and anger. Linehan's model also describes "relationship effectiveness" as balancing immediate goals with long-term relationship success. The focus is similar to the short-term gain/long-term loss exercise in batterer groups, but the focus is broader. The exercise also focuses on factors that can reduce interpersonal effectiveness: skill deficits, worry thoughts, and emotional reactions.

For borderline batterers who undergo abuse cycles, Linehan's work on emotion regulation skills is especially helpful. As with most cognitive-behavioral batterer treatment (CBT), Linehan's model starts with skill building in identifying and labeling emotions. Although not as focused on anger as CBT groups, DBT also works on identifying the functions and reinforcers of emotions. In addition, DBT focuses on another function of emotion rarely discussed in CBT groups: validating one's own perspective by communicating it to others and thereby obtaining their validation.

Most CBT groups contain some form of stress reduction treatment (we do breathing and stretching exercises in ours). DBT directs the participant to recognize that vulnerability to the "emotional mind" (as opposed to rational mind) is increased through stress. DBT focuses on holistic stress management (nutrition, exercise, healthy sleep habits). An excellent resource for stress management is Kabat-Zinn's *Full Catastrophe Living*, which outlines the stress reduction program of the University of Massachusetts Medical Center.[15] This book is especially helpful regarding the development of "mindfulness" through meditation exercises. "Distress tolerance" is another focus of DBT that Kabat-Zinn's book can help with. DBT presents four categories of "crisis survival strategy": distracting, self-soothing, improving the moment, and focusing on pros and cons. These are presented as crisis management strategies, not long-term solutions.

DBT teaches that long-term avoidance of emotional pain leads to rumination about painful events. Experiencing, tolerating, and accepting emotional pain are ways to reducing pain. Many batterers use anger and rage as a defense against other emotions—typically shame and fear. Most CBT groups do not explore the deeper negative emotions underlying the anger and its behavioral expression (control and abuse). Some treatment programs (such as the Duluth model) do not even probe beneath the control aspect of abusiveness, treating control as the primary need when, in fact, it is a behavioral manifestation of deeper emotions. For this reason, both the emotion regulation and distress tolerance modules of DBT can contribute to batterer treatment. Our CBT group asks men to monitor their anger and other predominant emotions on a daily basis, while DBT uses daily "diary cards" that generate extensive daily monitoring.

Even if there are no obvious borderline clients in a batterer group, DBT can be a useful adjunct to CBT. Both therapies focus on common skills (emotion regulation, crisis management, mindfulness, assertiveness) that can benefit all clients. In addition, if there are men who undergo abuse cycles, these skills can help in cycle management described above.

WORKING WITH ATTACHMENT ISSUES IN BATTERER GROUPS

Many of the issues of control by abusive men stem from intimacy anxiety. Intimacy anxiety, in turn, is an attachment issue. Men with fearfully attached and preoccupied attachment styles experience intimacy anxiety, which they convert into anger and controlling actions. These include monitoring their spouses' use of time and space and experiencing "conjugal paranoia" and pathological jealousy. Fearful attachment is also highly correlated with borderline personality. (The role of attachment in the formation of the abusive personality is reviewed in Chapter 7.)

Treatment of attachment problems in a batterer population has two main forms: (1) the development of insight into attachment-based fears so that abusive men will stop blaming their wives as being the source of their discomfort, and (2) the formation of a secure base in the therapist–client bond. A therapeutic objective is developing recognition of an anxiety reaction to anticipated loss and an ability to self-soothe. The therapist must provide the attuned soothing voice that was missing in early development. A diary of attachment fears (like an anger diary), including talk-up and talk-down (self-soothing), can be used here.

As a psychoeducational aspect of group therapy, the insight issue can be addressed by describing "abandonment" scenarios: You call and she's not home, she's late returning from work or shopping, she pursues a job or hobby that takes more of her time. It is possible to have men generate fear of loss diaries the same way they generate anger diaries. It is also possible to structure systematic desensitization exercises to fear of loss in the same fashion as other fear-based cognitive-behavioral interventions (e.g., fear of flying). An anxiety gradient is established, with the most fear-inducing scenarios at the top, the less serious at the bottom. The client then visualizes the less serious scenarios and is taught relaxation techniques to extinguish the anxiety at the lower levels. When these are mastered, the therapist moves on to a more anxiety-producing level.

At the "process" level, Bowlby[16] defined five tasks for the therapist working with attachment disorders: (1) to create a secure base or therapeutic bond for the patient to explore thoughts, feelings, and experiences regarding self and attachment figures, (2) to explore current relationships with attachment figures, (3) to explore the relationship with the therapist as an attachment figure, (4) to explore the connection between early childhood experiences and current relationships, and (5) to find new ways of regulating attachment anxiety and emotion regulation when the attachment system is activated. This latter goal dovetails into the emotion regulation module of DBT and the basis of anger management. This latter statement is based on the hypothesis that attachment arousal in batterers gets labeled as anger and contributes to subsequent jealousy and abuse.

By now the reader may have noticed some similarities among CBT, DBT, and attachment approaches (see Table 9.4 for a nonexhaustive list). Note, though, that each has a way of expanding other approaches or focusing it differently.

SPECIAL POPULATIONS: PSYCHOPATHS

There is some question, of course, of whether or not psychopaths are treatable at all.[17] Psychopaths lack the ability to develop emotional relationships with significant others and with therapists, do not see themselves as having a psychological problem, and according to some studies, are the worst recidivists. However, the research suggesting that psychopaths are completely untreatable is far from conclusive (see Table 9.5). Losel[18] reviews this literature and concludes that "structured behavioral, cognitive-behavioral, skill-oriented and multimodal measures based on social learning theories have better effects on antisocial behavior [characteristic of most

TABLE 9.4. Comparison of Treatments

CBT	DBT	Attachment
Therapeutic bond	Therapeutic consistency	Secure base
Acceptance of client (empathy)	Radical acceptance	Nonjudgmental attunement (empathy)
Anger diary	Emotion regulation exercises	Attachment-fear diary
Change anger/abuse	Change impulsivity	Change attachment anxiety

TABLE 9.5. Negative Indicators of Treatment Effect for Psychopaths

- Classical psychotherapy requires transference; transference requires emotional relationships with significant others and the therapist, but this is the central deficit of psychopathic personality (Hare, 1996).
- Tendency to engage in pathological lying disrupts the preconditions for free association or honest communication with a therapist.
- Grandiose sense of self-worth and lack of remorse or guilt do not permit deep motivation for change.
- Shallow affect and lack of empathy impede the central work of emotions in therapy.
- Glibness, superficial charm, and conning, manipulative behavior (along with the previous point's qualities) lead to superficial role playing in therapy.
- Inability to accept responsibility for one's actions impedes therapeutic progress.
- Need for stimulation and boredom-proneness not satisfied in repetitious therapeutic setting.

but not all psychopaths] than other modes of treatment." Losel recommends the approach taken by the concept of the therapeutic community (TC) (see Table 9.6). He describes a permanent TC in an incarcerated setting, lasting for at least 1 year. A 3-hour-a-week group is a poor substitute, and there is a risk that the psychopath will con the therapist, take advantage of another client, and recidivate anyway. All I can do is warn you. I would recommend reading Hare[19] so that you will know what you are dealing with.

TABLE 9.6. Recommended Treatment for Psychopaths

Caveat: Psychopaths do worse in treatment than control groups. Research shows they are the most difficult to treat group. The Psychopathy Checklist is the best predictor of violent failures (Ogloff, Wong, & Greenwood, 1990; Harris, Rice, & Cormier, 1991). However, what success has been achieved has occurred through the following treatment strategies:

- Of all treatment modalities, structured, cognitive-behavioral treatments based on social learning theories have better effects on antisocial behavior than other modes of treatment.
- Therapeutic community programs seem to work best with various personality-disordered and offender groups (Esteban, Garrido, & Molero, 1995; Andrews et al., 1990).
- Meta-analysis of punishment or deterrence show, at best, weak effects (e.g., Scared Straight, etc., showed negative effect).

Note. Data from Losel (1998).

DO TREATMENT GROUPS WORK?

The assessment of psychotherapeutic treatment efficacy is typically done as follows: Groups of treated and untreated men and their partners report on the man's abusiveness both before and after treatment (for the treated group) or for a comparable time period (for the untreated group). The "outcome study" assumes that the two groups are either randomized or matched for their level of previolence before any meaningful comparison can be made. The difference in reduction or cessation of violence between the two groups is called the "effect size." Effect size is the standardized difference between the mean recidivism rate of the treatment group and the mean of the untreated group, divided by the pooled standard deviation for the two groups' scores. The analysis is strengthened by combining these differences across a number of independent studies in what is called "meta-analysis."

Meta-analyses yield summaries of several studies and are believed to be superior to data offered by any single study. This method cancels out the interpretative problems, due to the methodological variation that exists between independent studies, associated with any single design. Eligible studies are viewed as a population to be systematically sampled and surveyed. Individual study results are then quantified, coded, and assembled into a database.

The strongest finding to emerge from meta-analytic studies is that psychological treatment is generally effective. In a broad-ranging review of 302 meta-analytic studies, Mark Lipsey and David B. Wilson[20] found only six that produced negative results (the control group showing greater improvements than the treated group), with 85% of the studies obtaining effect sizes of .2 or greater. By comparison, the effect size for coronary bypass surgery is .15 and for breast cancer chemotherapy it is .09.

To make effect size more intuitively understandable, psychologist Robert Rosenthal[21] suggests a "binomial effect size display" (BESD), a depiction of the proportion of treated versus untreated clients who reach or exceed a common success criterion. In practical terms, for the treatment success criterion, a "binomial" effect size of .4 translates into about a 24% spread between treated and untreated groups. A .2 binomial effect size translates into about a 10% spread. The importance of the spread size depends largely on the behavior in question. For example, in regard to lives saved through some intervention, a 5% spread size would be considered pretty important to clients or patients. Lipsey and Wilson report an effect size of .67 for cognitive-behavioral therapies, and for offender treatment programs it is said to be .20. How would wife assault treatment compare?

Barry D. Rosenfeld assessed the outcome of treatment programs for spouse abusers, examining 25 treatment outcome studies, five of which focused on court-ordered clients.[22] Although Rosenfeld did not do a formal meta-analysis, he reported aggregate outcome results that allow for the general assessment of effect sizes. He found, for example, that according to police recidivism data, 8.4% of treated men and 23.4% of untreated men with comparable prior spouse abuse rates reoffended. This translates roughly into a 15% difference, or about a .30 effect size. This midrange result is somewhat higher than offender treatment program results and somewhat lower than that of treatment outcomes in general. These findings, in turn, probably reflect differences in individual clients' motivation to change.

THE PROCESS OF CHANGE

Psychologist James O. Prochaska and his colleagues have examined the role of destructive addictions and of motivational factors in the process of change.[23] Essentially, by examining studies of change for a variety of addictions, Prochaska et al. were able to derive some general principles of change, outlined in Figure 9.10.

Abusiveness can be thought of as a destructive addiction; the perpetrator knows only one way to reduce tension and regain feelings of control. In this sense, the Prochaska, DiClemente, and Norcross model of change applies to abusive men as well as it does to cigarette addicts or to alcoholics. Prochaska et al. describe a "precontemplation" stage in which the person is not yet convinced that he or she has a problem. Friends and family may believe that the person has a problem, but the person him- or herself is not convinced. With addicts, a familiar phrase is "I know I can quit, I've done it a dozen times." Others include statements that classify the problem as minor. With abusive men, denial and minimization of the problem is commonplace. Men attending court-ordered therapy for wife assault are often catapulted from the precontemplation phase into the "action" phase; they often enter treatment with a

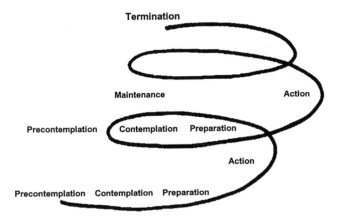

FIGURE 9.10. A spiral model of the stages of change. From Prochaska, DiClemente, and Norcross (1992). Copyright 1992 by the American Psychological Association. Reprinted by permission.

mixed motivational set. Experienced therapists know that some men will accept treatment as necessary and overdue, whereas others will still believe that the problem is with their wives, the courts, or the criminal justice system. According to Prochaska and colleagues' study, however, all these men will undergo a spiral process on the way to "termination" (permanent cessation of their abusiveness). This means that the expectation that one 16-week treatment group will automatically end abusiveness is somewhat naive or optimistic. Therapists should build in "relapse prevention" mechanisms, such as allowing men to drop in on new groups when they feel stressed, or emphasizing the importance of reentering treatment if relapse occurs. From the outcome research perspective, the implication of the model of Prochaska et al. is that some recidivism will occur in the treated group. As such, the emphasis should probably be on hastening the man's path toward cessation, rather than on expecting an "instant" improvement following treatment. In this light, my colleagues and I tracked men who had come to our treatment program for up to 11 years.[24] We used national police data to ascertain whether these men, after initial contact, had any repeat assault charges against them. These data are displayed in Table 9.7.

Some of these men had completed treatment (attended at least 12 sessions), others had dropped out (attended 0–11 sessions),

TABLE 9.4. Postcontact Crime Variables for Total Sample

	Total (N = 446)	Completers (N = 156)	Non-completers (N = 167)	Rejected (N = 32)	No shows (N = 91)
Average years at risk	5.19	5.20	4.85	5.91	5.59
Postcontact crimes					
Mean no. of crimes[a]	1.67	1.26	2.08	2.16	1.45
Mean no. of violent crimes[a]	0.61	0.47	0.74	0.88	0.49
Mean no. of assaults[a]	0.46	0.32	0.55	0.81	0.40
Percentage with at least one assault	25.3%	23.2%	28.0%	37.5%	21.0%
Mean no. of wife assaults[a]	0.26	0.23	0.50	0.29	0.23
Percentage with at least one wife assault		17.9%	22.2%	31.3%	16.5%
Total no. of wife assaults	116	36[b]	84[c]	9	21

Note. From Dutton, Bodnarchuk, Kropp, Hart, and Ogloff (1997b). Copyright 1997 by Sage Publications. Reprinted by permission.
[a]Statistically significant difference between completers and noncompleters.
[b]Six wife assaults by one man.
[c]Eleven wife assaults by one man.

some had been rejected for treatment (typically because of lack of motivation), and some had never even presented for assessment (no shows). These groups were followed for 5–6 years on average. Almost a third of the rejects reoffended, compared to 22.2% of the treatment group dropouts and 17.9 % of the completers. Since this was not a randomized design, we could not say whether these differences were due to treatment per se, or to motivational or psychological differences in the men. All groups demonstrated the following result pattern: the majority were nonviolent, a small minority were violent once, and an even smaller minority were serial batterers. One man in the dropout group had 11 repeat wife assault convictions, and one man in the treated group had 6 (the entire treated group of 156 men only had 36 repeat wife assaults, of which he accounted for 6).

These data seem to suggest that treatment works for most, but not all, abusive men. Who are the treatment risks? The man who completed treatment and reoffended six times had neurological problems as a result of head trauma. He was beyond the scope of our treatment model. Other psychological profiles that do not lend themselves well to treatment include those suggesting an antisocial or a borderline personality disorder. Extreme personality disorders simply require deeper, long-term or adjunct treatment.

One final point: Various attempts have been made to evaluate treatment groups for assaultive men. It is important to keep two things in mind in regard to outcome evaluation. The first is that appropriate controls are almost always lacking. The second is the result described above: treatment outcomes are extremely skewed. Most group completers have no recidivist offenses, a smaller group has one, and a tiny group continues to be chronic offenders. They are not normal distributions; hence, "significant" differences, based on statistical tests that assume normalcy, are hard to find. Although the data in Table 9.7 suggest that treatment groups work for most men most of the time, men with serious personality disorders are probably not good bets for wife assault treatment alone; they need further help focused on their personality disorder.[25]

THE PROPENSITY FOR ABUSIVENESS SCALE

Many professionals need to assess client populations for abuse potential. In the research described in the preceding chapters, we essentially used a strategy of comparing self-report scales supplied by treatment clients and control groups with their female partners' reports of each man's abusiveness. Eventually, I took the best 29 items (based on the strength of their individual Pearson correlation with the PMWI scores measuring abusiveness) and compacted them into one scale called the Propensity for Abusiveness Scale (PAS). These items came from the five scales comprising our predictive scales: the BPO, EMBU, MAI, TSC, and RSQ. The PAS has good psychometric properties[26] and has been cross-validated on several groups.[27] It has been shown to have three factors: recalled negative parental treatment (from the EMBU), affective lability (from the MAI and BPO scales), and trauma symptoms (from the TSC-33). The scale has a mean score of 49 (SD = 16.8) and a range of 12–95. It is highly correlated with women's reports of psychological abusiveness and significantly correlated with measures of physical abuse.[28] The PAS correctly classified 82.2% of men into high- or low-abusiveness groups based on their partners' reports. The PAS is displayed in Figure 9.11. Scoring is through simple addition of item responses. Scores above 57 indicate extreme likelihood of continuing psychological abusiveness.

Some of the results of the PAS are displayed in Figures 9.12 and 9.13. Use of the PAS is currently free. Once a larger normative sample is obtained, it will be sold by Western Psychological Services.

PART 1

For each of the statements below, please circle the number to the right of the statement that most accurately describes how the it applies to you, from 1 (completely undescriptive of you) to 5 (completely descriptive of you).

1	2	3	4	5
completely undescriptive of you	mostly undescriptive of you	partly undescriptive & partly descriptive	mostly descriptive of you	completely descriptive of you

1.   I can make myself angry about something in the past just   1 2 3 4 5
     by thinking about it.

2.   I get so angry, I feel that I might lose control.   1 2 3 4 5

3.   If I let people see the way I feel, I'd be considered a hard   1 2 3 4 5
     person to get along with.

PART 2

For each of the statements below, please indicate how true it is about you by circling the appropriate number.

1	2	3	4	5
never true	seldom true	sometimes true	often true	always true

4.   I see myself in totally different ways at different times.   1 2 3 4 5

5.   I feel empty inside.   1 2 3 4 5

6.   I tend to feel things in a somewhat extreme way,   1 2 3 4 5
     experiencing either great joy or intense despair.

7.   It is hard for me to be sure about what others think of   1 2 3 4 5
     me, even people who have known me very well.

8.   I feel people don't give me the respect I deserve unless I   1 2 3 4 5
     put pressure on them.

9.   Somehow, I never know quite how to conduct myself   1 2 3 4 5
     with people.

PART 3

Please read each of the following statements and rate the extent to which it describes your feelings about <u>romantic relationships</u> by circling the appropriate number. Think about all of your romantic relationships, past and present, and respond in terms of how you <u>generally</u> feel in these relationships.

Not at all like me		Somewhat like me		Very much like me
1	2	3	4	5

10.   I find it difficult to depend on other people.   1 2 3 4 5

11.   I worry that I will be hurt if I allow myself to become too   1 2 3 4 5
      close to others.

12.   I am somewhat uncomfortable being close to others.   1 2 3 4 5

(Figure 9.11 continued on next page)

FIGURE 9.11. The Propensity for Abusiveness Scale (PAS). From Dutton (1995d). Copyright 1995 by Plenum Publishing Corporation. Reprinted by permission.

PART 4

How often have you experienced each of the following in the last two months?
Please circle the appropriate number.

0	1	2	3
never	occasionally	fairly often	very often

13.	Insomnia (trouble getting to sleep)	0 1 2 3
14.	Restless sleep	0 1 2 3
15.	Nightmares	0 1 2 3
16.	Anxiety attacks	0 1 2 3
17.	Fear of women	0 1 2 3
18.	Feeling tense all the time	0 1 2 3
19.	Having trouble breathing	0 1 2 3

PART 5

Beside each statement, please circle the number of the response listed below
that best describes how often the experience happened to you with your mother
(or female guardian) and father (or male guardian) when you were growing up.
If you had more than one mother/father figure, please answer for the persons
who you feel played the most important role in your upbringing.

1	2	3	4
never occurred	occasionally occurred	often occurred	always occurred

		Father or Guardian	Mother or Guardian
20.	My parent punished me even for small offenses.	1 2 3 4	1 2 3 4
21.	As a child I was physically punished or scolded in the presence of others.	1 2 3 4	1 2 3 4
22.	My parent gave me more corporal (physical) punishment than I deserved.	1 2 3 4	1 2 3 4
23.	I felt my parent thought it was *my* fault when he/she was unhappy.	1 2 3 4	1 2 3 4
24.	I think my parent was mean and grudging toward me.	1 2 3 4	1 2 3 4
25.	I was punished by my parent without having done anything	1 2 3 4	1 2 3 4
26.	My parent criticized me and told me how lazy and useless I was in front of others.	1 2 3 4	1 2 3 4
27.	My parent would punish me hard, even for trifles.	1 2 3 4	1 2 3 4
28.	My parent treated me in such a way that I felt ashamed.	1 2 3 4	1 2 3 4
29.	I was beaten by my parent.	1 2 3 4	1 2 3 4

Note: The test is scored by adding the item scores.

FIGURE 9.11. *(continued)*

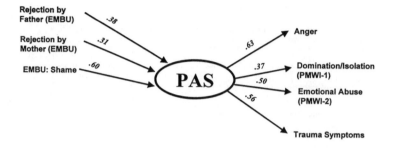

FIGURE 9.12. The centrality of the PAS in abusive men (N = 120): r > .31, p < .0001.

THE FUTURE

When I wrote the hardcover edition of *The Abusive Personality*, the death of the North American family was being predicted. Divorce rates had soared, and a population blip of fatherless boys threatened to drive up teenage crime rates. Most studies of dating violence found higher rates of abuse than those reported in the M. A. Straus national surveys on adults, and females seemed at least as aggressive as males.

The response to domestic violence in the United States was to invoke harsher penalties and in some states (e.g., California) to base court-mandated treatment on the Duluth model. After the hardcover edition was published in 1998, I began to conduct workshops with treatment providers in the United States and Canada. I found

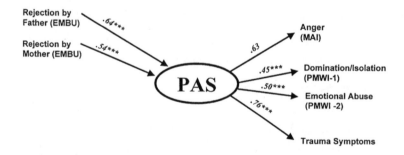

FIGURE 9.13. Zero-order correlations for the PAS in a nonalcoholic sample of clinical outpatients. PMWI, Psychological Maltreatment of Women Inventory. ***p < .001.

dissatisfaction with the Duluth model to be epidemic among this group, who felt they could not do psychotherapy but had to restrict themselves to "psychoeducational" groups. Outcome studies did not show favorable results for these groups, which in shaming men about "male privilege" were not empathic to the clients and, in return, got a guarded and defended clientele. Things are beginning to change. I sense a new openness to incorporating a variety of therapeutic techniques into batterer treatment. We are entering a second generation of batterer treatment based on a deeper understanding of the makeup of the abusive personality.

Notes

Chapter 1

1. Baron and Byrne (1977).
2. Zimbardo (1969).
3. Wiggins (1982).
4. Dutton (1995a).
5. Snell, Rosenwald, and Robey (1964).
6. Faulk (1974).
7. Bland and Orn (1986).
8. Rounsaville (1978).
9. Ibid., p. 17.
10. Ibid., p. 20.
11. Russo (1997), pp. 26–29.
12. Rounsaville (1978), p. 21.
13. Ibid., p. 22.
14. Ibid., p. 23.
15. Ibid., p. 28.
16. Dutton (1988).
17. Hamberger and Hasting (1986).
18. Saunders (1992).
19. Holtzworth-Munroe and Stuart (1994).
20. Jacobson (1993).
21. Hare (1993).
22. Porter (1996).
23. Tweed and Dutton (in press).

Chapter 2

1. Goleman (1995).
2. Schore (1994).
3. van der Kolk (1987), p. 46.

4. Elliott (1977).
5. Egeland (1993).
6. Rosenbaum and Hoge (1989).
7. Elliott (1977), p. 104.
8. Felthous and Bryant (1991).
9. Ibid., p. 73.
10. Elliott (1977), p. 104.
11. Bandura (1979).
12. Dutton, Webb, and Ryan (1994); Strachan and Dutton (1992).
13. Wilson (1977).
14. Brown (1965), p. 19.
15. Goldberg (1977), p. 19.
16. Simeons (1962).
17. Symons (1980); Buss (1994); Daly and Wilson (1988).
18. Guttenag and Secord (1983).
19. Buss (1994), p. 158.
20. Ibid., p. 157.
21. Daly and Wilson (1988), p. 205.
22. Dobash and Dobash (1992), p. 81.
23. Daly and Wilson (1988), p. 199.
24. Strachan and Dutton (1992).
25. Buss (1994), p. 157; Kasian and Painter (1992).
26. Renzetti (1992); Lie, Schilit, Bush, Montague, and Reyes (1991).
27. Hyde (1984); Frodi, Macaulay, and Thome (1977); Straus (1980); Stets and Straus (1990); Kasian and Painter (1992).
28. Coren and Mah (1993).
29. Wilson (1977).
30. Coren and Mah (1993); Buss (1994), p. 158.
31. Gelles (1975), cited in Straus and Gelles (1990a).
32. U.S. Department of Health and Human Services (1992).
33. Smith, Mercy, and Conn (1988).
34. Davidson (1978).
35. Ibid., p. 99.
36. Ibid., p. 99.
37. Dutton (1988), p. 10; Sprenger and Krämer (1486/1951).
38. Blackstone (1765–1769/1987).
39. Bograd (1988), pp. 11–26.
40. Ibid., p. 13 (emphasis mine).
41. Dobash and Dobash (1979), p. 24.
42. Bograd (1988), p. 14.
43. Goldner, Penn, Sheinberg, and Walker (1990).
44. Bograd (1988), p. 17.
45. Browne and Williams (1989).
46. Browne (1992, 1993).
47. Dutton (1995a).
48. Coleman and Straus (1986).
49. Renzitti (1992); Lie et al. (1991).

Chapter 3

1. Bandura, Ross, and Ross (1963).
2. Bandura et al. (1963); Bandura (1979).

  3. Eron, Huesmann, Lefkowitz, and Walder (1972).
  4. Huesmann (1988).
  5. Straus and Gelles (1990a); Kalmuss (1984).
  6. Widom (1989); Kalmuss (1984).
  7. Patterson, Littman, and Brickner (1967).
  8. Widom (1989).
  9. Egeland (1993).
 10. Ibid.
 11. Novaco (1975).
 12. Novaco (1976), p. 1124.
 13. Fromm (1963).
 14. Novaco (1976), p. 1126.
 15. Pollack and Gilligan (1982).
 16. Dutton and Browning (1988); Dutton (1988, 1995a).
 17. Arendt (1963).

Chapter 4

  1. Walker (1979).
  2. Zimbardo (1969).
  3. Baumeister (1990).
  4. Dutton and Yamini (1995).
  5. Rosenbaum (1990).
  6. Revitch and Schlesinger (1981).
  7. Wiggins and Pincus (1989).
  8. Gunderson (1984).
  9. Kernberg (1977).
 10. Millon (1981).
 11. Kraepelin (1896).
 12. Millon (1981); p. 348 (emphasis mine).
 13. Ibid., p. 348.
 14. Ibid., p. 348.
 15. Ibid., p. 350.
 16. Ibid., p. 349.
 17. Ibid.
 18. Revitch and Schlesinger (1981).
 19. Wertham (1966), p. 229, cited in Meloy (1992).
 20. Revitch and Schlesinger (1981), p. 137.
 21. Ibid, p. 136.
 22. Ibid.
 23. Crawford and Gartner (1992).
 24. Revitch and Schlesinger (1981), p. 137.
 25. Meloy (1992).

Chapter 5

  1. Huxley (1980), p. 15
  2. Oldham et al. (1985).
  3. Ibid., p. 14 (emphasis mine).
  4. A. Freud (1942).
  5. Oldham et al. (1985), p. 14 (emphasis mine).
  6. Saunders (1991).
  7. Dutton and Hemphill (1992); Dutton and Starzomski (1994).
  8. Dutton and Starzomski (1994).

9. Dutton and Hemphill (1992); Dutton and Starzomski (1993).
10. van der Kolk (1987); Herman and van der Kolk (1987); Zanarini, Gunderson, Marino, Schwartz, and Frankenburg (1989); Dutton and Hart (1992); Widom (1989).
11. Carmen, Rieker, and Mills (1984).
12. Widom (1989).
13. Starzomski and Dutton (1994).
14. Briere and Runtz (1989).

Chapter 6

1. Mahler, Pine, and Bergman (1975).
2. Shengold (1989).
3. Ibid., p. 24.
4. Straus and Gelles, 1990a, 1990b.
5. Klein and Riviere (1964). Copyright 1964 by W. W. Norton & Company, Inc. Excerpts reprinted by permission.
6. Ibid., p. 39.
7. Ibid., p. 11.
8. Klein and Riviere (1964), based on a lecture given in 1936, pp. 8–10.
9. Adam (1994); Dutton and Yamini (1995).
10. Winter (1973), p. 165.
11. Ibid., p. 166.
12. Trachtenberg (1988), p. 157.
13. Ibid., p. 161.
14. Ibid., p. 278.
15. O. Rank, quoted in Winter (1973), p. 168.
16. Ibid., pp. 170–171.
17. Klein and Riviere (1964), p. 19.
18. Ibid., pp. 20–21.
19. Ibid., p. 20.
20. Becker (1973).
21. Ibid., pp. 166–167.
22. Winter (1973), p. 171.
23. Mahler et al. (1975).
24. Ibid., p. 77.
25. Ibid., p. 95.
26. Ibid., p. 96.
27. Ibid., p. 101.
28. Celani (1994).

Chapter 7

1. Mahler et al. (1975), pp. 201, 205.
2. de Reincourt (1974), p. 5.
3. Dutton (1988), p. 107; Dutton and Painter (1993a); Bowlby (1977), p. 203.
4. Bowlby (1969, 1973, 1980).
5. Masson (1985); Freud (1896/1938).
6. Oppenheim (1991).
7. J. Bowlby (1940), cited in Karen (1990), p. 169.
8. Ibid., p. 169.
9. Bowlby (1977), p. 203.
10. Bowlby (1969), pp. 27–28.

11. Bowlby (1973), p. 284. Copyright 1973 by The Tavistock Institute of Human Relations. Excerpts reprinted by permission of Richard Bowlby.
12. Bowlby (1973), p. 285 (emphasis mine).
13. Ibid., pp. 287–288.
14. Ibid., pp. 289–290.
15. Ibid., p. 290.
16. Bowlby (1984), p. 11.
17. Bowlby (1973), p. 235.
18. Main, Kaplan, and Cassidy (1985).
19. Hazan and Shaver (1987); Collins and Read (1990); Adam (1994); Parker (1994); Dutton, Saunders, Starzomski, and Bartholomew (1994).
20. Ainsworth, Blehar, Waters, and Wall (1978).
21. Schore (1994).
22. Main et al. (1985).
23. Karen (1990).
24. Ibid.
25. Ibid.
26. Bartholomew (1990).
27. Ibid.; Sroufe and Waters (1977).
28. Ainsworth et al. (1978); Main and Weston (1982).
29. Margolin (1984).
30. Main and Weston (1982).
31. Karen (1992), p. 50.
32. Walker (1984).
33. Winter (1973); Trachtenberg (1988).
34. Sroufe (1988).
35. Bowlby (1977), p. 209.
36. Harlow and Harlow (1971).
37. Ibid., p. 206.
38. Crittenden (1988); Crittenden and Ainsworth (1989); Cicchetti (1984).
39. Straus, Gelles, and Steinmetz (1980); Kalmuss (1984); Widom (1989).
40. Silverman and Weinberger (1985).
41. Hazan and Shaver (1987); Shaver, Hazan, and Bradshaw (1988).
42. Shaver et al. (1988), p. 73.
43. Bartholomew (1990); Collins and Read (1990).
44. Bartholomew (1990), p. 149.
45. Crittenden (1988), p. 443.
46. Dutton et al. (1994).
47. Bowlby (1973), p. 289 (emphasis mine).
48. Starzomski (1993).
49. Dutton (1995a); Fincham and Bradbury (1992).

Chapter 8
1. Mones (1991).
2. Dutton and Painter (1981, 1993b).
3. Freud (1942).
4. Bettelheim (1943).
5. Dutton and Painter (1981).
6. Dutton and Painter (1993a, 1993b).
7. Ross, Campbell, and Clayer (1982).
8. Dutton (1994b); Dutton et al. (1996); Dutton and van Ginkel (in press).
9. Fromm (1963).

10. Briere and Runtz (1989).
11. Dutton (1995b).
12. Freud (1896/1938).
13. van der Kolk (1987).
14. Roberts et al. (1982); Hyer, Woods, Bruno, and Boudewyns (1989).
15. van der Kolk (1987).
16. Tangney, Wagner, Fletcher, and Gramzow (1992).
17. Wurmser (1981).
18. Terr (1990), pp. 113–114.
19. Katz (1988).
20. Ibid, p. 27.
21. Ibid, p. 29.
22. Daly and Wilson (1988).
23. van der Kolk (1987); Schore (1994).
24. Dutton and Holtzworth-Munroe (1997).
25. van der Kolk (1987); Cicchetti and Barnett (1991); Dodge, Petit, Bates, and Valente (1995).

Chapter 9

1. Linehan (1993a).
2. Maiuro and Avery (1996).
3. Cocarro and Kavoukian (1996).
4. Ganley (1981).
5. Wallace and Nosko (2003).
6. Pence and Paymar (1986).
7. Dutton and Sonkin (2003).
8. Bower and Bower (1976).
9. Reich (1945/1972).
10. Dutton and Winters (1999).
11. Arntz (1994).
12. Linehan (1993a), p. 32.
13. Rondeau, Brodeur, Brochu, and Lemire (2001).
14. Linehan (1993b).
15. Kabat-Zinn (1990).
16. Bowlby (1988).
17. Hare (1996).
18. Losel (1998), p. 136.
19. Hare (1993, 1996).
20. Lipsey and Wilson (1993).
21. Rosenthal (1984).
22. Rosenfeld (1992).
23. Prochaska, DiClemente, and Norcross (1992).
24. Dutton, Bodnarchuk, Kropp, Hart, and Ogloff (1997a).
25. Dutton, Bodnarchuk, Kropp, Hart, and Ogloff (1997b).
26. Dutton (1995d).
27. Dutton, Landolt, Starzomski, and Bodnarchuk (2001).
28. Ibid.

References

Adam, K. S. (1994). Suicidal behavior and attachment. In M. B. Sperling & W. H. Berman (Eds.). *Attachment in adults* (pp. 275–298). New York: Guilford Press.

Ainsworth, M. D. S., Blehar, M. C., Waters, E., & Wall, S. (1978). *Patterns of attachment: A psychological study of the strange situation.* Hillsdale, NJ: Erlbaum.

American Psychiatric Association. (1994). *Diagnostic and statistical manual of mental disorders* (4th ed.). Washington, DC: Author.

Andrews, D., Zinger, I., Hodge, R. D., Bonta, J., Gendreau, P., Cullen, F. T. (1990). Does correctional treatment work?: A clinically relevant and psychologically informed meta-analysis. *Criminology, 28,* 369–404.

Arendt, H. (1963). *Eichmann in Jerusalem: A report on the banality of evil.* New York: Penguin.

Arntz, A. (1994). Treatment of borderline personality disorder: A challenge for cognitive-behavioural therapy. *Behaviour Research and Therapy, 32*(4), 419–430.

Bandura, A. (1973). *Aggression: A social learning analysis.* Englewood Cliffs, NJ: Prentice-Hall.

Bandura, A. (1979). The social learning perspective: Mechanisms of aggression. In A. Toch (Ed.), *Psychology of crime and criminal justice* (pp. 298–336). New York: Holt, Rinehart & Winston.

Bandura, A., Ross, D., & Ross, S. (1963). Imitation of film-mediated aggressive models. *Journal of Abnormal Psychology, 66,* 3–11.

Baron, R., & Byrne, D. (1977). *Social psychology: Understanding human interaction.* Boston: Allyn & Bacon.

Bartholomew, K. (1990). Avoidance of intimacy: An attachment perspective. *Journal of Social and Personal Relationships, 7,* 147–178.

Baumeister, R. F. (1990). Suicide as escape from self. *Psychological Review, 97,* 90–113.

Becker, E. (1973). *The denial of death.* Glencoe, IL: Free Press.

Bettelheim, B. (1943). Individual and mass behavior in extreme situations. *Journal of Abnormal and Social Psychology, 38,* 417–452.

Blackstone, W. (1987). *Commentaries on the laws of England*. Portions reprinted in E. Pleck (Ed.), *Domestic tyranny: The making of American social policy against family violence from colonial times to the present*. New York: Oxford University Press. (Original work published 1765–1769)

Bland, R. C., & Orn, H. (1986). Family violence and psychological disorder. *Canadian Journal of Psychiatry, 31*(12), 129–137.

Bograd, M. (1988). Feminist perspectives on wife abuse: An introduction. In M. Bograd & K. Yllo (Eds.), *Feminist perspectives on wife abuse* (pp. 11–26). Beverly Hills, CA: Sage.

Bower, S. A., & Bower, G. H. (1976). *Asserting yourself: A practical guide for positive change*. Reading, MA: Addison-Wesley.

Bowlby, J. (1969). *Attachment and loss: Vol. 1. Attachment* New York: Penguin Books.

Bowlby, J. (1973). *Attachment and loss: Vol. 2. Separation*. New York: Penguin Books.

Bowlby, J. (1977). The making and breaking of affectional bonds. *British Journal of Psychiatry, 130,* 201–210.

Bowlby, J. (1980). *Attachment and loss: Vol. 3. Loss, sadness, and depression*. New York: Penguin Books.

Bowlby, J. (1984). Violence in the family as a disorder of attachment and caregiving systems. *American Journal of Psychoanalysis, 44*(1), 9–27.

Bowlby, J. (1988). *A secure base: Clinical applications of attachment theory*. London: Routledge.

Briere, J., & Runtz, M. (1989). The Trauma Symptom Checklist (TSC-33): Early data on a new scale. *Journal of Interpersonal Violence, 4*(2), 151–162.

Brown, R. (1965). *Social psychology*. New York: Free Press.

Browne, A. (1992). *Are women as violent as men?* Unpublished manuscript, University of Massachusetts, Worcester.

Browne, A. (1993). Violence against women by male partners: Prevalence, outcomes and policy implications. *American Psychologist, 48,* 1077–1090.

Browne, A., & Williams, K. (1989). Exploring the effect of resource availability and the likelihood of female perpetrated homicides. *Law and Society Review, 23,* 75–94.

Buss, D. (1994). *The evolution of desire: Strategies of human mating*. New York: Basic Books.

Carmen, E. H., Rieker, P. P., & Mills, T. (1984). Victims of violence and psychiatric illness. *American Journal of Psychiatry, 141,* 378–383.

Celani, D. (1994). *The illusion of love*. New York: Columbia University Press.

Cicchetti, D. (1984). The emergence of developmental psychopathology. *Child Development, 55,* 1–5.

Cicchetti, D., & Barnett, D. (1991). Attachment organization in maltreated preschoolers. *Development and Psychopathology, 3,* 397–411.

Cocarro, E. K., & Kavoukian, R. J. (1996) Neurotransmitter correlates of impulsive aggression. *Annals of the New York Academy of Sciences, 794,* 82–99.

Coleman, D. H., & Straus, M. A. (1986). Marital power, conflict, and violence in a nationally representative sample of American couples. *Violence and Victims, 1,* 141–157.

Collins, N. L., & Read, S. J. (1990). Adult attachment, working models and relationship quality in dating couples. *Journal of Personality and Social Psychology, 58,* 644–663.

Coren, S., & Mah, K. B. (1993). Prediction of physiological arousability: A validation of the Arousal Predisposition Scale. *Behaviour Research and Therapy, 31*(2), 215–219.

Crawford, M., & Gartner, R. (1992). *Woman killing: Intimate femicide in Ontario, 1974–1990.* Women's Directorate, Ministry of Social Services, Toronto, Ontario, Canada.

Crittenden, P. M. (1988). Relationships at risk. In J. Belsky & T. Nezworski (Eds.), *Clinical implications of attachment* (pp. 136–174). Hillsdale, NJ: Erlbaum.

Crittenden, P. M., & Ainsworth, M. D. (1989). Attachment and child abuse. In D. Cicchetti & V. Carlson (Eds.), *Child maltreatment: Theory and research in the causes of child abuse and neglect* New York: Cambridge University Press.

Daly, M., & Wilson, M. (1988). *Homicide.* New York: Aldine.

Davidson, T. (1978). *Conjugal crime: Understanding and changing the wife-beating pattern.* New York: Hawthorn.

de Reincourt, A. (1974). *Sex and power in history.* New York: Delta.

Dobash, R. E., & Dobash, R. P. (1979). *Violence against wives: A case against the patriarchy.* New York: Free Press.

Dobash, R. E., & Dobash, R. P. (1992). The myth of sexual symmetry in marital violence. *Social Problems, 39*(1), 71–91.

Dodge, K., Petit, G. S., Bates, J. E., & Valente, E. (1995). Social information-processing patterns partially mediate the effect of early physical abuse on later conduct problems. *Journal of Abnormal Psychology, 104*(4), 632–643.

Dutton, D. G. (1984). The social psychology of wife assault: Therapeutic, policy, and research implications. *Canadian Journal of Behavioural Science, 16*(4), 281–297.

Dutton, D. G. (1988). *Domestic assault of women: Psychological and criminal justice perspectives.* Boston: Allyn & Bacon.

Dutton, D. G. (1994a). Behavioural and affective correlates of borderline personality organization in wife assaulters. *International Journal of Law and Psychiatry, 17*(3), 265–277.

Dutton, D. G. (1994b). The origin and structure of the abusive personality. *Journal of Personality Disorders, 8,* 181–191.

Dutton, D. G. (1995a). *The domestic assault of women* (2nd ed.). Vancouver: University of British Columbia Press.

Dutton, D. G. (1995b). Trauma symptoms and PTSD-like profiles in perpetrators of intimate abuse. *Journal of Traumatic Stress, 8,* 299–316.

Dutton, D. G. (1995c). *The batterer: A psychological profile.* New York: Basic Books.

Dutton, D. G. (1995d). A scale for measuring propensity of abusiveness. *Journal of Family Violence, 10*(2), 203–221.

Dutton, D. G., Bodnarchuk, M., Kropp, R., Hart, S., & Ogloff, J. (1997a). Wife assault treatment and criminal recidivism: An eleven-year follow-up. *Journal of Offender Therapy and Comparative Criminology, 41*(1), 9–23.

Dutton, D. G., Bodnarchuk, M., Kropp, R., Hart, S., & Ogloff, J. (1997b). Client personality disorders affecting wife assault post-treatment recidivism. *Violence and Victims, 12*(1), 37–50.

Dutton, D. G., & Browning, J. J. (1988). Concern for power, fear and intimacy, and aversive stimuli for wife assault. In G. T. Hotaling, D. Finkelhor, J. T. Kirkpatrick, & M. A. Straus (Eds.), *Family abuse and its consequences: New directions in research.* Newbury Park, CA: Sage.

Dutton, D. G., & Hart, S. D. (1992). Evidence for long-term, specific effects of childhood abuse and neglect on criminal behavior in men. *International Journal of Offender Therapy and Comparative Criminology, 36*(2), 129–137.

Dutton, D. G., & Hemphill, K. J. (1992). Patterns of socially desirable responding among perpetrators and victims of wife assault. *Violence and Victims, 7*(1), 29–39.

Dutton, D. G., & Holtzworth-Munroe, A. (1997). The role of early trauma in males who assault their wives. In D. Cicchetti & S. L. Toth (Eds.), *Rochester symposium on developmental psychopathology: Developmental perspectives on trauma–theory, research, and intervention* (pp. 379–402). Rochester, NY: University of Rochester Press.

Dutton, D. G., Landolt, M. A., & Starzomski, A. J. (1995). *Validation of a scale for measuring propensity for abusiveness*. Final report for the Solicitor General of Canada.

Dutton, D. G., Landolt, M. A., Starzomski, A., & Bodnarchuk, M. (2001). Validation of the Propensity for Abusiveness Scale in diverse male populations. *Journal of Family Violence, 16*(1), 59–73.

Dutton, D. G., & Painter, S. L. (1981). Traumatic bonding: The development of emotional attachments in battered women and other relationships of intermittent abuse. *Victimology: An International Journal, 6,* 139–155.

Dutton, D. G., & Painter, S. L. (1993a). Emotional attachments in abusive relationships: A test of traumatic bonding theory. *Violence and Victims, 8,* 105–120.

Dutton, D. G., & Painter, S. L. (1993b). The battered woman syndrome: Effects of severity and intermittency of abuse. *American Journal of Orthopsychiatry, 63,* 614–622.

Dutton, D. G., Saunders, K., Starzomski, A., & Bartholomew, K. (1994). Intimacy-anger and insecure attachment as precursors of abuse in intimate relationships. *Journal of Applied Social Psychology, 24,* 1367–1386.

Dutton, D. G., & Sonkin, D. G. (Eds.) (2003). *The treatment of anger and abuse.* Binghamton, NY: Haworth Press.

Dutton, D. G., & Starzomski, A. J. (1993). Borderline personality in perpetrators of psychological and physical abuse. *Violence and Victims, 8*(4), 327–337.

Dutton, D. G., Starzomski, A. J. (1994). Psychological differences between court-referred and self-referred wife assaulters. *Criminal Justice and Behavior: An International Journal, 21*(2), 203–222.

Dutton, D. G., Starzomski, A. J., & Ryan, L. (1996). Antecedents of abusive personality and abusive behavior wife assaulters. *Journal of Family Violence, 11*(2), 113–132.

Dutton, D. G., Starzomski, A. J., & van Ginkel, C. (1995). The role of shame and guilt in the intergenerational transmission of abusiveness. *Violence and Victims, 10*(2), 121–131.

Dutton, D. G., Webb, A., & Ryan, L. (1994). Gender differences in anger–anxiety reactions to witnessing dyadic family conflict. *Canadian Journal of Behavioural Science, 26*(3), 353–364.

Dutton, D. G., & Winters, J. (1999). *A tracking study of cyclical batterers.* Unpublished manuscript, Department of Psychology, University of British Columbia.

Dutton, D. G., & Yamini, S. (1995). Adolescent parricide: An integration of social cognitive theory and clinical views of projective–introjective cycling. *American Journal of Orthopsychiatry, 65*(1), 39–47.

Egeland, B. (1993). A history of abuse is a risk factor for abusing the next generation. In R. G. Gelles & D. R. Loseke (Eds.), *Current controversies on family violence.* Newbury Park, CA: Sage.

Elliott, F. (1977). The neurology of explosive rage: The episodic dyscontrol syndrome. In M. Roy (Ed.), *Battered women: A psychosociological study of domestic violence.* New York: Van Nostrand.

Eron, L. D., Huesmann, L. R., Lefkowitz, M. M., & Walder, L. O. (1972). Does television cause aggression? *American Psychologist, 27,* 253–263.

Esteban, C., Garrido, V., Molero, C. (1995, November). *The effectiveness of treatment of psychopathy: A meta-analysis*. Paper presented at the NATO Advanced Study Institute on Psychopathy, Alvor, Portugal.

Faulk, M. (1974). Men who assault their wives. *Medicine, Science, and the Law, 14,* 180–183.

Felthous, A. R., & Bryant, S. (1991). The diagnosis of intermittent explosive disorders in violent men. *Bulletin of the American Academy of Psychiatry and Law, 19*(1), 71–79.

Fincham, F. D., & Bradbury, T. N. (1992). Assessing attributions in marriage: The Relationship Attribution Measure. *Journal of Personality and Social Psychology, 62*(3), 457–468.

Freud, A. (1942). *The ego and the mechanisms of defense*. New York: International Universities Press.

Freud, S. (1938). The aetiology of hysteria. In A. Brill (Ed.), *The basic writings of Sigmund Freud*. New York: Modern Library. (Original work published 1896)

Frodi, A., Macaulay, J., & Thome, P. (1977). Are women always less aggressive than men?: A review of the experimental literature. *Psychological Bulletin, 84*(4), 634–660.

Fromm, E. (1963). *The art of loving*. New York: Bantam.

Ganley, A. (1981). *Participant's manual: Court-mandated therapy for men who batter–A three day workshop for professionals*. Washington, DC: Center for Women Policy Studies.

Gelles, R. J. (1975). Violence and pregnancy: A note on the extent of the problem and needed services. *The Family Coordinator, 24,* 81–86.

Glass, G. (1976). Primary, secondary, and meta-analysis of research. *Educational Researcher, 5,* 3–8.

Goldberg, S. (1977). *The inevitability of patriarchy*. London: Temple Smith.

Goleman, D. (1995). *Emotional intelligence*. New York: Bantam Books.

Goldner, V., Penn, P., Sheinberg, M., & Walker, G. (1990). Love and violence: Gender paradoxes in volatile attachments. *Family Process, 29,* 343–364.

Gottman, J. M., Jacobson, N. S., Rushe, R. H., Short, J. W., Babcock, J., La Taillade, J. J., & Waltz, J. (1995). The relationship between heart rate activity, emotionally aggressive behavior and general violence in batterers. *Journal of Family Psychology, 9,* 1–41.

Griffin, D. W., & Bartholomew, K. (1994). The metaphysics of measurement: The case of adult attachment. In K. Bartholomew & D. Perlman (Eds.), *Advances in personal relationships, Vol. 5: Attachment processes in adulthood* (pp. 17–52). London: Jessica Kingsley.

Gunderson, J. G. (1984). *Borderline personality disorder*. Washington, DC: American Psychiatric Press.

Guttentag, M., & Secord, P. (1983). *Too many women?* Beverly Hills, CA: Sage.

Hamberger, K., & Hastings, J. (1986). Personality correlates of men who abuse their partners: A cross-validational study. *Journal of Family Violence, 1*(4), 323–341.

Hare, R. D. (1993). *Without conscience: The disturbing world of the psychopaths among us*. New York: Pocket Books.

Hare, R. D. (1996). Psychopathy: A clinical construct whose time has come. *Criminal Justice and Behavior, 23,* 25–54.

Hare, R. D., Forth, A. E., & Strachan, K. (1992). Psychopathy and crime across the life span. In R. D. Peters, R. J. McMahon, & V. L. Quinsey (Eds.), *Aggression and violence throughout the lifespan* (pp. 285–300). Newbury Park, CA: Sage.

Harlow, H. F., & Harlow, M. (1971). Psychopathology in monkeys. In H. D. Kinnel (Ed.), *Experimental psychopathology*. New York: Academic Press.

Harris, G. T., Rice, M. E., & Cormier, C. A. (1991). Psychopathy and violent recidivism. *Law and Human Behavior, 15*, 625–637.

Hazan, C., & Shaver, P. (1987). Romantic love conceptualized as an attachment process. *Journal of Personality and Social Psychology, 52*, 511–524.

Herman, J. L., & van der Kolk, B. (1987). Traumatic antecedents of borderline personality disorder. In B. van der Kolk (Ed.), *Psychological trauma* (pp. 111–126). Washington, DC: American Psychiatric Press.

Holtzworth-Munroe, A., & Anglin, K. (1991). The competency of responses given by maritally violent versus nonviolent men to problematic marital situations. *Violence and Victims, 6*, 257–269.

Holtzworth-Munroe, A., & Hutchinson, G. (1993). Attributing negative intent to wife behavior: The attributions of maritally violent versus nonviolent men. *Journal of Abnormal Psychology, 102*(2), 206–211.

Holtzworth-Munroe, A., & Stuart, G. L. (1994). Typologies of male batterers: Three subtypes and the differences among them. *Psychological Bulletin, 116*, 476–497.

Huesmann, L. (1988). An information processing model for the development of aggression. *Aggressive Behavior, 14*(1), 13–24.

Huxley, A. (1980). *The human situation.* London: Granada/Triad.

Hyde, J. S. (1984). How large are gender differences in aggression?: A developmental meta-analysis. *Developmental Psychology, 20*(4), 722–736.

Hyer, L., Woods, M. G., Bruno, R., & Boudewyns, P. (1989). Treatment outcomes of Vietnam veterans with PTSD and the consistency of the MCMI. *Journal of Clinical Psychology, 45*, 547–552.

Jacobson, N. (1993, October). *Domestic violence: What are the marriages like?* Paper presented at the meeting of the American Association for Marriage and Family Therapy, Anaheim, CA.

Kabat-Zinn, J. (1990). *Full catastrophe living.* New York: Delta.

Kalmuss, D. S. (1984, February). The intergenerational transmission of marital aggression. *Journal of Marriage and the Family, 46*, 11–19.

Karen, R. (1990). *Becoming attached.* New York: Warner.

Karen, R. (1992, February). Shame. *The Atlantic Monthly*, pp. 42–70.

Kasian, M., & Painter, S. (1992). Frequency and severity of psychological abuse in a dating population. *Journal of Interpersonal Violence, 7*(3), 350–364.

Katz, J. (1988). *Seductions of crime: Moral and sensual attractions in doing evil.* New York: Basic Books.

Kernberg, O. (1977). The structural diagnosis of borderline personality organization. In P. Hartocollis (Ed.), *Borderline personality disorders: The concept, the syndrome, the patient.* New York: International Universities Press.

Klein, M., & Riviere, J. (1964). *Love, hate and reparation* New York: Norton.

Kraepelin, E. (1896). *Psychiatrie: Eine Lehrbuch* (3rd ed.). Leipzig: Barth.

Leary, T. F. (1957). *Interpersonal diagnosis of personality: A functional theory and methodology for personality evaluation.* New York: Ronald Press.

Lie, G.-Y., Schilit, R., Bush, J., Montague, M., & Reyes, L. (1991). Lesbians in currently aggressive relationships: How frequently do they report aggressive past relationships? *Violence and Victims, 6*, 121–135.

Linehan, M. (1993a). *Cognitive-behavioral treatment of borderline personality disorder.* New York: Guilford Press.

Linehan, M. (1993b). *Skills training manual for treating borderline personality disorder.* New York: Guilford Press.

Lipsey, M., & Wilson, D. B. (1993). The efficacy of psychological, educational and behavioral treatment. *American Psychologist, 48*(12), 1181–1209.

Losel, H. (1998). Treatment and management of psychopaths. In D. C. Cooke, A. E.

Forth, & R. D. Hare (Eds.), *Psychopathy: Theory, research and implications for society* (pp. 118–142). Dordrecht, The Netherlands: Kluines.

Lynam, D. R. (1996). Early identification of chronic offenders: Who is the fledgling psychopath. *Psychological Bulletin, 120*(2), 209–234.

Mahler, M., Pine, F., & Bergman, A. (1975). *The psychological birth of the human infant.* New York: Basic Books.

Main, M., Kaplan, N., & Cassidy, J. (1985). Security in infancy, childhood, and adulthood: A move to the level of representation. In I. Bretherton & E. Waters (Eds.), Growing points of attachment theory and research. *Monographs of the Society for Research in Child Development, 50,* (1–2, Serial No. 209), 66–104.

Main, M., & Weston, D. R. (1982). Avoidance of the attachment figure in infancy: Descriptions and interpretations. In C. M. Parkes & J. Stevenson-Hinde (Eds.), *The place of attachment in human behavior* (pp. 31–59). London: Tavistock.

Maiuro, R. D., & Avery, D. H. (1996). Psychopharmacological treatment of aggression. *Violence and Victims, 11*(3), 239–262.

Margolin, G. (1984). *Interpersonal and intrapersonal factors associated with marital violence.* Paper presented at the Second National Family Violence Conference, University of New Hampshire, Durham.

Masson, J. M. (1985). *The assault on truth: Freud's suppression of the seduction theory.* New York: Penguin Books.

Meloy, J. R. (1992). *Violent attachments.* Northvale, NJ: Aronson.

Millon, T. (1981). *Disorders of personality DSM-III: Axis II.* New York: Wiley.

Mones, P. (1991). *When a child kills: Abused children who kill their parents.* New York: Simon & Schuster.

Novaco, R. (1975). *Anger control: The development and evaluation of an experimental treatment.* Lexington, MA: Lexington Books.

Novaco, R. (1976). The functions and regulation of the arousal of anger. *American Journal of Psychiatry, 133,* 1124–1128.

Ogloff, J. R. P., Wong, S., & Greenwood, A. (1990). Treating criminal psychopaths in a therapeutic community setting. *Behavioral Sciences and the Law, 8,* 81–90.

Oldham, J., Clarkin, J., Appelbaum, A., Carr, A., Kernberg, P., Lotterman, A., & Hass, G. (1985). A self-report instrument for borderline personality organization. In T. H. McGlashan (Ed.), *The borderline: Current empirical research* (pp. 1–18). Washington, DC: American Psychiatric Press.

Oppenheim, J. (1991). Shattered nerves: Doctors, patients, and depression in Victorian England. New York: Oxford University Press.

Parker, G. (1994). Parental bonding and depressive disorders. In M. B. Sperling & W. H. Berman (Eds.), *Attachment in adults* (pp. 299–312). New York: Guilford Press.

Patterson, G. R., Littman, R. A., & Brickner, W. (1967). Assertive behaviour in children: A step toward a theory of aggression. *Monographs of the Society for Research in Child Development, 32*(5), serial no. 133.

Pence, E., & Paymar, M. (1986). *Power and control: Tactics of men who batter.* Duluth, MN: Minnesota Program Development, Inc.

Pleck, E. (1987). *Domestic tyranny: The making of American social policy against family violence from colonial times to the present.* New York: Oxford University Press.

Pollack, S., & Gilligan, C. (1982). Images of violence in thematic apperception test stories. *Journal of Personality and Social Psychology, 42,* 159–167.

Porter, S. (1996). Without conscience or without active conscience?: The etiology of psychopathy revisited. *Aggression and Violent Behavior, 1*(2), 179–189.

Prochaska, J. O., DiClemente, C. C., & Norcross, C. C. (1992). In search of how people change: Applications to addictive behaviors. *American Psychologist, 47,* 1102–1114.

Reich, W. (1972). *Character analysis.* New York: Simon & Schuster. (Original work published 1945)

Renzetti, C. M. (1992). *Violent betrayal: Partner abuse in lesbian relationships* Newbury Park, CA: Sage.

Revitch, E., & Schlesinger, L. B. (1981). *Psychopathology of homicide.* Springfield, IL: Charles C Thomas.

Roberts, J. A., Ryan, J. J., McEntyre, W. L., Macfarlane, R. S., & Lips, O. J. (1985). MCMI characteristics of DSM-III post-traumatic stress disorder in Vietnam veterans. *Journal of Personality Assessment, 49,* 226–230.

Roberts, W. R. R., Penk, W. E., Gearing, M. L., Robinowitz, R., Dolan, M. P., & Patterson, E. T. (1982). Interpersonal problems of Vietnam combat veterans with symptoms of post-traumatic stress disorder. *Journal of Abnormal Psychology, 91,* 444–450.

Rondeau, G., Brodeur, N., Brochu, S., & Lemire, G. (2001). Dropout and completion of treatment among spouse abusers. *Violence and Victims, 16*(2), 127–144.

Rosenbaum, A., & Hoge, S. (1989). Head injury and marital aggression. *American Journal of Psychiatry, 146*(8), 1048–1051.

Rosenbaum, M. (1990). The role of depression in couples involved in murder–suicide and homicide. *American Journal of Psychiatry, 147*(8), 1036–1039.

Rosenfeld, B. D. (1992). Court-ordered treatment of spouse abuse. *Clinical Psychology Review, 12,* 205–226.

Rosenthal, R. (1984). *Meta-analytic procedures for social research.* Beverly Hills, CA: Sage.

Ross, M. W., Campbell, R. I., & Clayer, J. R. (1982). New inventory for measurement of parental rearing patterns: An English form of the EMBU. *Acta Psychiatrica Scandinavica, 66,* 499–507.

Rounsaville, B. J. (1978). Theories of marital violence: Evidence from a study of battered women. *Victimology, 3*(1–2), 11–31.

Russo, F. (1997). The faces of Hedda Nussbaum. *New York Times Magazine,* pp. 26–29.

Saunders, D. G. (1991). Procedures for adjusting self-reports of violence for socially desirability bias. *Journal of Interpersonal Violence, 6,* 264–275.

Saunders, D. G. (1992). A typology of men who batter: Three types derived from cluster analysis. *American Orthopsychiatry, 62,* 264–275.

Schore, A. N. (1994). *Affect regulation and the origin of the self.* Hillsdale, NJ: Erlbaum.

Seligman, M. E. (1975). *On depression, development and death.* San Francisco: Freeman.

Shaver, P., Hazan, C., & Bradshaw, D. (1988). Love as attachment: The integration of three behavioral systems. In R. J. Sternberg & M. Barnes (Eds.), *The psychology of love* (pp. 68–99). New Haven, CT: Yale University Press.

Shengold, L. (1989). *Soul murder: The effects of childhood abuse and deprivation* New York: Fawcett.

Silverman, L. H., & Weinberger, J. (1985). Mommy and I are one: Implications for psychotherapy. *American Psychologist, 40,* 1296–1308.

Simeons, W. (1962). *Man's presumptuous brain.* New York: Dutton.

Smith, J. C., Mercy, J. A., & Conn, J. M. (1988). Marital status and the risk of suicide. *American Journal of Public Health, 78*(1), 72–87.

Snell, J. E., Rosenwald, P. J., & Robey, A. (1964). The wifebeater's wife. *Archives of General Psychiatry, 11,* 107–113.

Sperling, M. B., & Berman, W. H. (Eds.). (1994). *Attachment in adults.* New York: Guilford Press.

Sprenger, J., & Krämer, H. (1951). *Maleus maleficarum* (M. Summers, Ed. & Trans.). London: Pushkin Press. (Original work published 1486)

Sroufe, L. A. (1988). The role of intent–caregiver attachment in development. In J. Belsky & T. Nezworski (Eds.), *Clinical implications of attachment.* Hillsdale, NJ: Erlbaum.

Sroufe, L. A., & Waters, E. (1977). Attachment as an organizational construct. *Child Development, 48,* 1184–1199.

Starzomski, A. J. (1993). *Attachment style, affect and construal of interpersonal conflict.* Unpublished master's thesis, University of British Columbia, Vancouver.

Starzomski, A. J., & Dutton, D. G. (1994). *Attachment, anger, and attribution.* Unpublished manuscript, University of British Columbia, Vancouver.

Stets, J. E., & Straus, M. A. (1990). Gender differences in reporting marital violence and its medical and psychological consequences. In M. A. Straus & R. J. Gelles (Eds.), *Physical violence in American families.* New Brunswick, NJ: Transaction Publishers.

Strachan, K., & Dutton, D. G. (1992). The role of power and gender in anger responses to jealousy. *Journal of Applied Social Psychology, 22*(22), 1721–1740.

Straus, M. A. (1979). Measuring family conflict and violence. The Conflict Tactics Scale. *Journal of Marriage in the Family, 41,* 75–88.

Straus, M. A. (1980). Victims and aggressors in marital violence. *American Behavioral Scientist, 23*(5), 681–704.

Straus, M. A., & Gelles, R. J. (1990a). *Physical violence in American families: Risk factors and adaptations to violence in 8,145 families.* New Brunswick, NJ: Transaction Publishers.

Straus, M. A., & Gelles, R. J. (1990b). Societal change and change in family violence from 1975 to 1985 as revealed by two national surveys. In M. A. Straus & R. J. Gelles (Eds.), *Physical violence in American families: Risk factors and adaptations to violence in 8,145 families.* New Brunswick, NJ: Transaction Publishers.

Straus, M. A., Gelles, R. J., & Steinmetz, S. (1980). *Behind closed doors: Violence in the American family.* Garden City, NY: Anchor/Doubleday.

Stuart, R. B. (1981). *Violent behavior: Social learning approaches to prediction, management and treatment.* New York: Brunner/Mazel.

Symons, D. (1980). *The evolution of human sexuality.* Cambridge, UK: Cambridge University Press.

Tangney, J. P., Wagner, P., Fletcher, C., & Gramzow, R. (1992). Shamed into anger?: The relation of shame and guilt to anger and self-reported aggression. *Journal of Personality and Social Psychology, 62,* 669–675.

Terr, L. (1990). *Too scared to cry: Psychic trauma in childhood* Grand Rapids, MI: Harper & Row.

Terr, L. (1991). Childhood traumas: An outline and overview. *American Journal of Psychiatry, 148,* 10–20.

Tolman, R. (1989). The development of a measure of psychological maltreatment of women by their male partners. *Violence and Victims, 4*(3), 159–177.

Trachtenberg, P. (1988). *The Casanova complex* New York: Poseidon Press.

Tweed, R., & Dutton, D. G. (in press). A comparison of impulsive and instrumental subgroups of batterers. *Violence and Victims.*

U.S. Department of Health and Human Services. (1992). Washington, DC: National Center for Health Statistics, Division of Vital Statistics.

van der Kolk, B. (Ed.). (1987). *Psychological trauma.* Washington, DC: American Psychiatric Press.

Walker, L. E. (1979). *The battered woman.* New York: Harper & Row.

Walker, L. E. (1984). *The battered woman syndrome.* New York: Springer-Verlag.

Wallace, R., & Nosko, A. (1993). Working with shame in the group treatment of male batterers. *International Journal of Group Psychotherapy, 43*(1), 45–61.

Wallace, R., & Nosko, A. (2003). Working with shame in the group treatment of male batterers. In D. G. Dutton & D. G. Sonkin (Eds.), *The treatment of anger and abuse.* Binghamton, NY: Haworth Press.

Wertham, F. (1966). *A sign for Cain: An exploration of human violence.* New York: Macmillan.

Widom, C. S. (1989). Does violence beget violence?: A critical examination of the literature. *Psychological Bulletin, 106,* 13–28.

Wiggins, J. S. (1982). Circumplex models of interpersonal behavior in clinical psychology. In P. C. Kendall & J. N. Butcher (Eds.), *Handbook of research methods in clinical psychology.* New York: Wiley.

Wiggins, J., & Pincus, A. (1989). Conceptions of personality disorders and dimensions of personality. *Personality Assessment: A Journal of Consulting and Clinical Psychology, 1*(4), 308–316,

Wilson, E. O. (1977). *On human nature.* Cambridge, MA: Harvard University Press.

Winter, D. G. (1973). *The power motive.* New York: Free Press.

Wurmser, L. (1981). *The mask of shame.* Baltimore: John Hopkins University Press.

Zanarini, M. C., Gunderson, J. G., Marino, M. F., Schwartz, E. O., & Frankenburg, F. R. (1989). Childhood experiences of borderline patients. *Comprehensive Psychiatry, 30*(1), 18–25.

Zimbardo, P. G. (1969). The human choice: Individuation, reason and order versus deindividuation, impulse, and chaos. In W. J. Arnold & D. Levine (Eds.), *Nebraska Symposium on Motivation* (Vol. 17). Lincoln: University of Nebraska Press.

Index

Polygamy, 20
Polygyny, 100
Posttraumatic stress disorder (*see* Trauma
    symptoms)
Power needs
    couples classification, 29, 30
    feminist analysis limitations, 30
    in sexual behavior, 100, 101
"Power wheel," 166, 167
"Pre-Oedipal" period, 94, 97, 110
Primitive defenses
    in abuse cycle, 87
    borderline personality, 73–75
    formation of, 94, 97
    and rage, 94–111
Projective identification
    in abuse cycle, 87
    borderline personality defense, 73–75
    developmental origins, 97
Promiscuity, males, 19, 20
Propensity for Abusiveness Scale, 187–190
Protective factors, abused children, 37, 38
Psychic murder, 95
Psychological Maltreatment of Women
    Inventory, 82–85
Psychopathic batterers
    characteristics, 9, 10
    classification, 6–8
    heart rate, 9
    treatment programs, 181–182
Psychotherapy (*see* Group treatment)

Q
Questionnaires (*see* Self-report scales)

R
Rage, 94–111
    humiliation link, 155, 156
    individual variations, 103
    in intimate relationships, 102, 103
    metabolic causes, 15
    and organic brain syndromes, 12–18
    primitive origins, 94–111
    separation anxiety as substratum, 120
    separation–individuation role, 105–108
    and splitting, 98
"Rapprochement subphase," 105–107, 110
Reality testing, 75, 76
Recidivism, 178
Rejection
    by fathers, 142–147
        contribution to spouse abuse, 144–
        147
    in maternal attachment relationship, 121,
        122
    psychological and physiological toll, 156,
        157

Relapse prevention, 174, 178
Relationship Attribution Measure, 90, 135–
    137
Relationship Style Questionnaire, 81, 132,
    133
Reproductive exclusivity, 20, 21
Reward, in habit formation, 33
Rounsaville, Bruce, 3–5
Rules of Marriage (Cherubino), 25
Rumination
    and catathymic crisis, 67
    murder-suicide perpetrators, 55, 56

S
Schizoid batterers, 6–8
Script learning, and aggression, 35
"Secure" attachment style, 123
The Seductions of Crime (Katz), 155
Self-deception, assessment, 78, 79
Self-management techniques, 172
Self-punishment
    individual differences, 49
    neutralization in abusers, 49–52
"Self-referred" men
    maladjustment, 76, 77
    questionnaire responses, 77–80
Self-report scales (*see also* Borderline
        Personality Organization Scale)
    borderline personality, 70–76
    completion of, compliance, 76, 77
    social desirability responses, 77, 78
Self-talk, 170
Separation anxiety
    and anger, 118–121
    and "optimal distance" from mother, 108
Separation–individuation
    and abused mothers, 106, 107
    and rage development, 105–108
Sex differences (*see* Gender differences)
Sex roles
    and aggression, 86
    and male blaming response, 43, 44
    male socialization into, 28
Sexual abuse
    dissociation in victims, 42
    in lesbian versus heterosexual
        relationships, 31
Sexual exclusivity, 20, 21
Sexual infidelity, 19, 20
"Sexual tantrums," 100
Shame (*see also* Shaming)
    in abused boys, emotional cover-up, 140,
        141
    group treatment detoxification of, 162
    guilt trade-off, 155
    neutralization in abusers, 49–52
    and questionnaire responses, 77–79